THE LIBRA SOLUTION

PRAISE FOR *THE LIBRA SOLUTION*

"In our studies, we find that people feel torn by everything they have to do at work and at home. *The Libra Solution* addresses this seemingly intractable problem by providing a perceptive analysis of how work needs to change and how we need to change too. Importantly, it shows that these problems may be less impervious to change than we may think by providing effective real life examples of how work can be redesigned in ways that benefit employers, employees, and their families."

Ellen Galinsky, President, Families and Work Institute, author, *Mind in the Making*

"*The Libra Solution* answers a fundamental question of major concern to today's working families—how can you have a satisfying job or career, a family, and a personal life? Levey offers strategies, examples, inspiration, and encouragement to families about how to create satisfying work and meaningful family lives."

Judi C. Casey, Director, Work and Family Researchers Network (WFRN)

"Insightful look at barriers that prevent women AND men from realizing greater balance in their work, family, and personal lives, with thoughtful recommendations for more effectively navigating all three critical spheres."

Ilene Lang, President, Catalyst

"*The Libra Solution* is a wise and helpful book for today's couples. I highly recommend this book!"

Joshua Coleman, psychologist, author, *The Lazy Husband: How to get men to do more parenting and housework*

"In *The Libra Solution*, Lisa Levey presents a new model of careers and family that much more clearly represents the needs and desires of most working couples and articulates an important future direction for work and family in the U.S. and elsewhere. Levey offers excellent insights into how we can make family systems and work organizations synergistic, not adversarial. From my own work with many leading employers, working fathers, and graduate students, I feel Lisa has "hit the nail on the head" in articulating the challenges and solutions (i.e. the Libra Solution) that will result in meaningful work and meaningful lives for today's dual-career families."

Brad Harrington, Executive Director, Boston College Center for Work & Family

"Most parents are taught to believe that a balanced life is a foolish dream. Lisa Levey wisely and warmly shows us the truth: that balance can be a practical and joyful reality for both parents. Bravo."

Marc and Amy Vachon, authors, *Equally Shared Parenting*

"Written in an engaging and informative manner, *The Libra Solution* speaks directly to many of the work and work-life issues that stymie women's advancement in the workplace. The heart of Levey's message is that men and women need to break out of tradition-bound and highly gendered ideas of success at home and at work so that all employees can have the opportunity to develop themselves as workers, partners, and parents."

Rosalind C. Barnett, Senior Scientist,
Women's Studies Research Center, Brandeis University,
co-author, *The Truth about Girls and Boys:
Challenging Toxic Stereotypes about Our Children*

"The author unflinchingly confronts a central work-life conundrum: the eerie sound of silence generated by talented workers everywhere who do what it takes to make their employers successful, yet balk at exerting their individual and collective power to negotiate reasonable rules of engagement at work. Levey's prescription of the Libra Solution as an actionable path out of this global dilemma is a bold, well-reasoned antidote. Bold, because it requires the courage to answer the most important questions that frame a meaningful life, like how much is enough? Antidote, because she has assembled an impressive array of evidence that reveals a brighter future: Libra workers are as good for business as they are for themselves, their families and communities."

Kathie Lingle, Executive Director,
Alliance for Work-Life Progress @ WorldatWork

"Written with common sense and optimism, *The Libra Solution* provides realistic models for prioritizing marriage and enjoying family time while recognizing that both parents need to provide economic stability for their children. A must read for couples, and for corporations who want to attract and retain top-notch talent."

Deborah Swiss, author, *Women and the Work/Family Dilemma*

The Libra Solution

Shedding Excess and Redefining Success at Work and at Home

Lisa D'Annolfo Levey

Baudin Press

The Libra Solution: Shedding Excess and Redefining Success at Work and at Home
Copyright © 2012 by Lisa D'Annolfo Levey.

All rights reserved. No part of this book may be used or reproduced in any manner whatsoever without permission from the publisher and copyright owner, except in the case of brief abstracts in articles or critical reviews.

First publishing, February 2012
Cover design and photography: Alicia Jylkka
Content editor: Jill Parsons Stern
Copy editor: Chip Cheek

Quotes without specific attribution are drawn from interview transcripts based on research conducted by the author for this book. In vignettes of women and men based on the author's interviews, small details have been altered in some cases to maintain anonymity.

For information, contact:
Baudin Press
440 Massachusetts Avenue
Lexington, MA 02420
www.baudinpress.com

ISBN 0-9839-8260-0
Library of Congress Control Number: 2011961693

Printed in the United States of America

For my mother, who never had the chance to live her dreams, and who will never know how prophetic her frequent reminders of *everything in moderation* would be in my thinking and in my life.

For Bryan, my deepest thanks for being a full partner in the juggle of life, raising children and managing careers. You inspire me every day and I feel so grateful to have you in my life.

For all the women and men balancing careers and parenting, trying to raise strong and resilient children, trying to create and live in egalitarian marriages that are deeply rewarding, and trying to leave the world a better place than when they came.

CONTENTS

INTRODUCTION	1
1. THE NEW "*PROBLEM WITH NO NAME*"	19
2. UNPACKING THE PROBLEM	27
3. SHE SAYS, HE SAYS: THE SELF-REINFORCING CYCLE OF GENDER	53
4. HOW WE WORK: DELUSIONS OF PRODUCTIVITY	91
5. WOMEN AND WORK: BEYOND WORK-LIFE CONFLICT	125
6. EXTREME PARENTING AND THE NEW FAMILY NORMS	153
7. THE LIBRA WORK AND LIFE MODEL IS THE SOLUTION	189
8. THE BENEFITS OF THE LIBRA APPROACH	213
9. BALANCE REDEFINED: FOCUS ON WHAT WORKS	253
ACKNOWLEDGEMENTS	261
NOTES	265
REFERENCES	283
INDEX	295
ABOUT THE AUTHOR	303

INTRODUCTION

WEAVING A SOLUTION TO THE WORK AND LIFE CHALLENGE IN THE 21ST CENTURY

I'm an idealist without illusions.

---John F. Kennedy

It seems like I've been preparing to write this book my whole life. I was a kid who was always observing and trying to make sense of what I saw. I was forever trying to figure out what made people do what they did—what made them happy, what made them sad, what motivated them, what inspired them. My drive to observe and understand eventually led me to a career as an organizational consultant on women's development and advancement and work-life integration, working with some of the most successful companies in the world. The alchemy of my professional work over two decades and my own life experience as a wife and mother have given me a powerful window into the topic of work-life issues and the experience of women and men putting together the pieces of their work and life solutions.

Work-life balance is a hot topic in the twenty-first century. Our lives are full to the point of overflowing; women, and increasingly men, struggle with combining their home and work lives, and we are inundated with polarizing discussions that pit women against men, working mothers against stay-at-home mothers, and permissive parents against authoritarian parents. We are inundated with messages of the precarious state of things, with particular attention to the instability of the modern work world. Many bristle at the concept of work-life balance, defining it as a zen-like state of perfect alignment and relegating it to a naïve, unrealistic fantasy. I see things as a lot more complex and also hopeful than all that.

I believe the great majority of us are looking for a work-life solution that, although not easy, is also not out of reach. I call this solution the *Libra approach*. It is defined by engagement in work we care about—seeking to add value in our jobs and simultaneously support ourselves and our families financially—all while enabling us to honor other important priorities in our lives. The Libra work and life approach offers an alternative to the pervasive twenty-first century norm of being excessively busy, feeling overwrought and overwhelmed, and often lacking time and space for what is most meaningful in our lives. The Libra model is based on a partnership approach to marriage and raising children that frees both women and men to seek professional fulfillment *and* deep involvement with their families. In a Libra family, people have made choices in their professional lives so as to ensure space for their priorities outside of work, both men and women remain highly engaged in the care and raising of the children, and both parents consider it their long-term responsibility to contribute to the financial well-being of the family.

In this powerful, twenty-first century way of living, women and men consider the trade-offs inherent in their choices and decisions, both personal and professional. They acknowledge the importance of the marital relationship—on par with the needs of children and career—as a central anchor of the family. Men and women practicing the Libra work and life model prioritize each other and value the abundance in their lives. I believe the Libra approach is a powerful model and we can learn a great deal from the men and women who practice this approach. This book shares many of their stories.

The word *metis* is defined as the ability to see patterns in the world and to derive a gist from complex situations.[1] My innate propensity to understand how systems work—combined with my professional training and experience as a consultant and researcher—enables me to bring a systems perspective to the work-life discussion.

When I talk about a systems perspective, I mean examining the relationships between many interrelated elements that together comprise the whole, and being able to isolate different contributing factors. You might think of it like peeling back the layers of an onion.

For example, the discussion about work-life conflict typically focuses on the individual rather than the family. Nevertheless, what happens at home within the unique dynamics of each of our families is at least as influential in our drive to find effective work-life solutions as what happens at work. By the same token, a focus on finding work environments that are flexible and embrace supporting the work-life needs of employees (an entirely wonderful thing by the way) is incomplete without taking into account our individual work styles and tendencies, which profoundly impact our ability to find sustainable work-life solutions. I bring fresh thinking to the work-life discussion by bringing together many elements that typically get treated as discrete pieces rather than as the complex ecosystem they are. This book will help to unbundle much of the complexity so that you can see with far greater clarity how to create a work-life solution that allows for your professional growth and development, active involvement in the activities which bring you fulfillment, particularly raising children, and a strong and enduring partnership with your spouse.

My career has been spent driving organizational change. This book broadens my focus to include driving change at the individual—and family—level. My primary goal in writing this book has been to illuminate a unique work and life solution which is often not seen as a viable option. The Libra work and life model is all about women and men making conscious choices, architecting their own work-life scripts, finding success at work and at home, practicing moderation, and combating the deeply ingrained gender norms that limit our creativity and perceived options.

One of my primary goals in writing this book was to avoid judgment on what *the* right work and life solution is, or to add to the already rampant, polarized dialogue. About this point, I want to be emphatic. I deeply believe there is no one best work-life model for every person or every family. Work-life decisions are deeply personal and private and take into account many variables. I also believe you can never fully understand all that goes into someone's decision-making process about such important matters until you walk in their shoes. Yet my research and my own life experience have underscored the numerous benefits of the Libra model, defined by partnership, gender equality, and moderation. It enables greater fulfillment, greater connection, and greater choice. Instead of judging "one right way," this book seeks to provide inspiration and guidance for those who want to practice the Libra work and life approach in their own lives.

The book is intended to function as a springboard for thinking about the work and life balancing act with fresh eyes. It is intended to help individuals get greater clarity on what is most critical for them as they devise their unique work and life solution. It is intended to promote discussion and conversation among couples—those planning for children in the future as well as those currently raising children—which will assist them in developing a joint work and life vision. It is intended to help women and men consider changes in how they integrate their work and personal lives that will bring them greater satisfaction and assist in their efforts to build strong, resilient marriages and families. The book is intended to provide "uncommon sense"—meaning it will explore and challenge many unexamined, current-day norms and assumptions that define our choices and our lives.

The Libra approach is laced with a combination of idealism and pragmatism. This mindset provides a compass for keeping your aspirational goals in mind while simultaneously dealing with the day-to-day realities of life in the modern world. Let me illustrate the many threads—both professional and personal—which have informed my thinking on work and life integration, gender issues, and the creation of the Libra work and life solution.

The First Thread: The Legacy of Family and the Surprising Gift of Adversity

My experience of growing up in a large and complicated family system has profoundly impacted my thinking. I am one of seven children from a Catholic Irish/Italian family. My parents split up when I was three and I was the youngest child of six. My father then went on to remarry and I have one younger brother from that marriage.

The only memory I have of my parents being together on purpose—as opposed to when they had to pick us up or drop us off—was when I was about eight or nine years old and my mother and I were grocery shopping at a local shopping center in my town. We bumped into my father in the parking lot and the three of us got an ice cream at a Brigham's nearby. I don't remember specifics about what was said or how long it lasted or what flavor of ice cream I ordered, but I do remember the feeling of us being together—me with both my mother and father—and what an unusual experience that was in my life.

Perhaps this is why I wasn't a little girl who spent a lot of time thinking about getting married. I didn't think I wouldn't get married—or that I would—I just didn't think about it that much one way or another. What I did think a lot about was how I could get a good education so that I could be financially independent. In my family of origin it always seemed to me that financial independence went hand in hand with power and control, and to me, that meant choice. My mother was born in a generation—and in a situation—where she never got to live or to even understand her dreams. She seemed forever overwhelmed with the clearly very difficult job of trying to raise and care for six children. I knew that I wanted not only to figure out my dreams but also to help others figure out theirs.

My father's parents were Italian immigrants, and like many children from that experience, my father saw education as the road to success and emphatically stressed its importance. I was a natural student and education became my conduit, my way to open doors and get a window into a bigger world. There was much about my early years that was difficult and that I would not necessarily want to repeat, but at the same time I will forever feel like much of the adversity in my younger life was a precious gift. It enabled me never to take things for granted, to work hard for what I believed in, and to understand diversity in a visceral way, not as an academic concept but as a way of being in the world.

The Second Thread: Learning the Customs in a Foreign Land

I was an economics major in college partly because I was a girl who was "good in math" and partly because my father told me it would be good preparation for a business career. I was a very hard-working student and had excellent grades, so I was chosen by several investment banks to be on their interview schedules when they came to the Cornell University campus. I didn't really know what I wanted to do career-wise, and getting a good job in commercial banking or the investment field seemed like as good a choice as any. After one of the recruiters asked with a clear sense of swagger how I felt about working hundred-hour weeks, I declined my other investment banking interviews, thinking even then that the machismo seemed ridiculous and unnecessary. I eventually joined the investment subsidiary of a large insurance company and used my technical and financial expertise to model complex financial instruments that I could no longer describe today—unless I did some brushing up. My next position, in my midtwenties, was working as a research analyst for the CEO of a boutique investment management firm analyzing capital market data, helping to design a new investment product for the firm, and managing a several-million-dollar investment portfolio. My last investment stop before changing careers was with a major mutual fund company.

My interest in observing systems followed me into my early career in the investment field, where I was as intrigued by the way people treated each other—who had power and what got rewarded—as I was with the substance of my research and portfolio management work. I felt like some of the environments I worked in were truly toxic; the emphasis on posturing, the tendency to hoard information, and the theatrics around being seen as "someone important" struck me as counterproductive to getting the job done. In order to still be at their desks at six or seven p.m., when the big boss would walk the floor, people would waste time during the day, only to be frantically busy when I expected them to be thinking of heading home. I never minded working late if needed, but these shell games that people played with their time seemed disingenuous, if not detrimental, to them, their colleagues, and the firm.

In my early career in investment management, it was not unusual for people to be publicly humiliated in meetings. I didn't like the way women were treated, sometimes in disparaging and disrespectful ways. The mostly male portfolio managers seemed to talk down to women in marketing and other non-technical roles and there were occasional comments about more senior women who had slept their way to the top. At one organization where I worked, it was rumored that one of the few women portfolio managers had left because she had a nervous breakdown. I don't know any of the facts, but based on the way I saw people were treated, it certainly seemed in the realm of possibility.

My values conflict continued to grow until one business trip helped crystallize my frustrations. I was attending a conference to demonstrate an investment model that I had helped develop. I was asked by my manager—a woman—to go to the airport and collect the luggage for a company executive who needed his bags (two of which turned out to be golf bags) for a major client event that evening. I was in disbelief. I was indignant. I asked myself, Is this why I worked so hard in college and business school: to run errands? As I've thought about this incident with the hindsight of many years, I've often wondered if a man would have experienced this request in the same way. Would he have seen it as a personal affront, or as an opportunity to connect with this executive about a hobby? All I know for sure is that it reinforced for me as a young woman early in her career that this industry was not a place I wanted to be.

In addition to the challenges I saw and experienced around being a woman, there was another equally important issue at hand. Despite doing a highly competent job and getting excellent feedback, I couldn't deny that this wasn't work that mattered deeply to me. I had a male colleague who clearly felt great joy and interest following the constant permutations of the markets. For me the market permutations just weren't all that exciting and I couldn't see myself doing this work for the next several decades of my life. The problem was I didn't know what I wanted to do.

The Third Thread: Finding Work I Loved

The inspiration came one day when I saw an article, "A New Vision of Corporate America," in the *Boston Sunday Globe Magazine*. The article highlighted Lotte Bailyn, a professor of organization studies at the Sloan School of Management at the Massachusetts Institute of Technology, and Fran Rodgers, an entrepreneur whose company Work/Family Directions consulted with organizations to help them support the work-life issues of their employees. These two women spent their days trying to make the corporate world a better place for women—and men. I was hooked—this was what I wanted to do.

Until that moment, I thought that the way to succeed in a career was to choose a path and follow it. From training programs, to the listings in my college and graduate school career-office job binders, to plotting my next step for advancement in financial services because "that's where the jobs were," my career vision was linear and my creativity greatly lacking. I had not considered stepping off the beaten path. Reading the article inspired me. I saw that the job market was wider than I had imagined, and, more important, people actually got paid for doing work that was meaningful to me. As I think back, it is particularly ironic that I had not made this connection before. I attended the Simmons School of Management, a business school that trains women leaders and has developed a reputation for principled leadership, attracting students interested in social aspects of management such as ethics. At the time, my attraction to Simmons was far simpler than principled leadership; I was looking for a different experience than my undergraduate years. Many business schools—at least in the late 1980s, when I was contemplating this next step—were filled with people like me, a few years outside of college, many with backgrounds in financial services and consulting and expecting to return to these industries. Most were men.

The average age of students at Simmons was older—about thirty-three at the time—and the women harkened from a broad range of backgrounds and professions. I remember discussing in class one day a case study about marketing birth control to women in Bangladesh. It turned out one of my former classmates had direct experience with this issue prior to business school, having done health care planning with women in developing countries. I loved that diversity.

In the early 1990s, I decided I wanted to find a way to combine my interest in women in business with my experience in investment management and forge a new career. I began to research the work-life field in earnest. I read, I called people, I did informational interviews galore. I took an unpaid internship where I researched and reported on the appalling state of pay and benefits for child care workers in the U.S.

The Fourth Thread: Making the Work Environment Better for Women and Men

I was hired as a researcher on a gender-issues study for one of the major Wall Street investment banks. It was the perfect way to bring together my deep understanding of the investment field and blend that with my desire to better understand gender and work-life issues in organizations. One of my strongest memories was the incredible well of emotion that was tapped during focus groups with women at the investment bank. They were angry. They were frustrated. They had so much to say. Once they got in the room, they didn't want to stop talking and they seemed to feel great comfort in being with other women discussing these issues and feeling heard.

I became the lead writer on the client report for the investment bank. I was elated. Here I was, being paid in my day job to do what I did so naturally throughout my investment career, noticing how people were experiencing their work environments. After nearly two years of networking and doing contract project work, I finally got my dream job as an associate consultant in the consulting arm of Work/Family Directions, the same company highlighted in the *Boston Globe* article. I did extensive employee research during my several years at Work/Family Directions (eventually renamed WFD). It was a great privilege and a powerful learning experience to listen to men and women talk candidly about putting together the pieces of their home and work lives.

Our research helped clients answer questions about their workforce and the family characteristics of their employees. We looked at how employees experienced their work environment and what they needed to be successful in integrating their work and home lives. We studied the business implications of work-life issues for the organization, and analyzed the differences and similarities in how different groups of employees experienced the organization. We asked employees questions about what first brought them to the organization and what would make them stay or would make them leave. We asked them what behaviors were rewarded in their workplace, how supportive managers were regarding work-life issues, how much control they believed they had over their work, and what got in the way of being effective in their jobs. Finally we asked workers what they thought would help in removing obstacles to their efficiency and satisfaction.

I spoke to hundreds of employees in one-on-one interviews and employee focus groups and easily surveyed thousands, building a wealth of knowledge in identifying macro trends that applied across many organizations and represented hundreds of thousands of employees. At this point I was in my early to midthirties and I was having far greater appreciation for the role of gender in the lives of women and men. Like many women of my age, I had gone through college feeling as though gender was a nonissue, the world was the same for men and women of my generation, and that the women's movement had removed whatever barriers women might have faced in earlier times. Now, I was finding out that things were not that simple by a long shot.

I was also discovering the impact of work-life issues on people's lives and families. Men and women talked about the need for their families to be invisible at work. They talked about wanting to advance in their careers but being worried about the additional time away from their families that greater responsibility would require. They shared their concerns that many of the people they managed were at risk of getting completely burned out because they were so driven and would try and continue at an unsustainable pace.

Women talked about the guilt they felt when they had to work late. Younger women without children would often comment about not knowing how they could possibly do their job and manage the additional responsibility of having children. Men talked about the toll work took on their family lives, commenting, "My spouse thinks I am married to my job," and, "I worry that I am missing precious time with my children." Both men and women talked about the great difficulty of trying to juggle it all, the unrelenting and potentially debilitating pressure to drive results, and the potential of long hours to ruin families.

I joined Catalyst in 2000, becoming a director in the Advisory Services group in 2001. Catalyst is a prestigious research and advisory organization with a long history of supporting women at work. Founded in 1962 by a visionary woman named Felice Schwartz, their initial focus was on helping women enter the workforce. In the early 1970s, Schwartz published a book titled *How to Go to Work When Your Husband Is Against It, Your Children Aren't Old Enough, and There's Nothing You Can Do Anyhow*. By the 1980s Catalyst had changed its focus from providing services for individual women to partnering with organizations in helping them create work environments that better suited the changing workforce, including increasing numbers of women and minorities.

My work at Catalyst involved continued employee research, with a greater focus on advancement issues, and I began to develop a particular expertise understanding the work cultures and business models of professional service firms such as law and accounting firms. The issues were very similar to those I had seen at the investment bank a decade earlier, when I was first entering the work-life field.

At Catalyst, I would often work with groups of employees to help them drive culture change in their organizations. For example, women leaders at a client company would seek assistance from Catalyst in determining how they could act as change agents and improve the situation for all women in their organizations. I would meet with the group and help them clarify the salient issues they were trying to address and what role they could, and should, play to have the greatest impact. A cornerstone of Catalyst's consulting work is a focus on efficacy—how to be strategic and streamlined—while determining what would drive substantive and lasting change. This perspective greatly informed my work with clients.

I became very involved with, and eventually led, the network consulting practice at Catalyst. Employee networks are a means for people from a particular dimension of diversity—such as gender, race, or sexual orientation—to come together, learn from one another, and help collectively influence the work environment. For example, a women's network might initiate and provide input on the design and development of a new women's leadership mentoring program in their organization, or members of a gay and lesbian network might participate in a panel discussion helping to educate others at work about particular challenges for gay and lesbian employees. Another core piece of my consulting became working with leaders at Catalyst's member companies, basically a who's who of the Fortune 1000 and leading professional service firms, to help them understand their role in creating work cultures that promoted work-life effectiveness, or WLE. We defined WLE as simultaneously benefiting employees *and* the business by identifying practical solutions that allow strong performance over the long term.

It was fascinating to have conversations with senior executives, with employees of both genders, and particularly with women at every level in the organization about the work-life conflicts they faced, their approach to integrating their work and personal lives, and what messages about work-life priorities were communicated in their organizations.

During my many years at Catalyst, I worked with numerous clients to help them drive change in their organizations, and felt that in so doing, I was playing my small part in helping to create the world Catalyst's vision statement describes: "Catalyst seeks a world that supports and encourages every woman in her career aspirations and places no limits on where her skills and energy can take her."

The Fifth Thread: Marrying and Becoming a Parent

Serendipitously in 2010—at which time I was writing this book—I celebrated my twentieth wedding anniversary. I met and married my husband, Bryan, in my midtwenties. I laugh when I think about my many incorrect assumptions upon first getting to know him. He was three years older than I, just old enough to start having that grown-up and slightly settled feeling that seems a world away for most of us at twenty-four. He owned his own condo, managed more than thirty people at a high-tech company, and drove an Audi. I jumped to the conclusion that he was a yuppie (remember that term—the young, upwardly mobile professional?) and thus not my type. But as I got to know him, it became clearer and clearer that my snap judgments were not on target.

The car in particular has made us chuckle for all these years. I assumed Bryan bought the car as a status symbol, but what I later came to find out was that he bought the car because it was a deal, a discontinued model that was discounted by several thousand dollars. My bias that he must be a workaholic, as evidenced by his very responsible job at a reasonably young age and the fact that he was more than half an hour late for our first date because a work meeting had run long, was also wrong. He had joined a small high-tech company after college. The company was growing quickly and Bryan's good work and dedication brought opportunity and increasing responsibility. I later came to understand that he, like many of us early in our careers, spent most of his time at work because that's where his friends were and that's where his social life was. But as we continued to date and became a couple, it was clear to see that I was a priority in his life, too.

By the way, I didn't expect him not to work hard, but I was clear that I wasn't willing to always be on the short side of work. When Bryan was making his toast at our wedding, his manager at the time was in attendance and Bryan proceeded to say, "When I met Lisa, I was always at work because that was what I did with my time, but since being together, I am working less because I have somewhere else I want to be." We joked that it was a good thing he didn't get fired with his boss listening from the front row. In all seriousness, it reinforced yet again that our relationship was a priority in his life.

We were married for several years before we even thought about having children. When we got married, I was ambivalent about whether I ever wanted to have children. I was focused on growing in my career—even as it was becoming clear the investment field was not my lifetime stop. More important, I was concerned about wanting to—or more accurately, being able to—handle the intensity of raising children. Having lived through some difficult childhood years and having seen my mother overwhelmed with the clearly challenging job of raising six children, I was very unsure about taking that seemingly enormous step. A few things were really clear to me. One was that I would not become a parent until I felt like I had worked through some of my own stuff and could bring much stronger skills to the job than I knew I had at twenty-six. Another was, if we had children, we would be partners in this endeavor—through and through—because I knew I needed that support to be effective and happy as a parent.

As part of my preparation for writing this book, I interviewed Bryan with my research hat on (and a glass of wine in hand). I told him that in retrospect, I was surprised he was willing to marry me knowing I might not ever want to have children. For me, his response was profound. He said that he had hoped I would change my mind as I grew older because he was worried that if he never had a child, he might feel like he missed out on something really important. I asked, "Would you have wanted to get divorced if it had become clear that I did not want to have children?" He said, "No, because even if I got married to someone else and had children, it's not like I wouldn't have lost something equally important—my relationship with you."

I was thirty-three when I had our first son, Skylar, and our second son, Forrest, was born when I was thirty-six—what I came to know was referred to as advanced maternal age! Raising my sons over the last fourteen years with my husband as my copilot has given me countless opportunities to learn, and grow, and figure out what it means to be in a partnership marriage that makes space for work, children, love, and me. Bryan and I are the youngest in our sibling groups, and our parents are older than many of our peers' parents, so elder care has long been a part of our juggling act.

I always thought I would have daughters, because four of my six siblings are female and all of Bryan's and my siblings were parents of girls when we started having children. The XX chromosome seemed deep in our family's DNA profile. I always imagined I would share all I had learned through my own life experiences as part and parcel of raising wise and strong and competent daughters. What I've come to believe is that raising sons is an important part of my journey as I ponder gender equality and think about new work-life models. What I know is that one of my greatest life goals is to raise sons who grow into caring, thoughtful, and responsible men who embody gender equality in their thinking and in their actions. Men who will become the kinds of fathers, husbands, and leaders at work that we need more of in the world.

Tony Schwartz, one of the sons of Catalyst founder Felice Schwartz, came to speak to the Catalyst staff about how his research on world-class athletes applied to—as he called them—corporate athletes, or managers and executives trying to deliver great performance over time. His work has been very effective with men who respond far more to the concept of a corporate athlete than to the language of work-life balance. As Tony talked about being a little boy sitting at the dinner table while his mother was formulating her ideas for what would become Catalyst, I imagined the power of him hearing those discussions and those ideals as he was in the process of forming his own. My hope is that both my work and the road that my husband and I are walking together will play an important role in raising sons who believe in and demonstrate shared responsibility and equality.

A few years ago, when my son Skylar was nine, Drew Gilpin Faust was named president of Harvard University. One day I pointed out to Bryan that the presidents of the Massachusetts Institute of Technology and Harvard were both women and what an incredible milestone this was for someone like me, having grown up in the Boston area and long aware of the power of education. During this discussion Skylar, playing nearby—yet apparently listening to the conversation—turned to me and gave an emphatic thumbs-up. That small gesture became a special moment where I thought that maybe, just maybe, my goal of raising feminist sons was on its way to being realized.

Over the course of my consulting career, I have been very fortunate to work in environments where work-life integration was obviously a priority. As a management consultant doing sophisticated and demanding work, managing clients and deadlines—often on the road—I have had probably every work arrangement under the sun. I've telecommuted, worked reduced workloads at 60, 80, and 90 percent, been employed full-time, and worked remotely from another state. Through it all, I have consciously used my own life as a mother, wife, and businesswoman as a testing ground for what I was espousing in my consulting. For me, authenticity is nonnegotiable, and if I was going to consult about work-life issues, women's advancement, and diversity, I was going to do my very best to live them in my own life. At times it worked exquisitely, and at other times not so well. Luckily I believe in continuous improvement and have used the opportunities to retest and refine what I was learning.

The Final Thread: Framing and Naming a Unique Work-Life Model

Along my journey of consulting on work-life issues, I met Jessica DeGroot, founder of ThirdPath Institute, who gave a name (shared care) and frame to the way Bryan and I had been seeking to set up our lives. We met at a major work-life conference, both asking questions of the speakers and panelists that revealed a different way of approaching the work-life conversation. Our questions referenced the role of men both at work and at home and a work-life model where both parents were very involved with the care of the family as well as with pursuing their professional goals and dreams. Jessica founded ThirdPath Institute soon after this conference in the early 2000s with the stated goal of helping individuals and organizations in making more time for life. It was in my conversations with her that I was able to articulate the work-life approach that I had been following. Her work continues to inspire and inform mine.

The Libra Approach: Women and Men Writing New Work and Life Scripts for the 21st Century

This book pulls together key threads—early life experiences, formative career experiences working in a male-dominated field, years of research and consulting, and my own very personal story of being a working parent in a dual-career marriage and a member of the sandwich generation, raising children while simultaneously managing elder care responsibilities.

These threads are not only part of my story, but also part of the stories of many other couples and families who have and are seeking to construct a more sustainable and more fulfilling work and life approach. The Libra model aims to ensure that both men and women are able to pursue both their professional and their personal goals, prime among them to be intimately involved with raising their children. The Libra model includes making the marital relationship a priority so it can endure long past the child-rearing years, and it includes a focus on the individual that allows for continuous personal growth and fulfillment in areas that matter most for each person.

Stories throughout this book, of women and men practicing the Libra approach, come from multiple sources. I conducted in-depth interviews with dozens of men and women over more than eighteen months. I conducted a discussion with a father's group that met monthly for more than twenty years, beginning in the late 1970s, from when their children were newborns until they were young adults, and I connected with a father's group that started in 2008 and has swelled from a handful to several hundred members. Some of the stories come from written profiles published by ThirdPath Institute, as well as ThirdPath teleconferences, of men and women pursuing a highly shared approach to parenting and seeking to ensure space for their lives outside of work. The book also references many research studies of men and women in dual-career marriages.

This book shares what I have learned throughout my consulting career working with organizations that are leaders in their industries, as well as those identified as among the best companies to work for in the U.S. and the world. I've conducted secondary research on a wide range of related topics including feminism, parenting, marital trends, work design and productivity, among others. I hope you find the book rigorous and provocative. Mostly I hope the book is a vital resource for helping you craft your very best twenty-first century work and life solution.

CHAPTER 1

THE NEW "PROBLEM WITH NO NAME"

And when women and men think, the first step in progress is taken.

---Elizabeth Cady Stanton

In the late 1950s Betty Friedan attended her college reunion at Smith College and conducted a survey of fellow alumna, inquiring about their post-college experiences and their satisfaction with their lives. She started writing about what she called "the problem with no name." This research was eventually expanded and became the core of her extraordinarily successful 1963 book, *The Feminine Mystique*, a revolutionary wake-up call that many say ushered in the second wave of the women's movement (the first being women getting the right to vote in the 1920s). In the beginning of the book, Friedan described "the problem that has no name":

> The problem lay buried, unspoken, for many years in the minds of American women. It was a strange stirring, a sense of dissatisfaction, a yearning (that is, a longing) that women suffered in the middle of the 20th century in the United States. Each suburban wife struggled with it alone. As she made the beds, shopped for groceries ... she was afraid to ask even of herself the silent question—"Is this all?"[1]

Fast-forward nearly fifty years, and the debate about women and work rages on. Despite great progress, women continue to struggle mightily with finding a way to combine their professional ambitions and family aspirations in ways that feel satisfying and sustainable. Younger women contemplating their futures worry about their ability to "do it all," and many women with children continue to feel pushed to make a choice between paid work and family. Fifty years after Betty Friedan's book, a woman's rightful role in the workplace and at home remain highly controversial.

Added to the equation is the confusion about the changing role of men relative to work and home. Men want to be involved fathers but they feel the incredible pull of the provider role. Many men are conflicted about not wanting to fully shoulder the economic load as the only or primary wage earner, but our deep cultural biases about men as providers allow virtually no forum for that conversation. Men also struggle with conventional work demands that don't allow them to be the parents they want to be, and those who walk a different path—assuming the more primary parent role—remain in the margins, fighting for a place in a still deeply mother-centric parenting world.

Media headlines capture (and contribute to) the collective angst about women's and men's ambitions, desires, and roles at work and at home. A series of stories, kicked off by the *New York Time*s article "The Opt-Out Revolution" in the fall of 2003, heralded a return to a focus on home and family among highly educated and talented women. The *Washington Post* highlighted "The Mommy War Machine," emphasizing the divide between working and stay-at-home mothers. The *Atlantic*'s cover story in the summer of 2010 trumpeted "The End of Men" and questioned whether postindustrial society was simply better suited to women. The *Wall Street Journal* brought us "Why Chinese Mothers are Superior," highlighting a highly disciplined approach to raising talented and high-achieving children, a trend story soon refuted in another *Journal* article, "In Defense of the Guilty, Ambivalent, Preoccupied Western Mom."

While the 1970s heralded an era of exploring gender roles and questioning long-held norms, in the new millennium, gender roles can seem part of an academic or quaint discussion rather than a central tenet of how men and women live their lives. In the 1970s and 1980s, managerial and professional couples were the most likely to share family work, however by the 1990s and 2000s, the most change—and sometimes the most sharing—occurred among couples with blue collar or pink collar jobs.[2] Many young women bristle at the label "feminist," and men, who by all accounts are playing a more active role at home than their fathers ever did, are now feeling more of the work-life stress that working women have felt for years.

While younger men and women may say they want egalitarian marriages, they lack the confidence to make them a reality in their lives. In a study of more than 120 men and women aged eighteen to thirty-two who were raised in a wide variety of family structures, including dual-earner, traditional, and single-parent families, the large majority, no matter their childhood experience, identified an egalitarian marriage as their ideal.[3] The women in the research identified their fallback position as eschewing marriage and children if it meant they would need to return to more traditional roles. For the men, their fallback plan—if they were not able to achieve their egalitarian ideal—was a more traditional model whereby, while their wife would work outside the home, his career would be primary, and she would assume the lead role in caring for the family.[4]

Despite women's rising tide of accomplishment and despite men's rising involvement at home, we still deeply question even the possibility of creating a work-life solution that enables meaningful work and deep family involvement for both women *and* men. Feminists never envisioned the definition of success as women (or men) having to make a Solomon-like choice between a complete work focus or a complete home focus. The real goal of the women's movement was to transform workplaces and gender roles—not simply to create black and white, either-or alternatives. The real goal was to break the gender shackles and allow women and men to devise more creative, more flexible, and better solutions to live full and meaningful lives.

Has Betty Friedan's "problem with no name" been resolved? I would argue yes—and no. Women have been able to identify their dissatisfaction and the desire to contribute professionally as well as in their roles as wives and mothers. Across the last several decades, women have stormed into the workforce with the goal of having it all, intent on professional and personal satisfaction. Yet the solution—combining professional achievement with raising children—has spawned a new struggle, with women supposedly *able* to have it all, yet feeling a similar yearning, a similar dissatisfaction and discontent that they battle to understand. As men have increasingly identified far more strongly with their role as caretakers, and attempted to integrate this new vision into their role as providers, they too have begun to viscerally experience the struggle.

And so, half a century later, we face the *new* problem with no name. There are two core pieces to this problem that cannot be divorced from one another:

- *The gravitational pull of gender.* This force pulls couples—most with the best intentions of equality—to quickly and precipitously slip into highly stereotypical gender roles once they have children. As mothers' and fathers' lives diverge, the sense of equality is lost and many marriages weaken through time.
- *The frenetic new normal.* There is a collective sense of powerlessness—and a resultant perceived inability—to wrest control of our lives from the seemingly endless demands swirling around us. The intensity of work leads the way for men and women in professional roles, with or without children. For parents, the extra layers of demand and strain drive them to feel continually on edge, drained, overwhelmed, and unable to manage it all.

These underlying paradigm shifts are formidable obstacles, but we can address them by starting to ask new questions, by taking a new approach. We can pull apart the threads of the "new problem" and examine and name each one to gain clarity and energy in determining how we want to shape our lives. By evaluating many pervasive norms and hidden assumptions that perpetuate gender roles and profoundly influence how we work, how we parent, and how we live in the twenty-first century, this book will help you follow an alternative work and life model—the Libra approach—that enables greater fulfillment, more choice, and more flexibility. The Libra approach assumes a long view and enables women and men to write new work and life scripts that reflect their most deeply held priorities. The Libra mindset engenders sustainability, intentionality and appreciation, and supports people, not in "having it all," but in having *the best of it all.*

For most couples, the tipping point in needing to acknowledge the impact of the problem with no name comes when they decide to have a child. Having a child is a critical inflection point with implications for your career, your finances, your priorities, and your relationships. Becoming a parent brings with it a whole series of adaptations, and it can be a game changer in a couple's relationship, for good or ill. Several decades of research have discovered a decline in marital satisfaction after the birth of a first child and subsequent smaller declines over the next several years. Researchers from the University of California at Berkeley found that the reduction in marital satisfaction was nearly totally explained by lack of planning, extreme ambivalence about parenthood, and men or women going forward with having a child despite never coming to clear agreement as a couple. Strikingly, they found that among couples in which one of the parents did not want to have a child but went forward anyway, *all* of them were no longer together by the time the child reached kindergarten.[5] The good news is that thinking and talking with your partner about what having children will mean in your lives goes a long way in helping you better prepare for and adapt to this joyous and challenging change. By the way, among the highest levels of marital satisfaction are those reported by spouses living together in their later years, many having deepened their bond through the experience of raising a family together.[6]

During the period of time leading up to having a baby, couples are flooded with information. They receive information about childbirth and the care of the baby in the first year or two of his or her life. Women receive information about taking a maternity leave or getting back into shape after the baby. Men get the jokes about the impending lack of sleep and sex but little useful information about finding support to adapt to this critical new role in their lives or about the particulars and considerations of taking a paternity leave.

But where are the resources to help couples think through the big questions that will redefine their new life *together* as parents? There are important questions to consider, independently and in partnership, questions like how can you combine your old life with a whole new set of responsibilities as a parent? How will being a parent change your relationship and your marriage? How are your choices about income and work-life solutions related? What is most critical to help you feel strong and able to meet the growing demands of your family? The goal is not to have all the answers but to start asking the questions and for each new parent to start a dialogue about his or her real hopes and dreams, concerns and worries. This conversation is the beginning of one you will have many times and in many ways as you design the solution that is right for your family.

When, as a younger woman, I was contemplating how my husband and I would combine parenting and work, I was struck that none of the choices on the conventional list appealed to me. To my mind they included:

- *Traditional,* with a father highly focused on work and the mother highly focused on caring for the children and managing the home;
- *Semi-traditional,* with a father highly focused on work and the mother working part-time or full-time outside the home yet still the predominant home and family manager;
- *Classic dual-career,* with both the father and mother highly career focused, struggling mightily to manage their lives outside of work.

I was looking for a fourth option, seemingly not a choice on the menu. It included both my husband and me working outside the home to jointly meet the economic needs of the family—at a more manageable pace and workload but still pursuing professional growth in careers we cared about—as well as both of us playing a central role in the care of the home and family. As a couple we would work as a team to manage it all, and intentionally slow down the velocity to enjoy these multiple roles.

This book offers that fourth option—the Libra approach to life, work, and relationships—and illuminates how we can shift our thinking and our lives in powerful, positive directions. The Libra approach is the twenty-first century work-life model for men and women wanting to write their own scripts. It is defined by greater sustainability, greater equality, and greater satisfaction. It is defined by men and women together crafting their unique work-life solution in that vast middle ground between working all the time and not working at all, between mothers do this, fathers do that, and everything needs to be split precisely down the middle. Instead couples define, and redefine, roles based on skills and life goals, evaluating, strategizing, calibrating, and recalibrating as they move together through the weeks, months, and years.

Women and men are searching for something different— another way to put together the puzzle pieces of their lives—but they lack a roadmap and they don't know how to get from here to there. This book will show you how it is possible to create lives characterized by both satisfying work and deep family involvement, prove that it is possible for couples to model a strong and enduring partnership for their children that grows and deepens rather than erodes through time, and help you to take back control of your life by creating time and space for what energizes and strengthens you, even in the midst of so many demands.

While the provocative headlines swing us from one extreme to the other, behind the drama, behind all the fuss, there are the many quiet, untold stories. They are the stories of men and women who are finding their way, who are breaking the shackles of gender, who are creating time for their families and their work and their lives, and who are living their lives in a way that many say can't be done. While we seem to be stuck in the old scripts, there are many powerful journeys of men and women finding a new way through the work-life gauntlet. This book shares many of their stories.

This book will help you understand the challenges that come together and drive us toward highly gendered norms and overextended lives. It will explore how these forces profoundly impact our perceived options and choices, and most importantly, it will illuminate an alternative, the Libra solution. You will come to understand the abundant benefits of the Libra work-life model—for individuals, for couples, for children, and for workplaces. Through the real-life experiences of men and women, you will come to deeply understand this work-life model and see how obstacles to living a Libra life can be recognized, managed, and overcome.

When you look back on your life—as a professional, as a parent, and as part of a couple—in five years, ten years, twenty years, you should not be left with the vague question that is the hallmark of the *new problem with no name*: "How did I get here?" Following the Libra approach will enable you to say with satisfaction, "I have played a key role in creating the life I always wanted."

CHAPTER 2

UNPACKING THE PROBLEM

Perplexity is the beginning of knowledge.

---Kahlil Gibran

Lisa Belkin, a long-term writer on work-life issues and the originator of the Motherlode blog, remarked in a February 2010 radio show, "What's fascinating is that even couples who state [equality] as their goal find themselves having to knock their heads up against obstacles that they didn't realize were going to be there." She goes on to say, "They insist they will be more equal ... They insist they will not sell their souls for work ... We'll have to wait and see if life gets in the way."[1]

Despite improvements, when it comes to how parents spend their time, the division of labor remains skewed, with women continuing to do a disproportionate share of the housework and child care, even in dual-earner families where both parents work full-time, and men consistently registering longer hours at work.[2] Research among nearly 1,000 fathers of children under age eighteen highlights the disconnect between aspirations and reality, with nearly two-thirds indicating both parents *should* provide equal amounts of care for their children and less than a third reporting this was actually the case in their households.[3] Mothers in dual-career households have the least leisure time of women or men in any family configuration, and time for leisure pursuits decline as education increases, for both men and women.[4] Men spend more time in the paid labor force, working longer hours on average than women, with the gender difference increasing when men and women become parents.[5] According to a nationally representative sample, fathers worked 47 hours per week, men without children reported 44 hours on average, while women, whether or not they lived with children, reported working between 40 and 41 hours weekly at their jobs.[6] The sense that working parents are fighting to keep up with all the demands coming at them is pervasive. In her book *Mind in the Making*, Ellen Galinsky reports, "When I asked a group of parents to describe how they felt about 'life these days,' many used images of floods—of sinking, feeling overwhelmed, finding it hard to come up for air or to think clearly when there's such an onrush of everything to do."

Why is this paradox so persistent? Why do women and men wanting and fully intending to create egalitarian marriages revert, a few short years and a child or two later, to highly gendered norms that seemed out of the question earlier in their lives? And why, despite clearly articulating a desire for greater balance in their lives, do so many parents push themselves to their very edge, a life filled with so many commitments and yet so little joy?

A confluence of powerful forces—gender norms, the way we work, the way we live, the things we fear, and the resignation that things will never change—has given rise to a modern-day tidal wave that pushes us toward a life of constant busyness. Once we have children, that wave sweeps us into highly gendered roles. Lacking the perspective that allows us to recognize the approaching tidal wave and therefore intentionally make different choices and decisions, we are, more often than not, swept up in the powerful cultural currents.

Being able to surf the wave, rather than be swept along with it, means using strategies that will set you up for success as you seek to be engaged professionals and parents as well as to purposely ratchet down the intensity. It also involves questioning some deeply entrenched assumptions that may obscure the real story of how we work and live at the beginning of the twenty-first century. This chapter unpacks the modern-day problem with no name and explores the forces that individually and collectively lead us down a road that we never intended to travel.

Gender Norms: Powerful and Pervasive

In the personal versus the professional sphere, I first noticed how gendered things were when I started planning my wedding. Bryan and I began thinking about the various decisions that needed to be considered throughout the process. While attending a bridal show, where purveyors of wedding services had set up their booths, it quickly became abundantly clear that I was the target customer. The people seemed to look past Bryan as if he were irrelevant in these decisions. Perhaps we were unusual in that we, not my mother or his mother, were planning the wedding. Nevertheless, I soon came to realize that there was enormous machinery, as relentless as a roller coaster, fueling the decisions of millions of couples on the endless details required for that "perfect day"—sarcasm intended. This was, perhaps, Bryan's first taste of having to fight for a seat at the domestic table, the way women have had to fight for a seat at the conference-room table for many years. Throughout the book, I will illuminate many ways in which men are not invited to the domestic table and provide ideas for how we can ensure that the domestic table remains as gender neutral as possible.

According to social science research scholars, society tends to define a good wife and mother as someone who is "nurturing," "warm and welcoming," and the person primarily responsible for the care of the children, while good husbands and fathers are first and foremost economic providers, along with acting as the "authority figure" in the household.[7] If, after a day spent at a bridal trade show, any doubt about the prevalence of gender norms still remained, living through one day as a parent in most middle-class communities would dispel that doubt. Yes, men are more likely to do drop-off or pick-up at school or at day care, and there are some men—typically few—at PTA meetings or parent education workshops, but the weight of evidence clearly shows that mothers continue to own the domestic space. They are predominantly the ones who volunteer in the classroom, organize the endless school activities, and attend the many talks and lectures on everything ranging from special education issues to stress in school to discipline.

On any newsstand, the articles on parenting are overwhelmingly targeted to women. I did a highly unscientific study and went into our nearby Barnes & Noble, one of the giant stores with a full café, children's play area, and comfy chairs scattered throughout. The store had a large magazine section, and in or next to the women's section there were fashion magazines, magazines on cooking, home decorating and gardening, and, yes, all the magazines related to parenting.

In the men's section were magazines on transportation (who knew there were so many magazines about boats, cars, and the like?), sports, pornographic and semi-pornographic magazines (e.g., *Maxim*), and *Men's Health*, which seems the closest men come to what I would call a general interest magazine. At least the *Men's Health* website brought up several articles about parenting and being a good father and even had a tab on their navigation bar titled "Family Guy"—now that's progress. I do look forward to the day when parenting magazines aren't slotted into women's interest but instead are universal for anyone playing a role in raising and caring for children. While there has been substantial progress in recent decades regarding gender roles, with fathers assuming greater responsibility at home and women having entered the workforce en masse, our ambivalence about working mothers and stay-at-home fathers and our assumptions about powerful women and nurturing men remain deeply embedded.

Research among middle school students highlights the depth and persistence of gender norms. The researchers found that while both boys and girls overwhelmingly state men and women are equal, many gendered norms remain the reality in their lives. Middle school girls were much freer to excel academically and in sports—in fact these were encouraged for many girls—yet they still indicated acute pressure to be thin and beautiful, as well as smart and strong. Sadly, middle school boys continued to struggle with highly gendered norms. They reported being teased, left out, and called gay for acting like girls in any way. Boys characterized "boy" behavior in the highly traditional ways—liking sports, being competitive, hating to lose to a girl, liking to play video games, and being rowdy. In an exercise asking the middle school students to identify which of several occupations were more likely to be held by men, women, or by both men and women, their responses were highly gendered despite their professed beliefs in equality. Gender norms may evolve but they also clearly endure.[8]

Gail Collins, a leading thinker on women's roles at work and at home, chronicled the journey of women, from the first settlers to the 1980s. In *America's Women: 400 Years of Dolls, Drudges, Helpmates and Heroines*, she highlights the degree to which gender norms are a social construction—wrought with paradox and irony—and have changed dramatically through time:

> The history of American women is about the fight for freedom, but it's less a war against oppressive men than a struggle to straighten out the perpetually mixed messages about women's roles that was accepted by almost everybody of both genders. Southern matriarchs aspired to be the image of the helpless female, then ran the plantations while their husbands went to Congress—or luxuriated at a spa. Pioneer women rode sidesaddle and wore gloves to protect their soft hands, then crawled up the side of mountains with a newborn baby in one arm. Everyone believed that married women were obliged to stay home with their children, while everyone bought factory goods produced by poor working mothers, made from cotton picked by female slaves. When slavery ended, nothing irritated white Southerners—or visiting Northerners—more than the idea that ex-slave women wanted to stop working and become homemakers.[9]

How We Work:
Changes in the Employee-Employer Value Proposition

By the time I graduated from college in the mid-1980s, the evolution from an expectation of lifetime employment to another career paradigm was well underway. I never entered the work world with the expectation of working for an organization for life—or even a very long time. When I first started my consulting career, there were numerous articles about how lifetime employment was no longer an option and work was about a mutually beneficial relationship between employers and employees for whatever period of time it lasted. While the employer-employee value proposition was once predicated on trading reasonable work and loyalty for job security and comfort during retirement years, the new value proposition was a far more transactional model predicated on trading time and skill for money and experience.

Starting in the 1980s and into the 1990s, organizations were explicitly clear that the expectation of job security was no longer part of the employment equation. Simultaneously, many of these same organizations lamented the opportunistic approach of employees—particularly younger employees—toward work. Keeping the best employees became a central business challenge. In my consulting engagements, managers would express frustration that younger employees felt entitled to raises and promotions much more quickly than in past generations. They would comment that even in the best of situations, employees would leave at the drop of a hat for a bigger paycheck or a more interesting job. Many clients would hire a diversity consultant such as me with the express goal of helping them figure out how to retain high-performing employees, particularly men of color and women.

My take was that organizations were now getting just what they had asked for. We had trained employees, particularly younger generations, to believe that longer-term employment was no longer a realistic option, and that they should expect to be in charge of their own career development. Their goal became to extract the maximum gain from the employment relationship, in both experience and pay, during whatever time they worked for an organization. I always believed that given the option, many employees, even younger ones, would choose longevity over movement, but the need to always be looking for the next thing had become the expected norm.

In the Catalyst research report *Next Generation: Today's Professionals, Tomorrow's Leaders*, men and women in their midtwenties to midthirties reported they were more likely to leave their jobs when particular conditions were not met. Of those reporting an intention to leave within three years (one third of respondents), 45 percent felt their expectations for being able to balance their work and personal lives were not met, while 47 percent indicated their expectations for advancement opportunities were not realized. Yet the study also found that nearly half of those in their midtwenties to midthirties would be happy to spend the rest of their careers with their current organizations.[10] Among nearly 1,000 fathers raising children, and ranging in age from their midtwenties to over sixty, half reported job security as an extremely important job characteristic, greater than for any other item tested including advancement, high income, and workplace flexibility.[11]

Given the nature of competition and the increasingly global world we live in, I don't expect to see a return to former notions of job security anytime soon. Employees today know that, in good times and in bad, for reasons they can control, and for reasons they cannot, job loss is a constant possibility. Like most things, there are pros and cons to this. Employees understand, to a much greater degree, the role they will need to play in shaping their career paths, and with this responsibility comes freedom and choice. On the other hand, the lack of security can exact a heavy toll. Once couples have children, the need for predictability is greatly heightened, and identifying which parent will be job-centric, focused on moving up in his or her career, making more money through time, and delivering crucial health benefits seems a prudent strategy. Furthermore, the sense of insecurity leads people to avoid, or to feel they cannot, put up boundaries at work. A consistent theme in my consulting work has been the perception that setting boundaries would negatively impact your career by making you seem less committed and thus not as deserving of advancement, as well as rendering you more vulnerable to job loss.

How We Work: The Mismatch Between Career Paths and Active Family Involvement

Among the clearest contributors to highly gendered marriages is the misalignment in the timing of careers and raising children. In two research studies conducted by Catalyst—one with attorneys and a second with women and men who had earned MBAs—results showed that approximately two-thirds of women *had not* followed the typical career path (working full-time continuously since completing graduate school) while the great majority of men had. Women attorneys were three times as likely to have worked a reduced schedule and four times as likely to have taken a leave of absence as their male colleagues.[12] A survey of women alumni of the Harvard Business School who graduated in the classes of 1981, 1985, and 1991 found that less than 40 percent were working full-time.[13] For the most highly educated women, the timing of starting to ramp up in their careers a few years after completing their graduate training is in direct conflict with the very intensive stage of raising young children.

In their book *The Career Mystique: Cracks in the American Dream*, Phyllis Moen and Patricia Roehling underscore that while both men and women continue to believe that total commitment to the job, putting in long hours, and working hard hold the best promise for advancement and maintaining job security into retirement, this model no longer fits the realities of most people's lives.[14] They describe the career mystique as "a false myth standing in the way of creating new, alternative workplace and career flexibilities."[15]

There exists a continuing disconnect between the typically linear career paths in many organizations and professions and the far more complex family structures that are relevant in this new millennium. Day-to-day flexibility is seen as permissible and available to many women and men in professional roles, but architecting new career paths—such as less than full-time work, sabbaticals and leaves, or periods of time in and out of the workforce—remains anathema to advancement in the minds of most employees. In a study of executives in U.S. corporations, over 90 percent felt they could be flexible with their schedules when they had family or personal matters to attend to, but less than one in five believed they could use a flexible work arrangement without jeopardizing their career advancement.[16] Similarly, less than a quarter of law firm associates reported believing that flexible work arrangements were a viable option for someone aspiring to the partnership.[17]

There has been much written about the "opt-out revolution"—the idea that highly educated women *choose* to stop working outside the home once they have children. Much was made of a small decline in the late 1990's in the percent of moms with children under the age of one working outside the home after the long-term increase of women's labor force participation rate over several decades.[18] The articulation of an opt-out revolution ignited fierce debate, underscoring just how strongly we all feel about doing our best on behalf of our families and thus wanting and needing to defend our personal work-life choices, whatever those might be.

Multiple research studies have challenged the notion of the opt-out revolution. A study in the June 2008 issue of the *American Sociological Review* indicated that the opt-out revolution had been overblown and that fewer than 8 percent of professional, college-educated women born since 1956 left the workforce for a year or more during their prime childbearing years.[19] Furthermore, the study indicated that women with young children were working longer hours than ever before. Researchers at the Center for Gender in Organizations at the Simmons School of Management surveyed 500 professional and managerial women in 2003 and 2004 and concluded: "The issue of mothers 'opting-out' of the workplace has been overplayed in the media. ... In contrast to the assertion of the 'Opt-

Out Revolution' that women with children are turning away from leadership and power to become full-time parents, we found no significant differences between women with children and those without in terms of their attitudes toward leadership and power."[20]

Some critics of the opt-out revolution argued this phenomenon represented the experience of only the most elite women, with graduate degrees, high-powered careers, and husbands who earned substantial incomes. Anecdotally, my experience within my own social circles suggests far more complexity than that. I see women friends and acquaintances, all with college degrees, some with and others without graduate degrees, and with varying income levels, choosing to leave the workforce at least for several years while raising their children. What remains indisputable in the endless coverage of women's thinking and decisions about work and family is that rigid, linear career paths lead to far more gendered roles *after* having children, whether women choose to stay at home or continue to work outside the home. In either case, the woman becomes the de facto family manager. It is well documented that after having children, women tend to decrease their work hours and men tend to increase theirs. This polarization can be explained by the different roles that men and women play at home and are highly consistent with the model of the primary career holder who gives work full focus and few boundaries. These primary careers—which seem antithetical to putting up limits at work—feed into the increasing hours, always-on, 24/7 culture that has become far more of the work norm for both men and women.

These rigid career paths, clearly so misaligned with the rhythms of women's lives, don't support the incredible resurgence of many women in their careers after the intense phase of raising children. Women in their fifties and sixties are often ready to focus on their work lives in a different way, while men who have been giving their all at work for the last thirty years or more are understandably ready to ramp down. Sandra Day O'Connor, the retired Supreme Court justice, shared that she'd spent ten years at home while her children were small. Imagine: a woman of her incredible professional success spent a full decade out of the workforce. Her story reinforced what I had always believed—that fundamental skills and talents may dull to some degree if unused, but they also endure and are at the ready to reinvigorate.

In several professions characterized by particularly long hours (e.g., law, consulting, investment banking, academic medicine), endurance and stamina are critical and the career-path mismatch is even more pronounced. Professionals in these fields are driving full steam ahead until their forties and fifties, perhaps early sixties, when the hope is they have accrued enough wealth to retire early and live the good life. For any woman or man who seeks to be highly involved while raising children, the mismatch is stark.

How We Work and Live: The Technology Explosion and Our Changing Experience of Time

Perhaps none of the forces outlined in this chapter impact our experience of constant speed and lack of balance more than the seismic changes in technology. The fact that it is possible to be technologically accessible, even if not psychologically so, at any time and nearly any place, makes many of us feel the need to be always available and responsive. People mistakenly equate accessibility with the ability to actually pay attention and thoughtfully respond. Feeling overwhelmed by their daily lives leads many couples to specialize once they have children; one person focuses on making money, and the other focuses on managing at home. In this way they mistakenly believe they can regain some sense of order over the plethora of daily responsibilities and demands.

The norms we've created around using technology have profoundly reconfigured our experience of time. It is difficult to remember how relatively recent these seismic shifts have been. At the beginning of my investment career in the mid-1980s, electronic spreadsheets (Lotus 123 at the time) had been available for only a few short years. It was a huge milestone in the mid-1990s when my colleagues and I were able to communicate with clients via email. I distinctly remember walking down Boylston Street in Boston before cell phone use became ubiquitous and thinking, as I walked by a young woman seemingly talking to herself, that she was a little off—until I spotted the small device tucked next to her ear.

The technology wave has continued and accelerated over the last thirty years. Electronic connectivity is now considered by many homeowners as indispensible as working plumbing. New developments in technology have brought capabilities that we could only have dreamt about a few decades ago. At times I find myself trying to help my children understand how incredible the power of the Internet has been, especially for someone like me, who is drawn toward research and information. For them, seeing real-time videos of sharks via live cam in the Pacific Ocean is interesting, but not extraordinary.

Yet the constant overload of information and the ability to be always connected come at a very high cost, robbing us of concentration, focus, any feeling of completion, and a sense of mastery. There is always another communication to respond to or another source of information to manage and process. In all my years of consulting, I have *never* conducted an employee research study where work overload was not a dominant theme. The extent of perceived and experienced overload varies by organization, and more broadly by industry or profession, but the sense of feeling overloaded at work has become the rule rather than the exception in the twenty-first century, particularly for knowledge workers, whose primary value emanates from their expertise and from managing large amounts of often complex information.

Technology is impacting both how we work and how we experience our work environments. The Families and Work Institute (FWI) found in their 2004 study *Overwork in America* that "one in three U.S. employees experienced feeling overworked as a chronic condition," while 44 percent of U.S. employees reported feeling overworked often or very often.[21] The study reported that employees who experienced more frequent interruptions that made it difficult to get their work done were far more likely to report being overworked; more than half of the study respondents indicated having to work on too many tasks at the same time and/or having interruptions that made it difficult to get their work done.[22] Furthermore, the one in three employees who were in contact with their work outside of normal work hours were substantially more likely to report feeling overworked.[23] Across many employers, representing hundreds of thousands of employees, my colleagues' and my research found that the reported experience of burnout increased exponentially, rather than linearly, as hours increased.[24]

Technology, contributing to our distracted—yet seeking to be ever-responsive—way of working in the twenty-first century, has negative consequences for both individuals and their workplaces. The FWI researchers found that those experiencing high levels of overwork were not only more likely to make errors at work and to feel angry at their employer and resentful of their coworkers, they were also, perhaps not surprisingly, more likely to report signs of clinical depression, to be in poorer health, and to neglect caring for themselves.[25]

How We Live: Home Is Work

In addition to how we work, many norms we've created in our home lives, coupled with the use of home as an alternative work site, exacerbate the sense of feeling rushed and overwrought. Many parents rush home from work to juggle dinner and homework and then fire up their computers, returning to work for several hours before bedtime. In a focus group discussion I conducted for an insurance company as part of a comprehensive work-life needs assessment, one mother of three poignantly described walking though her front door night after night to face a tsunami of responsibilities—dinner, homework, laundry, cleaning up the clutter, and on and on—before settling back down to fielding email, typically getting to bed too late, and getting up the next morning, not feeling well rested, to face it all over again.

At the time I was not a parent myself and I remember the chilling feeling that came over me as I listened to her story. It wasn't like I hadn't heard various permutations of that story before, but there was something about the depth of her resignation that struck a chord with me, the sense of "this is my life and there is nothing I can do about it." The cumulative messages I heard, the despair and resignation of so many employees regarding the work and life struggle, made me long to find another way.

For many of us, home no longer functions as a refuge but rather as a loading station before going on to the next activity. In addition to long and intense hours at work, for many parents, particularly of school-age children and teenagers, work is followed by a mad dash, with a rushed dinner at home or in the car, en route to a lesson, a practice, a performance, or a game. Weekends are no longer sacred, with children's events regularly scheduled at all times of the day and night, even on holidays and during vacations. We have defined a constant stream of enrichment activities for our children as the baseline for good parenting.

It is no secret that being busy is a prized value in American culture. We associate being busy with being important and adding value. Casual conversations with friends, neighbors, and relatives often start with the throwaway comment, "I'm sorry I haven't been in touch but I've been so busy." To say otherwise—"I don't have much going on"—signals a lack of achievement. In modern work environments it is abundantly clear that not being busy is a bad thing because it might mean that your job is unnecessary and thus vulnerable. Finding something to be busy at becomes paramount, whether or not it adds value for the organization.

When I was making a career change from the investment industry to consulting on work-life and diversity issues, there was a hard adjustment period where I lost the sense of day-to-day structure and predictability. I felt an acute need to prove my worth and fill my days with checks on my to-do list—read X number of articles, make

Y number of phone calls, do Z number of chores around the house. For many accomplished women who have made the choice to leave the workforce and stay at home with their children, the stark contrast between the rhythms of work (where getting something done is the goal) and home (where sometimes just passing time is the goal) can be profound. For some women, "professionalizing" the home environment by creating constant activity and measurable outcomes may be a way to replicate the familiar rhythms of a working day.

How have recent advances in technology, and our evolving expectations about accessibility and connection, influenced our experience of home and our ability to function intellectually, socially, and spiritually? In her newest book, *Distracted: The Erosion of Attention and the Coming of the Dark Age*, Maggie Jackson provides a compelling look at how "our near-religious allegiance to a constant state of motion and addiction to multi-tasking are eroding our capacity for deep, sustained, perceptive attention—the building block of intimacy, wisdom, and cultural progress—and stunting society's ability to comprehend what's relevant and permanent." During the last several years of my mother-in-law's life, as she needed to slow down considerably, I often thought about how the beginning and the ending of our lives are very similar and require far more time and patience to navigate. I also thought about how young children and elders have not necessarily bought into this notion of being busy, and pondered when it is that we start to pick up the social cueing that having a lot going on is a good thing. The pace of life has clearly sped up, but at the same time, the currency of appearing busy has risen substantially as well.

Technology has unleashed a whole set of new challenges for how we live our lives that we, as a society, have just started to sort out. Our new, fast-paced world of 24/7 access calls for developing new skills to manage the volume and velocity of information we face daily. As our brains get used to constant stimulation, our capacity to attend fully to anything diminishes. One psychiatrist labeled this condition "attention deficit trait," or ADT—a self-created form of ADD arising from the environments in which we live and work. The sad result is that the plethora of information and stimulation moves us into a modern-day survival mode where fear and impulses dominate. Black-and-white thinking becomes the standard, and people struggle with the ability to see nuance and shades of gray.[26] These conditions are not the recipe for thoughtful decision-making or long-term planning, the very things that make a Libra life possible.

How We Live: Lacking a Sense of Enough

The concept of diminishing marginal returns is a central one in economics. In layman's terms, it is the point at which the incremental cost outweighs the incremental benefit. Perfectionism goes hand in hand with diminishing marginal returns. When I think about how I spent my time in college and graduate school, this concept clearly comes to mind. The extra time required to get an A or even A+ was great when compared to the ultimate benefit, and I probably could have spent a whole lot less time, been more relaxed and had more fun, and done not quite but nearly as well.

I see the question "How much is enough?" everywhere around me. How large a house is necessary for three, or four, or five people? How much money does a family need to live comfortably? How many communities (e.g., work, school, church, temple, social justice causes) are enough to support with your time and money? How many fundraisers are necessary to make up for the lack of public monies being funneled to public schools? How many flavors of cereal, or yogurt, or beer do you need to be satisfied? How many extracurricular activities are enough for a child to feel enriched? How many networks—personal and professional—are enough to maintain? It seems we have lost common sense about what is enough in so many parts of our lives.

As I entered my life as an adult in the mid-1980s, my world was one of upward movement. Between 1980 and 2007, the median house price in the United States increased four-fold. The Dow Jones Industrial Average, a major financial marker, skyrocketed from approximately 800 in the summer of 1982 to more than 14,000 by the fall of 2007. Over these nearly thirty years the proportion of disposable income spent on the mortgage and consumer debt increased by more than a third and the percent of disposable income reserved for savings declined from 11 percent to less than 1 percent.[27] The book and PBS television show *Affluenza* have brought attention to overconsumption in our society. "Affluenza" is defined by the authors as "a painful, contagious, socially-transmitted condition of overload, debt, anxiety, and waste resulting from the dogged pursuit of more."[28]

I've often pondered what is required to raise a middle class family and how that has changed through time. When I hear concern that the next generation of children may not be materially better off than their parents, I think, *What's wrong with that?* I am acutely aware that having enough is a real concern and hardship for families at a certain income level, but for highly educated men and women, the real issue seems to be one of having too much rather than too little. Many of us have clearly entered into the space of diminishing marginal returns when it comes to possessions that we need to buy, manage, insure, clean, and finally dispose of, and to my mind, for many of our children, having less would be positive rather than negative. Research bears me out. Increases in income track with increases in happiness primarily at poverty levels where added resources have the greatest impact. Beyond a middle class lifestyle, further moves up the income ladder do not equate with increases in happiness. Instead, other factors, such as strong relationships, a feeling of meaning and purpose, enjoyable work, and involvement in civic groups correspond with continued increases in life satisfaction. One hypothesis is that increased incomes fuel rising expectations, and consequently the baseline adjusts upward, removing the psychological benefits of economic growth.[29]

The sense of "not enough" extends far beyond money and consumption. As a working parent I struggle with what is necessary to raise children. The requirements for involvement and engagement have skyrocketed, as have the demands for extracurricular stimulation and material goods. I've had many, many conversations with other adults about how their own parents had limited or no involvement in their schoolwork throughout their entire secondary education. We recently had a school science fair and my neighbor reminisced about the annual science fairs when she was a child. Her parents' role was to help get necessary supplies and transport her and her project to and from the event. That's it, end of story. Parents of my generation recall as youngsters simply being outside for most of the day and then coming home for meals when it got dark. That was certainly the situation for both me and my husband when we were growing up. Today, the conversation goes, the world has changed and it's too dangerous for kids not to be closely supervised. It is simply not seen as an option for caring, modern parents to give their children a lot of autonomy. Yet perceptions of heightened danger stand in stark contrast to the reality that violent crime against children has declined precipitously in recent decades.[30]

Women face rising expectations of what is "enough" on many fronts, whether externally or self-imposed.[31] Young women responding to the cultural norm of intensive mothering feel the need to be skilled and loving mothers. They feel the need to be successful in their careers as well as to be trim and attractive. Accomplished modern women feel the need to be socially conscious and to give back to their communities and, oh yes, to be all these people *at the same time.* "When researchers ask teenage girls what is important to them—finding a successful job, staying close to their friends, having a family, looking good, and so on—they discovered that their answer was 'everything.' They ranked nothing as less important."[32] In the arena of doing and being "enough," men are catching up to women, as their reported stress and difficulty trying to balance work and life has risen alongside rising expectations of the role they will play in caring for their children.[33]

Many, perhaps most of us, struggle with how to be comfortable with enough in many different parts of our lives. The inability to define enough feeds quite directly into our drive to work harder and to earn more so as to afford the expanding list of requirements for a middle class lifestyle. Our fear of *not keeping up* and of *being left behind*, both for ourselves and our children, runs deep, particularly among successful, highly educated men and women in the twenty-first century. For new parents, the heightened sense of expectation on the home front collides with typically already intense work demands. We feel unable to put up the boundaries anywhere and life becomes all about the juggle. This intensity leads to the decision, for women, to cut back at work, or to stop working altogether, and we are left living lives that don't match our modern-day expectations. All the while, we rarely step back to consider, *What is enough?*

Resignation and Fear: We Don't Trust It Can Be Different

The instability of the job market and the lack of clarity about the new rules of engagement for professionals lead many people, even those who appear to have substantial negotiating power, to experience the world as though they have few options with regard to choices about work-life integration.

In the mid-2000s I conducted a workshop at a work-life symposium for a top-ten business school. The conference was focused on managing work-life issues, and in partnership with a colleague, I had developed, and was facilitating, a workshop to help students think about their goals and concerns as well as strategies for integrating their work and personal lives after business school. I was struck during the workshop by the overwhelming sense of resignation among the participants; I returned to my hotel room that evening with a heavy heart. These obviously accomplished, very bright students seemed fully ready (particularly the men) to accept that there was little hope of putting up any boundaries at work, because that was what the work world demanded in the types of jobs they would inhabit. Simple, clear, end of story. I was left thinking how strange it was that even these students, the ones companies clamor to hire, and who are in arguably a powerful position to negotiate their rules of engagement, seemed to see no connection between their professional bargaining power and their ability to prioritize balance in their lives.

Through many years of consulting, in which I was retained specifically because the organization sought to more effectively address the work-life issues of employees, the vast majority of workers remained very reluctant to ask for something different. I heard a great deal about the perceived risks and organizational norms that prevented people from wanting to appear less committed in any way. I understood the vulnerability employees may have felt, but at the same time they were also emphatic about acknowledging their own contribution to overwork and seemed powerless to stop working, even when there was not external pressure to do so. The Society for Human Resource Management reported in a 2009 study of over 600 employees that more than half indicated self-imposed pressure was responsible for their working beyond their normal workweek.[34]

With headlines such as "We've Run Out of Work/Life Balance," "Work-life imbalance: Farewell to the flexibility fad," and "Balance is Bunk," the media certainly feeds the constant insecurity about any notion of working and living differently. But media headlines, while powerful and compelling, often don't tell the whole story. For example, similar to our fears about safety for our children, we as adults perceive the world as less safe, despite a long decline in the crime rate beginning in the mid-1990s and recently reaching levels not seen since the 1960s. This decline continued despite the economic difficulties of recent years, yet the trend in public opinion has gone in the opposite direction, with nearly three-quarters of respondents to a Gallup poll in 2009 reporting an increase in crime over the last year.[35]

During the entire time that Bryan and I have been raising our sons, whenever we've discussed doing something out of the ordinary relative to work, such as us both working reduced schedules, or taking a leave of absence to travel, or taking a joint parental leave, particularly for Bryan, who works in the technology industry, the common reaction has been, "You're so lucky that your company lets you do that." Even in the years before the technology bubble, when millionaires seemed to sprout up overnight and technology jobs seemed a dime a dozen, the mention of negotiating around schedule or workload was treated as strange at best, unrealistic at worst. It always seemed peculiar to me that employee-employer relationships regarding work and life integration were treated more like a parent/child relationship—with permission sought and subsequently granted or denied—than adults coming together to solve business problems, including workload and scheduling constraints.

Fear and resignation, independently and in combination, drive couples to more traditional roles by making them feel they don't have the will and/or the ability to write a different script. We are bombarded with so many messages about what we need to be doing—to stay healthy, to raise successful children, to excel at work, and on and on and on. This messaging, along with the realities of more tenuous employment and the need to be highly self-sufficient in American culture, managing the cost of health care, retirement, and higher education, spurs us to push harder and do more and never feel able to rest.

Resignation and Fear: Can We Tap the Power and Energy of the Women's Movement in Earlier Years?

One of the greatest joys for me in doing research for this book has been better understanding the energy and power of the women's movement in earlier decades. Through the years, I had come to deeply appreciate the doors that were opened for women of my generation, but I don't think I truly understood the collective force of women and men coming together—as they had during earlier periods in history, such as the 1960s and 1970s—to change the world. Judith Warner, in her provocative book, *Perfect Madness,* describes the generation of women born between the late 1950s and the early

1970s (I would fit in that demographic) as a blessed group who came of age when most of the major battles of the women's movement had been won. She characterized them as a strikingly apolitical group who have been bred to be independent and self-sufficient, to rely on their own initiative and personal responsibility, and to privatize their problems. She reported, "It almost never occurs to them that they can use the muscle of their superb education or their collective voice to change or rearrange their social support system." Her description captured my experience both of ambivalence and of not fully understanding the power of a collective voice in driving change during earlier decades of the women's movement.[36]

My emerging awareness sparked in the fall of 2008, when I attended a conference, "Gender Equality in a Time of Economic Stress," at Suffolk University Law School in Boston. The Honorable Judge Nancy Gertner, appointed by President Clinton in 1994, gave the keynote address, and her remarks both educated and moved me. She talked about how the women's movement was a revolution about changing the workplace and about changing families, *not* merely about choice. She shared that, in many ways, neither workplaces nor families had been transformed. She pointed out that choice ultimately means meaningful alternatives; without these, we are left with false choices—organizations that remain unfriendly to family issues, and continuing gendered roles on the home front. Judge Gertner spoke of "The Revolution of Declining Expectations" and how it was necessary to reignite consciousness-raising for women and men. Her remarks certainly raised my consciousness. I was so energized that at the conference's completion I sat in the law school foyer filling several pages of notes, outlining the myriad forces that contribute to women and men slipping into highly stereotypical gender roles once they become parents. These notes became the foundation of this chapter.

In a conversation with feminist scholar Stephanie Coontz, I asked her why she thought the word "feminist" does not resonate with many younger women. She replied, "It's a very complicated issue. We have faced these attacks over many years with feminists labeled as anti-man, as anti-family. It was a complete caricature. This has been going on since the early twentieth century. Every time women make a gain, it takes years to be slightly accepting, and then it's the feedback, 'Now you've gone too far.' There is a relentless campaign to redefine feminism and to put it on the margin."[37]

Lillie Margaret Lazaruk, a family friend and women's advocate for more than forty years, started her career with the YWCA in Atlanta, helping to develop and train college students and others in social action concepts. Many years later she launched and ran a women's center at a community college, substantially changing the lives of many women by putting them on the path to independence. I asked her what her definition of "feminist" was, and she said, "I see it as someone who advocates for the rights of women as equal human beings—social, political, everything. I was horrified when I began to examine things and see how unequal it was for women. You end up with job discrimination; you end up with less pay. Why is it that teachers—mostly women—get paid so little, while rocket scientists—who are mostly men—get paid so much? And without teachers you wouldn't have rocket scientists."[38]

When I asked her why she thought younger generations of women had not embraced feminism to the same extent as in the past, she said, "You had this whole thing about bra-burning that never really happened. Younger women had opportunities that were based on the success of the women's movement and they were not willing to recognize that. They thought they had gotten there on their own steam. I don't think they realized how hard it was for women to get where they are today—things like the first woman in law school and the first woman in medical school. Those are things that women now take for granted."[39] She went on to say, "I think a lot of women did not want to identify as a feminist. They thought it was a red-flag word—that you are some wild-eyed bra-burner. They did not have time for the histrionics, but there had to be a lot of noise about the victories of the women's movement. They were hard won."[40]

Her words certainly resonated with me. If I had not changed careers and spent more than a decade talking directly with women about their present-day work experiences, I very much doubt I would have come to appreciate on a deep level just what the women's movement meant in terms of paving the way for women of my generation. Furthermore, I would not have understood that the women's movement had not solved all the issues and was thus not just an artifact of history and no longer relevant. That was what I thought earlier in my career.

To provide some sense of how profoundly conditions have improved for women in recent decades, consider this powerful data. As recently as 1963, homemakers had legal claim to her husband's income in only eight states, the notion of marital rape did not exist, white male dropouts earned more than female college graduates, and the help-wanted ads were segregated by gender. Since that time, women are more likely to graduate from college than men, women (and men) have community property rights enabling them a share of the household income while raising children, even if they are not working outside the home, and sexual harassment is a serious issue in most workplaces.[41]

My interviews for this book with couples who had practiced the Libra approach while raising their children—who are now adults, some with very young children of their own—furthered my understanding of the power and energy of earlier stages of the women's movement. In speaking with several of these couples, I saw a pattern emerge in the interviews, with many references to feminism and the women's movement. One interviewee remarked that it was a time of cultural explosion and that both women and men were actively experimenting with gender identities and what the roles of both women and men were and could be. Through these interviews, with women and men who came of age during the second wave of feminism in the late 1960s and 1970s, I came to appreciate the sense of active experimentation, of challenging the norms and trying to write a different script that I rarely hear expressed or see demonstrated by women or men today.

In a focus group conversation with a group of fathers who came together monthly over two decades from the late 1970s to the early 1990s while raising their children—a parenting group entirely organized by the men and without any involvement from their wives—I was struck by the men's commitment and vision. For this group, it was extremely important to share with other men the joys and struggles inherent in fatherhood and to actively challenge one another. They sought to learn together about being far more engaged and involved fathers than in earlier generations. Their drive to create a new model of parental partnership was palpable.

This is not to say that there isn't incredibly good and important work being done every day around gender roles, active parenting for both fathers and mothers and the like. But having spent most of my career working on these issues while simultaneously being a typical parent experiencing the day-to-day juggle of kids and careers, I can say there is not the strong sense of a movement, of the best and brightest women and men wanting to proactively wrestle with these issues, or of understanding that there even are any issues, until they are well down the road in their careers and raising children. For most young couples, having grown up with girls and boys playing sports, working side by side in college and graduate school, launching their careers together, it is understandably difficult for them to realize just how gendered most marriages become after children—even in the twenty-first century.

Powerful Forces Interacting

Each of these factors contributes independently—and in interaction with one another—to challenge the best intentions of very smart and thoughtful people as they seek to balance work and life. Job insecurity moves us to cling to the primary job, resplendent with health insurance and 401(k) benefits, as do rigid career paths that no longer fit. The constant overflow of information raises our anxieties about the safety of our children, piques our perceived need for things, and keeps us in constant motion so we have little time to stop and contemplate a different reality. The endless list of things to do—both at work and at home—reinforces a sense that specializing and moving into highly gendered roles after children is a simple way to cope with the cacophony of demands. Deeply ingrained gender norms that we may not even know are there, reinforced by systems that define our lives—at work, in schools—contribute to the traditionalism of parents who thought they would write a different script than in past generations.

In the end, the confluence of forces powerfully impacts our choices and decisions, and each of us, coping with our individual situations, wonders, "How did I get here?" It is possible and desirable to follow a different path—not as an extraordinary gesture, not as a romantic notion—but as a commitment requiring greater awareness and intentionality, some new assumptions, and the development of new skills and norms that all contribute to the reality of a Libra life.

CHAPTER 3

SHE SAYS, HE SAYS:

THE SELF-REINFORCING CYCLE OF GENDER

We shall not cease from exploration and the end of all our exploring will be to arrive where we started and know the place for the first time.

---T.S. Eliot

There are many societal norms that reinforce stereotypical gender roles. Women are supposed to be pretty and nurturing. Men are supposed to be strong and good providers. Despite our sense that those norms are old-fashioned and no longer relevant, they remain embedded deep within our psyches, based on countless experiences throughout our lives that reinforce them. There are few places where these norms are played out more explicitly than in the workforce. Consider Tom Brady, the New England Patriots quarterback, beloved by many (and reviled by others not living in New England). They say women adore him and men want to be him. He's attractive, talented, rich, and yet sweet, with that boy-next-door personality. Of course he's also married to a stunning supermodel. In the local Boston press Brady was lauded for showing up to *practice* bright and early the day after his wife, Giselle Bundchen, gave birth to their first son. Brady said, "I owe it to the guys in the locker room to really focus on what I need to do for this team, and put all these emotions aside and kind of come in here with a great sense of determination on what we have to do as a team. So as a captain and leader of this team, the last thing they need from me is to be really not focused on the job at hand. There's plenty of things for me to really be doing here this week."[1]

Lest we wonder what men are supposed to be doing, Brady drives home the message that commitment to work is number one. Seminal research on fathers by the Boston College Center for Work and Family and the Families and Work Institute highlights the work-life pressure men increasingly experience as a result of escalating work demands (and the need to be a successful provider) coupled with evolving expectations of fathers as highly engaged parents.[2] The report *The New Male Mystique* describes the conflict: "The 'ideal' man today is not only a good employee working long hours to be a successful breadwinner, but is also an involved and nurturing husband/partner, father and son."[3]

Women, on the other hand, face persistent questioning about both their ambition and their competence for leadership. Countless women—highly accomplished young women who are professional equals with their male peers—continue to worry that letting colleagues know they are expecting will signal that they are no longer committed to their professional work. Men don't get asked if they "plan to come back to work after the baby is born." Rather, it is assumed they will be *more* committed to success in their career once they become a "family man."

Catalyst reported the dilemma working women face in expressing their ambition and leadership abilities in a study aptly titled *The Double-Bind Dilemma for Women in Leadership: Damned If You Do, Doomed If You Don't*. It's fine for women to be smart and accomplished, but first they must be seen as nurturing. Based on research conducted across several countries, Catalyst found that women are evaluated against a masculine standard of leadership. If women behave in ways that are consistent with gender stereotypes of caretaking behaviors, for instance being supportive as well as focusing on team-building and mentoring others, they are seen as "too soft" and less competent as leaders. Alternatively, if they behave in ways that are perceived as inconsistent with these stereotypes, such as being assertive and focusing on managing upward and solving problems, they may be perceived as competent but characterized as "too tough," unfeminine, and lacking interpersonal skills. Unlike Goldilocks, for women, no leadership style is ever just right.

Our collective ambivalence regarding gender roles was evident in a Pew Research Center poll conducted in collaboration with *Time* magazine. In the fall of 2010, fully 30 percent of respondents in this nationwide poll perceived the ideal marriage as one in which the husband provided financially and the wife took care of the house and children. The Pew Research poll also documented 37 percent of respondents reporting their belief that more mothers of young children choosing to work outside the home was bad for society.[4] Even among those who identify strongly with the notion of equality, gender biases persist in sometimes unexpected ways. A father I interviewed, who works part-time and is the primary daytime caretaker of his two-year-old son, expressed his complete surprise at his own father's reaction to his caretaking role. This young father regarded his own parents as role models for a very egalitarian approach to parenting. He said:

> My dad was always very involved in my childhood growing up. I have always wanted to be a dad because I loved my dad so much and he looked like he was having so much fun doing it. ... I always had the shared parenting idea. Since both of my parents worked, they were very equal in the time they spent with us. I felt like both of them wanted to spend time with us.

In questioning this young father about what kinds of reactions he gets to his family's work-life approach, he said:

> My dad has made several comments about how he didn't think he would raise a son who would not support his family. My behavior right now does not fit in with his definition of success.

A woman living the Libra model—both she and her husband work reduced schedules in their corporate jobs as engineers and split the care of their infant (along with one day per week of care by a relative)—explained how deeply entrenched gender norms can thwart our ability to find good solutions:

> We were not comfortable with day care or with giving up our careers. I wanted to contribute to the household income. I was not comfortable with being a stay-at-home mom. It would have meant giving up an identity I had built up my whole life. For a long time I thought we would not have kids. It never occurred to me that we could both work part-time. We went to school together and equality is at the core of who we are as a couple. I was shocked that I didn't think past that [of only reducing her schedule].
>
> I told my husband, "I want to do this but can't figure out how," and he said, "We can both work part-time." That was it; we had a solution. From there it was pretty easy.[5]

Both women and men feed into gender norms, creating and reinforcing a powerful cycle. Gender norms keep us stuck and do not allow us to come up with better and more creative solutions for putting together the work and caretaking elements of our lives. For many years it was easy for me to see what men were "doing wrong." They weren't organized enough, they weren't focused on the right things, they didn't get what it meant to be a parent, they didn't care, etc., etc. But after years of observation, listening and learning, I have come to see and much more clearly understand the challenges, complexities, and heartaches men face in integrating their work and family lives. I have also become far more sophisticated in my understanding of how women contribute, often unknowingly, to creating marriages that are not the egalitarian vision they say they want.

How Women Contribute to the Cycle of Gender Norms

1. Over-managing at home and not allowing their husband/partner to share control and responsibility. Among the biggest challenges women struggle with is their instinct to over-manage in the home environment. Many women see their role as defining the standards relative to home and family. While they indicate wanting help and support from their partners, often they define that support on their terms and are reluctant or unwilling to share control. Maternal gatekeeping is the term used to describe this phenomenon.

Academic research has found that the behaviors and attitudes of the mother influence the role fathers play at home. A study of approximately 100 families with infant children found that, no matter what their reported attitudes about the proper paternal role, fathers played a greater role in the care of their children when encouraged by their wife or partner. Even men who saw women as more natural parents, or thought the mother should be the primary nurturer, played a more active parenting role if they received positive messaging from their spouse. On the other hand, criticism eroded their participation. Understandably, when men feel their input doesn't count or they feel negatively judged in their interactions with their children, eventually many start to disengage. It is easy to see how criticism would especially deter men who felt ambivalent about or lacked confidence in their caretaking role from the outset. In the research, men's desire to be involved parents translated into actual behavior only when their wife or partner also perceived the father's involvement as important.[6]

Another study, of 1,023 couples with preschool-age children from twenty large cities across the U.S., additionally illustrates the maternal gatekeeping phenomenon. The researchers found that, while mothers were open to sharing playtime activities with their partners, they remained protective of their role as caretaker and in driving the educational experiences of their children.[7]

It is easy to understand why many women struggle with sharing the caregiving role. Many women perceive their mothering skills as core to how they see themselves, and sharing that role can feel uncomfortable or threatening, even for women who wholeheartedly support shared parenting. The maternal instinct is deep, and women continue to feel responsible for their children's behavior and success. For women, active parenting is an expectation, while men, though not as much as they used to, are acknowledged and rewarded for assuming an active parenting role.

Amy Vachon recalled the first time she left to go to work after the birth of her first child. Despite strong ideals of equality, she handed her husband, Marc, a list with details of her daughter's napping and feeding schedule. In response, he immediately ripped the list up, sending the clear message that he was quite capable of caring for their daughter. Amy and Marc have since spent the last decade honing their ability to fully share their parenting journey, and they share their experiences in the book they coauthored, *Equally Shared Parenting: Rewriting the Rules for a New Generation of Parents*.[8] Professor Sarah Schoope-Sullivan, one of the lead researchers on the influence of mothers' behavior in relation to the active parenting of their partners, believes deeply in the value of co-parenting. In sharing her personal challenges with ceding parenting control to her husband, she describes the struggle for many women:

> I have certainly felt ambivalent about relinquishing control over what my daughter wears or eats. There are times when my husband dresses her in an outfit and I think, "What is he doing?" I try to bite my tongue. The way your children look, a lot of mothers feel like it reflects on them. The way I would describe it is, in the end, society is still not going to come down on the father. Society is going to come down on you.[9]

Women need to understand that when they assume the "expert role" and relegate their husband or partner to helper status rather than acknowledge him as a competent, fully capable co-parent, they are actively erecting barriers to his full involvement. Allowing fathers to develop their own, independent relationships with their children is among the greatest gifts a woman can give to both the man and the child. It is imperative for fathers to have time alone with their children, time when they are fully in charge, because it is during these periods they build and develop their parenting competence and confidence. When a father's contributions are micromanaged and overshadowed by the mother, he is denied the opportunity to appreciate the gift of parenting in all its complexities, challenges, and rewards.

It is important to note that the contributions of fathers to the care of their children is determined by several factors, not only by the attitudes and reactions of their wife or partner. Certainly, men's beliefs about the proper roles of mothers and fathers and their interest in being an active parent are critical. Selecting a partner who is open to being an involved parent is an extremely important element in living a Libra life. Women can also benefit by considering what role their encouragement or discouragement might be playing in realizing their goal of co-parenting.

2. Not defining new standards. Another way in which women contribute to the gender cycle is by rigid adherence to the status quo and failure to create new norms—or by their reluctance to even consider new norms—at work and at home once they become parents. This is not to imply that changing long-term habits and practices, which typically are comfortable and familiar, is an easy process. For most of us, it is not. But children command so much of our time, energy, love, and capacity that it is unrealistic to think you do not need to develop *a new normal* once you become a parent. The house probably won't be as clean or orderly, the laundry probably won't get done as efficiently, the bills may not get paid as expeditiously, and the holiday cards may not be as personalized or be sent at all. But what is most important will likely get done, and if you are anything like me, you will see that some things slipping through the cracks is not the end of the world—although it might feel like it in that moment.

As someone who long prided herself on being on top of the details, I faced a particularly low moment one morning when I was getting gas in my car and the person at the station informed me that my inspection sticker was six months overdue. I drove away and started to cry. What bothered me more than the sticker being overdue was that not even a hint of needing a new sticker was on my radar. Somehow forgetting that one task was emblematic of my feeling out of control and unable to keep up with all the details of my expanded life as a parent and professional and, at that time, elder caregiver. The next day I went back to the gas station to get my new sticker, and in the big picture it really wasn't such a big deal. But in that moment, it loomed large and felt highly symbolic.

I do believe it's possible, and sensible, to make sure what is most important to you remains a priority. If an extremely clean house is important to you, or getting to the gym several times a week really matters, your energy and resources should be spent there. At the same time, the reality is that once you become a parent, your life does change in wonderful and challenging ways, and you don't have the luxury of time or the level of control you used to. It is wise to identify and streamline your priorities, and critical to do so if you intend to follow the Libra model.

Having children—compelling as they are—has been the most effective way for some of us highly driven types to actually put the brakes on and stop the constant working, striving, and doing. A woman with a very successful academic career told me that her daughter was an important catalyst in helping her recalibrate her standards of success. She said:

> Being a parent has really helped me see the big picture. I think, Do I really want to be this parent who is always tired, always working? I notice the effect it had on my daughter. Also I don't want her to get the impression that working is bad. I want her to think work can be a fun and fulfilling part of someone's life. I do enjoy my work, but cutting back

allows me to look forward to coming to work and not like I am missing things [at home].

While some women discover that becoming a parent helps them put limits on work, for others having children and trying to mix work and home feels untenable. One of several reasons women choose to stop working outside the home is because they do not want to—or cannot—adapt their standards. For this group of women, mixing the roles of parent and professional leaves them feeling unsatisfied and like they are not meeting their expectations in any part of their lives. They prefer the ability to focus rather than dilute their efforts. But there can be a danger to this type of all-or-nothing approach. One mother shared the story of a close woman friend, an Ivy League educated attorney and Fulbright scholar, who stopped working to raise her children. She described this friend as having made a very conscious choice to put her career on hold. A decade later, and now very eager to get back into the workforce, this woman cannot see a way to manage the logistical complexities of her mothering role with a paying job. What started as a choice has morphed into what feels like a lack of options.

In her research with accomplished women professionals who stopped working in order to stay home with their children, sociologist Pamela Stone has found that these women internalize their choice to focus on home as a reflection of their own perfectionism. Stone interprets the link these women make between their perceived high standards and their decision to stay home as being compatible with their drive for achievement (as well as compensating for the loss of their professional identities.)[10] In *Perfect Madness*, author Judith Warner, catalyzed first by her own journey into high-intensity parenting and subsequent extensive research with mothers across the country, dramatically captures the intense pressure many mothers experience in their quest for the mothering gold medal. She writes, "Some of the mothers appeared to have lost nearly all sense of themselves as adult women ... They were so depleted by the affection and care they lavished upon their small children that they had no energy left, not just for sex, but for feeling like a sexual being. It all reminded me a lot of Betty Friedan's 1963 classic, *The Feminine Mystique*. The diffuse satisfaction. The angst, hidden behind all the obsession with trivia, and the push to be perfect. The way so many women constantly looked over their shoulders to make sure that no one was outdoing them in the performance of good Mommyhood."[11] But striving can go too far and lead to unrealistic goals and eventually a sense of failure.[12] Rigid standards that don't flex to accommodate the added complexities of being a parent are a major obstacle to combining professional work and active family involvement.

A critical component of the Libra solution is doing your best to find peace with what is and is not realistic—and pondering what is and is not helpful at this stage of life, especially when your children are small. The Libra model is not right for every couple, but if this highly shared approach—which allows for professional expression and deep family engagement—is your ideal, getting clear on where you can bend is an important part of the equation.

3. Not sharing financial ownership. A central way in which women perpetuate the gender status quo is by not assuming shared ownership for meeting the economic needs of the family. Women seeing themselves as "helpers" rather than full partners in the financial sphere is the mirror image of men seeing themselves as "helpers" rather than full partners in the parenting and home spheres. One of the characteristics that distinguish the Libra work-life model is that both the man and woman feel a shared sense of responsibility to provide financially for the family.

The importance of women's financial role at home is growing. According to the Census Bureau, women professionals contribute over forty percent of household income, and one in four women earns more than their husbands.[13] However, while the majority of mothers work outside the home, many more women than men choose to stop working for at least some period of time. According to 2008 and 2009 data from the Bureau of Labor

Statistics, approximately 70 percent of women with children under eighteen, in comparison with 94 percent of men, are employed outside the home.[14]

My many years of conducting employee research revealed patterns that applied across multiple organizations, representing hundreds of thousands of employees. One of the clearest patterns was the vast discrepancy in family composition by gender. Among men and women with children under thirteen working in client companies, a majority of men—and in some of these companies, up to two-thirds of male employees—had wives who were not in the workforce and contributing financially to the family.[15] The Boston College study of fathers working across several large companies found that more than 40 percent of their spouses were contributing less than $25,000 per year to the household income.[16] More than half of the dads indicated they would feel okay not working outside the home if their spouse or partner made enough money to comfortably support the family.[17] Among this group of nearly 1,000 fathers raising children, those in the primary breadwinner role spent less time with their children and attached greater importance to the need for high income and job security in comparison to men whose wives and partners were also primary breadwinners.[18]

For younger women, the word "choice" is central to their definition of feminism (even if they don't label themselves as a feminist). In work-life focus groups, I heard frequent comments from younger women that symbolized their perception of the work-life struggle. A typical sentiment was, "I am thankful that I don't have to make the trade-offs that women before me have had to make. What's important to me is that I have the choice." Younger women identified the *choice* as the key differentiator for their generation. Yet feminists never envisioned success as women (or men) having to make a Solomon-like choice between a complete work focus or a complete home focus. The real goal of the women's movement was to *transform* workplaces and family roles.

In her research with professional women who made the choice to stop working outside the home, sociologist and author Pamela Stone explores this paradox. Women interpret their choice to stop working as a privilege, a reflection of their husband's career success and a symbol of their own high standards (being able to focus on being the best parent they could be and not having to dilute their focus—and potential contribution—at work). Stone describes a disjuncture between the rhetoric of choice and the reality of constraint that shapes women's decisions to go home. She writes that, between trying to be the ideal mother (in an era of intensive mothering) and the ideal worker (a model based on a man with a stay-at-home wife), these high-flying women faced a double bind. Fundamentally, they faced a "choice gap": the difference between the decisions women could have made about their careers if they were not mothers or caregivers and the decisions they had to make in their circumstances as mothers married to high-octane husbands in ultimately unyielding professions. This choice gap obscures individual preferences, and thus reveals culture, jobs, society—the kinds of things sociologists call "structure."[19]

The notion of women "having choice" about working outside the home is evidence of a deep inequality, because most men don't feel they have any choice about this role. Two-thirds of the respondents in a 2010 Pew Research Center poll reported that to be ready for marriage, it is very important for a man to support his family financially, and 41 percent of respondents reported that providing a good income is a very important quality in a good husband. The comparable figures for women were 33 percent and 19 percent. An evolution in the marriage demographics has resulted in people marrying others at the same educational and socioeconomic level, so that professional couples are managing two careers.[20] In the twenty-first century, doctors marry lawyers, bankers marry scientists, and professors marry business executives. In the absence of changing roles at home and finding ways to contain work, the best choice often seems to be to specialize and have someone, usually the woman, focus her energies at home.

Women typically underestimate the difficulty of stepping out of the workforce, especially for an extended period of time, and then trying to reenter. I am the last person who wants to feed into the fear and unease that surrounds many people's feelings about job security, and I certainly think most women and men who have left the workforce and have a strong desire to return can find a way to do so. That said, the weight of evidence is that leaving the workforce for an extended period of time with no plan for reentry is just not a prudent decision.

A poignant article highlights one woman's changed thinking about the issue of economic dependence. In the late 1970s Terri Hekker wrote an Op-Ed piece in the *New York Times* on the satisfaction of being a full-time housewife in the new age of the liberated woman. This article went on to become a book by Ms. Hekker titled *Ever Since Adam and Eve* and was followed by a national speaking tour and much publicity. In a follow-up piece in the *New York Times* more than twenty-five years later, Ms. Hekker wrote, "In the continuing case of Full-Time Homemaker vs. Working Mother, I offer myself as Exhibit A." She went on to explain that her husband—with whom she had five children and six grandchildren—served her divorce papers on their fortieth anniversary. She described herself as not feeling divorced but more like "canceled"—along with her credit cards, health insurance, and checkbook. She wrote, "I read about the young mothers of today—educated, employed, self sufficient—who drop out of the work force when they have children, and I worry and wonder. Perhaps it is the right choice for them. Maybe they'll be fine. But the fragility of modern marriage suggests that at least half of them may not be."[21] The statistics today continue to give credence to Terri Hekker's fears. Women's standard of living declines while men's increases after divorce. In 2009, the average age of widowhood was sixty for women, and more than a third of women in their forties—as well as more than 40 percent of women in their fifties—were divorced.[22]

It is easy to understand why women who are unsatisfied at work and simultaneously struggle with the demands of work and family are moved to leave the workforce. I've long advised clients that this combination—dissatisfaction at work and unrelenting work-life stress—constitutes a toxic mix and is anathema to retaining women professionals. For organizations seeking to retain these women, the prescription must include both proactive career development and the provision of a more flexible work culture. Women do not leave their jobs casually or cavalierly; many feel conflicted about their choice to stop working. I conducted many exit interviews with employees whom the client companies identified as highly effective and whom they were disappointed to lose. These interviews were completely confidential so that the individuals could be totally candid; only aggregate themes were reported back to the client company. Through this process, women revealed the multifaceted nature of their decisions to leave. The stories often contained elements of job dissatisfaction in addition to work-life conflict, yet a woman's decision to leave would get justified as a decision to be home with her family. The reality was typically far more complicated and nuanced.

While women do feel conflicted about leaving the workforce, there is another element at play as well. Women leave work because they believe they can. They feel a freedom to leave jobs that don't meet their emotional needs in a way that most men do not. It is also highly socially acceptable—even encouraged—for women to be at home with their children. It seems easier than finding another, similar work situation that is a better work-life fit, or identifying what type of paid work they do want to do. Some women leave the workforce because they are dissatisfied with the initial career paths they've chosen, and in the absence of feeling compelled at work, staying home is a good alternative. Since men don't typically feel they have this choice, they persevere because someone needs to pay the bills.

From an equality perspective, if I want my husband to do all of the things I do to care for our family, then I think it is only fair that I should likewise be sharing the economic load. The goal in the

Libra model is to create enough flexibility so that neither person feels trapped in a work situation that does not meet their needs over the long term. There are periods of ups and downs and all jobs have trade-offs, but in this model, meeting the economic needs of the family is a joint endeavor. Over time, couples work to ensure that both can identify work situations they can live with and optimally desire. This kind of financial fluency allows couples to weather economic ebbs and flows and provides opportunities for both individuals to maintain a connection to the workforce. There may be times—as the major economic recession of 2008 illustrated with great drama—when people are out of work by no choice of their own. Sharing the financial load makes such unexpected events somewhat less scary.

Though I identify strongly with working, and consider providing income as one of the important ways in which I take care of my family, I think I would struggle being the only earner in our household. This thought sometimes surprises me. I could imagine taking on this role for a few years, so that Bryan could take a sabbatical or potentially change careers, but having the full weight of the financial responsibility without end would not feel like a comfortable long-term solution for me. I greatly admire the men and women who are the sole or primary earners in their families, but for me the shared approach to meeting the economic needs of the family is the right one.

4. Not prioritizing the marriage. Raising children is all consuming. They need you for so many things. As babies, they need their caretakers to do everything for them: feed them, clothe them, protect them, entertain them, love them, comfort them—everything. Even though my children are well past the physically intense stage, I can see how they still rely on our help and our presence in many ways. At the same time, I believe a strong marriage is one of the greatest gifts that parents can give to their children, and for a couple's relationship to thrive, it needs time, attention, and effort.

Paying attention to your relationship means ensuring you and your spouse's needs are being met professionally and personally, to at least some degree. Professionally, that translates to doing work you feel good about. I am not talking about some pie-in-the-sky fantasy of a perfect job without any struggles or trade-offs, but a work situation that is at least neutral and ideally a positive, generative experience. Long-term work situations that feel toxic and don't allow people to maintain reasonable physical and emotional health should prompt the development of an exit strategy. Feeling stuck in a work situation that is a bad fit, without any plan for change, is not a recipe for success—for the individual, the couple, the children, or the family. The shared sense of financial ownership that I described earlier enables both members of the couple to feel a certain measure of professional freedom that allows them to adapt and customize their work situations. Prioritizing a marriage in relation to work means committing to ongoing conversations and support so that both partners feel capable of making a change in their professional lives—or starting down the path toward a change.

Prioritizing the marriage also means making space for intimacy. I am defining intimacy broadly, ranging from talking without being constantly interrupted, to having fun together doing whatever you both enjoy doing, to making time for maintaining your sexual connection. Many Libra couples I spoke to admittedly struggled to make as much time and space for one another as they would like, particularly in the very intense stage of caring for preschool children. But they were all very cognizant of the importance of investing that time and energy into the relationship and took steps to do so. A Libra dad with a six-month-old said, "We are just arranging to have a babysitter so we can have some time to have adult conversation." Another dad, teaching part-time and caring for his preschool child on some days during the workweek, said, "When my wife comes home and she's had a hard day at work, she might need me to listen about her day for a while. Just because we have a child does not mean I stop being a husband." He also shared that his wife was a very good listener, and in fact he had to work much harder at that skill because it did not come as naturally. A woman attorney said that she and her husband incorporate time together into their lives through everyday activities such as walking their dogs and commuting to work together on several days of the week.

What happens in many relationships is that, in addition to the pressure exerted by the sheer volume of everything that feels like it needs to get done, each person holds resentment that makes them pull away. It is a classic scenario: he feels resentful because of all the pressure he experiences around earning money, while she feels resentful because she perceives he is not doing his share at home. The cycle is self-perpetuating and the end result is an erosion of the marital partnership. In the Libra model, the sense of shared ownership in financial and all other matters goes a long way toward preventing and disrupting this cycle. Shared ownership is the *secret sauce* for embedding gender equality in work-life solutions.

Because motherhood is such a visceral experience, I think it is easier, especially in those earliest years of raising children, for moms to be subsumed by their children's physical and emotional needs. The cultural norm of mother-intensive parenting—defined by the mother's complete devotion to meeting the needs of her children—is highly regarded. As a result, many women lack long-term perspective, becoming completely absorbed in their mothering role without paying sufficient attention to the importance of nurturing their marriage—a key factor in the equation of raising a family.

5. *Feeding into the adrenaline high of being superwoman.* I recently spoke with a dynamic and accomplished young woman who is very much in the throes of trying to integrate her career as a successful entrepreneur with her role as a new mother. She shared how the women in her new mother's group often discuss their perceived need to be good at so many things all at once: devoted, caring, and skilled mothers, accomplished professionals, attractive and fit, connected to family and friends, socially conscious—the list goes on. She spoke honestly about the intense high they admit getting from doing it all—and how it motivates them to prove they can be a generation of overachieving, handle-it-all, modern women.

There has been rampant discussion about the superwoman syndrome, and I've been guilty at times (perhaps even frequently) of buying into this cultural phenomenon. When I reflect on my own arrogance—and while I hate that word, it feels like the right application here—about being able to handle so much, I have to admit there is a whole lot of self-satisfaction that comes with feeling as though you can juggle all the balls and be the strong and powerful twenty-first century woman. When I was traveling a great deal for work, I could be very pleased with myself for getting all my work materials in order (since I was typically presenting and/or running the client meeting) and making sure my stuff was back from the cleaner, my hair was colored, all the ducks were lined up relative to school stuff, the dog, etc. Much of this preparation was necessary but much was not. Bryan could have easily handled many home-related things on my pre-trip to-do list, but somehow I got a kick out of doing it all—and then of course sharing all I had done. Many women, not just me and my young mother friend, feed into these gender norms because, quite frankly, there is great power in feeling like you can do it all. Not to mention the bonus "relationship points" you rack up by being able to point to all that you've accomplished (sarcasm intended). An accounting approach to who's doing what does not typically engender the spirit of the Libra approach, but long-term perceptions of fairness are critical. Considering how we might be feeding into the superwoman syndrome is a means to disrupt the self-perpetuating gender cycle so as to create more flexible and better work and life solutions.

While I've outlined overarching themes characterizing gender struggles, the experience of women of color differs greatly in some respects. Women of color are often in different family structures than white women. Among families, approximately 80 percent of Caucasian and Asian women are in married couples, while nearly 70 percent of Hispanic women and less than 50 percent of black women are in married-couple families.[23] Historically and currently, women of color, particularly black women, are far more likely to have economic responsibility for the family. As a result, one might hypothesize that women of color would report greater work-life difficulties than white women, but in my consulting work, I have seen just the opposite. Women of color tend to be more matter of fact about the work-life struggle. A senior-level African American woman had this to say about trade-offs in balancing her work and family lives:

> My family is important, very, very important, and I make loud, active statements about what I'm going to do if work interferes with my family. ... I cannot go for a week and not see my family. My male peers go for two weeks, no problem! I think that most of their spouses do not work. Women still are the primary care providers for our children, even if we are executives.
>
> I make work trade-offs and family trade-offs as well. There are imbalances that are strange. We are expected to pay attention to our kids in school, but we are also expected to be away in Europe on the opening day of school.[24]

My theory is that, because being a working parent is just a reality of life for many women of color, they are very pragmatic about doing what needs to get done. Black women provide a particularly strong example of long having combined paid work with raising their children, and often the care of parents and other extended family members.[25] We could learn much by better understanding their stories, about how they adapt and remain flexible as they juggle these multiple priorities in their lives.

The Flip Side of the Gender Story

Men are facing seismic cultural shifts as they seek to define their evolving roles at work and at home. Being a provider has long been the definition of a good husband and father, and men still very much feel that pull. But the expectations for modern fathers have expanded beyond being able to focus his energies on financially supporting the family. While more than twice as many respondents in the Pew Research poll indicated a man, as opposed to a woman, needs to be a good provider in order to be a good partner, more respondents also reported that a man (82 percent versus 74 percent for a woman) needs to put family before anything else to be a good partner.[26]

These days, men are increasingly on the hook for both providing financially *and* being involved at home, and the statistics suggest that men are stepping up at home: the amount of time fathers spend with their children under thirteen increased by 50 percent (from two to three hours per day) between the late 1970s and 2008.[27] I am one of the people who have written about the fact that women still do more at home—and it's true that women continue to devote more time than men to child care and household chores—but the gap is narrowing. Perhaps not surprisingly, men's reported experience of work-life conflict is also growing as they assume a more central role at home. In the late 1970s, approximately one-third of fathers in dual-earner couples indicated significant work-life conflict compared with 60 percent in 2008.[28]

In a phone interview with Josh Coleman, who has written extensively about relationships and parenting, he said, "The cultural ideals of the breadwinning father and the stay-at-home mother are still extremely powerful for people. There is almost programming that remains an active part of our culture. The influence of how we think of ourselves as women and men goes to the question of gender identity: this is right for a man to do and this is wrong for a man to do. For the longest time, men developed their sense of masculinity from being a provider and a protector. Many men are wondering what makes them a man now, so they cling to a career which makes them the provider. [But] men feel like they can't be happy anywhere. Before, if you were working hard and you were a good provider, that was enough, you had done your duty as a man. Now, men work more hours because of the economic insecurity, and also have this intensive parenting model where all of your free time is dedicated to parenting."[29]

One could debate if the trend of increasing male work-life stress was a bad thing (because heightened stress can be detrimental and have numerous health consequences) or a good thing (because it signals that men are playing these dual roles to a greater extent and are beginning to experience what working mothers have felt for some time). The silver lining is that experiencing the visceral pull of both is a catalyst for men to drive change in their workplaces as women have been doing for decades.

For example, a financial executive who played the far more traditional role as the provider when his children were growing up hit a turning point in his life at the prospect of becoming a grandparent. His own parents passed away when his children were quite young, and his children never had the chance to get to know them very well. Thus, when his grown daughter and her husband were contemplating care for their first child, the grandfather-to-be offered to help, changing his own work schedule in order to spend a day per week caring for his granddaughter. He told his wife, "My granddaughter and I are going to have our own relationship. She is going to know who I am." While he encountered initial resistance from his boss, he was given the leeway to experiment and prove it could work. The executive reported that four years later, while his boss was from the "old school," he had gotten used to the arrangement and could see it was working and his team had developed substantially through the process. He went on to say, "Caring for my granddaughter has been the greatest thing in my life. It has been everything that I wanted it to be."[30]

How Men Contribute to the Cycle of Gender Norms

1. Not sharing their true feelings about money. Despite men identifying very strongly with their role as providers, I believe many men truly welcome sharing the economic load and the sense of freedom and flexibility it provides. Like Betty Friedan helping women give voice to their feelings that being solely responsible for child care and homemaking left them wanting, my hope is that this book plays some role in helping men share their voices far more freely about the pressures they feel as providers, leaving them wanting in other areas of their lives. Not only do men feel the need to work ever harder in this insecure, fast-paced work world that we live in, but they are left with increasing guilt and frustration about not being able to spend more time with their families or on activities that bring them joy and replenish them. (This is similar to the stress that many mothers have felt for some time.) Among a nationally representative sample, men report increasing job insecurity, rising perceived work demands, and a desire to work fewer hours. Yet they don't cut back because they report that they need the money.[31]

A mirror image of women feeling frustrated and resentful because their husbands are not helping enough to care for the children and family is men feeling frustrated and resentful because their wives are not helping enough in shouldering the financial load. Many men experience conflict between their desire to allow their wives the choice about working outside the home and their desire to share the financial responsibility more equitably. Because the expectation of men as providers is so pervasive and automatic, they have little to no forum to struggle with or even to discuss this conflict, in many cases even with their wives.

The greater the financial needs of the family, the less able men feel to consider other work and life possibilities which might not exact such a high personal toll. One of the men I interviewed shared that his wife's interest in potentially moving into a bigger house and sending one of their children to private school made him feel more trapped in a job situation he had started to loathe. He brought this issue up with his wife. Fortunately, she was receptive to the conversation and openly listened to his concerns. They discussed how to work together to be more thoughtful about money decisions and the interaction became an important and positive step forward in their relationship. Men marshalling the courage to candidly discuss their true feelings about work, money, and trade-offs serves to dismantle the gender shackles and allows for the development of more creative and less gendered work and life solutions.

2. *Positioning himself as the helper, not a full partner, at home.* Similar to women not sharing ownership for the monetary well-being of the family, instead perceiving herself in a helper role, many men don't assume the full responsibility for all that needs to be managed after having children. From the outset, it is the responsibility of both parents to ensure that the child is cared for at all times. So when men (or women) think they can stay late at work, or head out on Saturday morning to the gym, or do anything else without checking with their partners to see that the child care is covered, they are not sharing the load. This sounds dramatic, but in the Libra model, both parents see themselves as the default in caring for the child or children unless they have made other plans. The couple may work out that the more accessible parent is the default person in certain situations, such as if the school calls because the child is sick and needs to go home. But too often this default simply happens without much—or any—discussion at all. And before long, mom is doing all the flexing.

Men who don't see themselves as the default parent—and in Libra families, both parents share this default parental role to a much greater extent—perpetuate the gender stereotype that the mother is in charge. According to research, over 50 percent of men take less than a week off when their child is born, providing very little time for them to get comfortable with caring for their newborn or to support their partner with this vast new responsibility.[32] In the Libra model, mothers are not in charge, *parents* are in charge.

A father shared with me his experience of needing to work at being the full "other parent":

> One of the things I've noticed about my own tendencies is that it's easy for me to let it slide, so if the baby starts crying, I'll let my wife deal with it. There is a built-in expectation that she will manage it and a built-in expectation that I don't have to. It's built into her and me—it's built into all of us, I

think—so I have to be constantly aware of that and not fall back on my laziness. The truth about getting up to get your kids in the middle of the night is that there is something wonderful about it. Not at that instance when it is a pain in the neck, but I believe we get much closer to our children through those tiny little things that seem like annoyances. In overcoming that, in being vigilant about not falling into a trap of expectations, I get much closer relationships to my children than otherwise I would have.

Some men rationalize that their wives do more of the child care because moms want to and/or are more natural at it. In any given family, that may be true, or it may not be true. In either case, having an open discussion about the roles each of you want to play will get you much closer to authentic choices for both of you, however you ultimately end up determining the best fit for your family.

3. Not pushing back on a wife or partner who is taking over at home. I admit that I'm expecting a lot here, but by men not pushing back on their mates who become overly dictatorial in the home space, they are contributing to these deeply gendered norms that constrain us all. Women should not deny their children the full participation of their fathers, and at the same time, men need to assert their right and privilege as a parent. If you feel your wife or partner does not make room for your contribution, then it is your job to initiate that conversation. The mother has no more right to dictate the father's role than the father has to behave like a 1950s stereotype and waltz out on a Saturday morning to play eighteen holes of golf because "he had a long week at the office." Negotiation and discussion are at the heart of the Libra approach so that the parents are working as a team to care for the family. The benefit of having two parents deeply involved in this way is enormous for children. They get to see two different takes on the world and two different ways of approaching things. The broader portfolio of skills you collectively bring to bear as parents provide an even stronger foundation for your children than if one parent is always in the lead role.

Of course, there are situations in which either parent may feel the other is detrimental to the well-being of their children. That is a much more serious situation and beyond the scope of this book. But in many cases, I think parents, especially mothers, simply have strong preferences for the way they like things and don't realize that overmanaging the parenting and home space doesn't leave room for their husbands to be true partners in the endeavor.

When I asked one of the dads in my research what he saw as benefits of the Libra approach, he shared that he had not been very close to his father growing up, not only because his father worked long hours, but because it seemed more difficult for his dad to stake out his place as a parent. He said, "The mother situation is so strong, it eclipses everything around her. Taking care of my daughter is an opportunity for me and I love this sense of being a father, of being involved in her life."

It can be easy for whichever parent spends more time with the child during waking hours to move into the dominant parent role, leaving the other parent to feel like a second-class citizen. It is the attitude of the parents, and how they respond to the situation, that makes all the difference. One father I spoke with, who works in the music business and is the primary caretaker of his young child during the day, shared his experience in minimizing the second-class parent situation:

> I have talked to other dads I know and one guy said, "I had to tell my wife, 'You are not here during the day and this is how I do things.'" I thought, This is just crazy. The basis for everything in our relationship is communication. If I do something new [with our son], I'll say that I've started doing it that day. There have been times when my wife feels like the second-class parent, and that she is being forced to do what I've decided. I try to listen and change my behavior. We both made it clear to each other that we were interested in being

equal parents in the stewardship of our son. We both made clear we wanted to do this together.

4. Not redefining work norms after becoming a parent. One of the most significant ways in which men unwittingly perpetuate gender norms is by not being more candid about the demands and challenges of being both an involved professional and an involved parent. Men tend not to push back at work when necessary or define new norms that allow more space for this major new role in their lives. There are many compelling reasons men don't do this. The strong pull of the breadwinner role remains, even in families where both partners work. Many men feel disproportionately punished for emphasizing their family needs and priorities. The work world does not expect men to prioritize family needs, and the default norm is that becoming a family man means a man will work hard—or even harder—because now he is in a far more responsible role. Feelings of increased job insecurity and escalating work demands heighten the struggle. The more pressure men feel as the only, or primary, financial provider, the less comfortable they will likely feel putting up boundaries around work. Whether or not both the husband and wife work, if the family tends to live beyond their means and is in constant catch-up to manage their expenses, he is going to feel far less flexibility to keep work in its rightful place.

The Boston College research on fatherhood highlights the complexity of men and their relationship to work vis-à-vis work and life integration. The researchers found that among a group of thirty-three new fathers, with children ages three months to eighteen months, and in dual-career situations with both partners working full-time, the self-reported definition of a good father included being a primary (not sole) breadwinner, as well as playing an active role in their children's lives. Most of the participants indicated that co-parenting was their goal and gave themselves a rating of 4.2 on a 5-point scale regarding being an involved caregiver for their children.[33] In a second phase of the research, the great majority of the nearly

1,000 fathers surveyed similarly perceived their parenting role as providing *both* financially and as a nurturer for their children.[34] Two-thirds of fathers believed that they and their spouse or partner should equally share the care of their children.[35]

Both phases of the research explored the extent to which fathers felt supported in their work environments, and the results were overwhelmingly positive. Among the survey respondents, over 80 percent indicated their manager was supportive when they had a problem or needed to manage family issues, and the majority perceived their supervisors as supportive of employees using flexible work practices. Similarly, they reported their coworkers as understanding when they needed to attend to personal business.[36] There were additional benefits that accrued to fathers in their new role as parents. The first report stated:

> Another very important dimension of becoming a father was the view that being a father granted an individual a greater aura of credibility, maturity and responsibility. This theme was echoed by many participants. They felt they were viewed as more serious (in a career sense) by their peers.[37]

Yet the fathers' beliefs about sharing at home as well as their perceived support at work did not translate into action in many cases. More than three-quarters of the fathers took one week or less away from work and 16 percent took no time at all after the birth of their most recent child. Only 6 percent of fathers negotiated a formal flexible schedule and virtually none of the fathers worked reduced hours. Conversely, four of five fathers surveyed had asked to work on challenging assignments and sought opportunities to increase their knowledge, clearly negotiating on behalf of career advancement.[38] The fathers were characterized as "willing to invest a lot of time and effort into their work." Based on interviews with nearly three dozen new fathers, surprisingly not a single participant indicated that fatherhood negatively impacted his career focus.[39]

This paradox between intention and action, and the enduring belief that parenthood will not affect work, are fundamental ways in which men perpetuate the gender cycle. I am left to ponder how men can believe that becoming a parent—among the greatest milestones in a person's life—will not affect their relationship to their career in any way. Fathers did make use of informal flexibility, flexing their start and end times, working from home, and in some instances working on a compressed schedule, but often their use of flexibility was under the radar, hidden, perpetuating the notion that it's work as usual for new fathers. These results crystallize the continued challenge of evolving attitudes and realities at work and illustrate the need for dads, in addition to moms, to help adapt work cultures that are out of step with our modern family structures.

What became clear in my employee research through the years was that men were far less likely to use their social capital at work to drive change around work-life issues. While men had far fewer struggles than women with asking for a raise or seeking a promotion—whether they were qualified or not—the idea of formally seeking flexibility was anathema to most. Men were far less likely to push against the system or even question the norms. I remember interviewing the general counsel of a large corporation whose wife had passed away in recent years. This man suddenly found himself a single parent raising two school-age daughters. He was quick to emphasize in the interview that this major life event—the death of his wife and his daughters losing their mother—had not impacted his work negatively in any way. I finished the interview saddened that even under such extreme life circumstances, this man—and many men—perceive the need to put family first, even for a finite period of time, in opposition to the notion of a committed, successful professional. These two roles are *not* mutually exclusive.

Men tend to erect far fewer boundaries at work in part because they define the scope of their role at home in a narrower, typically more predictable way. Based on time data from the Bureau of Labor Statistics, women in dual-career households spend more time on the physical care of children, while men spend more time playing with their children and doing hobbies together. Also, among household duties, women spend much more time on food preparation and cleanup, while men spend more time on lawn and garden care.[40] In the Boston College research, fathers were asked to identify the most important aspects of being a good father and the lowest score was given to *doing your part in the day-to-day child care tasks*.[41] Many men in focus group discussions and interviews I've conducted cite involvement with extracurricular activities—such as coaching a sports team—as their way of being involved with their children. I thoroughly applaud this involvement, but I also know that needing to get to the field by 4:30 p.m. is not the same as the unpredictability of managing when your child has their third earache in two months, or you need to go on frequent business trips and still coordinate all the changing details of child care in your absence. You have much more discretion about when you get around to lawn work, while hungry children at the end of a long day don't wait. Small children and the tasks involved in managing their lives are messy in both the literal and the figurative sense. In the Libra model, both parents are far more involved in all the bending and flexing at work *and* at home that is required to raise children.

I'm not suggesting that it is easy for men to redefine their work norms, but I can tell you as a veteran organizational consultant that men are a critical key to the continued evolution of work environments. People are constantly on the lookout for role models in their organizations who give credence to dual centrism—the ability to place equal importance on work and home. While many men are very supportive of the people who work for them, and can act as advocates regarding work-life issues, the greatest power I've seen is when they model these behaviors themselves. A key flexibility marker in any work environment is not only the prevalence of people working more flexibly but who the people are who comprise that group. The extent to which men—and people in leadership (often still disproportionately men)—work more flexibly, verbalize the importance of their family lives, and erect boundaries at work is highly emblematic of how employees experience the work culture.

Men need to partner with women to continue to make major shifts in gender norms in our workplaces that then extend into our family spheres. As long as mothers, but not fathers, curtail their employment as a response to overwhelming demands from work and home, it will ensure gender inequality in both realms.[42] Women play a vital role in promoting this shift by *not* doing it all at home, which perpetuates the ideal worker with no boundaries myth and does nothing to help create the far more flexible and balanced work cultures that we want our sons and daughters to inherit.

5. Adopting the limiting mindset that his wife needs to earn the right to work. The typical economic discussion a couple has when having a child is, will her income cover the child care, and if not, does it make sense for her to continue working outside the home? To limit the discussion to just that perspective is shortsighted. For educated men and women, a career spans decades, not years, and to make a black-and-white decision about leaving a career based on the preschool years, when the need for care is greatest, does not take the big picture into account. Among a nationally representative sample of women and men professionals, the researchers found that women lost a substantial amount of their earning power after being out of the workforce for three or more years.[43]

Staying in the workforce, even if to a reduced degree, is an important investment in future earnings. A study of participants at a women's leadership conference with an average salary of over $100,000 annually reported among the key findings that "women are using flexible work options not to opt out of work, but to make employment work in their complex lives." The survey respondents took advantage of both full-time (48 percent) and reduced flexible work arrangements. The researchers reported, "Whether they negotiate boundaries around the job, telecommute, stay in a job that permits balance, or make a lateral move instead of a promotion, women are trying to "make work work."[44] In addition to the compelling financial argument for continuing to work, a substantive body of data underscores that women who remain in the workforce are happier and healthier over the long run than those who stop working altogether.[45] It is far better to consider the collective incomes of both adults as the family revenue and child care costs as one (albeit a major one) among many family expenses in thinking about the financial repercussions of staying in versus leaving the workforce.

    6. *Not seeking support to assist with adapting to fatherhood as a major new stage in life.* Through the years I've had a growing understanding of and appreciation for how men's approach to connecting with friends and seeking support can look very different than women's. A *Wall Street Journal* writer did a great piece titled "Friendship for Guys (No Tears!)" in which he illuminated why, despite differences in approach and style, men's friendships are no less valuable or important than those of the women in their lives. He shared a funny story about how he often joked that his poker buddies of twenty-plus years didn't even know the name of his kids and then one night he decided to test it out. He turned to his friend at the poker table and asked, "Hey Lance, could you name my children?" His friend shrugged, paused to think, and then smiled sheepishly and said, "I could rename them."[46]

    I laughed out loud when I read this story because my husband, Bryan, has also been playing poker for over fifteen years with the same group of men, and while they have been to our house many, many times over the years, Bryan knows what I would consider quite little about the context of their lives. He probably couldn't tell me what kind of work their wives do or the approximate ages of their children—things I would consider basic information. Bryan and I have had many conversations about the differences in our ways of connecting with same-sex friends. In the earlier years of our marriage, after Bryan's yearly get-together with a group of male college friends, I'd be bubbling with lots of questions and his stock reply would be, "We really didn't talk about that." I'd be incredulous. How could he have spent four days with these guys and not talked about how one friend's child is doing in middle school, or how another friend is doing in his new job?

Research with nearly 400 men focused on how men make, nurture, and maintain their friendships through time underscores that men derive great support from their relationships with male friends, even though they are more likely based on doing things together rather than expressing their deepest felt thoughts, hopes, and fears.[47] Experiential bonds stand in for the verbal connection that typifies the female approach to friendship. I've come to appreciate how deeply men connect through shared experiences, particularly with friends they have known for a long time, through observing Bryan, my brothers, male friends, and the husbands of female friends. Part of my deep motivation is to better understand how my sons experience the world. I try to stay mindful as the mother of boys of the value for my sons of sharing activities as a way to deepen our emotional bonds. As a verbal sort, I can't resist talking as a main mode of connection, but I can clearly see the power of experience in my sons' lives. I seek to provide plentiful opportunities for shared experiences. A family trip to Alaska, allowing ample opportunities to hike, bike, and see spectacular wildlife together, was one such experience that I believe my sons won't ever forget.

When men become parents, there are typically few avenues to help them in adapting to this major new role in their lives. While mothers' groups are ubiquitous, fathers' groups remain in their infancy. During my research for this book I met with a group of dads of grown children who had been getting together monthly for *twenty years* while they were raising their children. They spoke of the value of talking to other men who were going through the same thing. These men shared that, while their wives seemed to have many opportunities to talk about and integrate their new role as mothers—from talking about it with friends, colleagues, family members, and neighbors—they themselves did not feel like they had many places to talk in a meaningful way about being a new father.

One of the perennial issues, and a topic they categorized as one of the most important through the years, was the professional career demands placed on them as men. They described their workplaces as often requiring a commitment of time and energy that did not leave them enough time to be the parents they wanted to be. (Does this sound familiar to thirty-something new dads?) One of the men said, "We were always figuring out how to parry these demands, how to get around the pressures to ignore our families and focus on career advancement. We were always undergoing changes at work that needed to be processed and vetted with the group and that is what we talked about."

This kind of opportunity for men to share their frustrations and reflections about fatherhood is critically important. As the Boston College fatherhood study reported, "At the close of our interviews, many of the fathers thanked us for allowing them to participate. Some relayed that the interview provided the first structured opportunity they had been given to reflect on and discuss their new and important roles. It seems that men want to have opportunities to discuss fatherhood, as well as their challenges in balancing their work and home lives. Providing more venues where this conversation is welcomed, both in and out of the workplace, would be beneficial as men strive to adjust to their new, more complex lives."[48]

The New York City Dads Group, formed in early 2009, provides an example of such a forum where dads can connect and share the many aspects of their lives as fathers. The two fathers who started the New York City Dads Group, Lance Somerfeld and Matt Schneider, both had business careers and subsequently retrained to become public school teachers through a New York City Teaching Fellowship program. Lance—who was home full-time for the first two years of his son's life and subsequently returned to teaching part-time—shared with me the story of how the group formed. He said that Matt, his fellow teacher, was a role model for him when he decided to stop working for a time to be home with his infant son. While on parental leave, Lance found that typically he would be the only male among many mothers and nannies at daytime activities for young children. His online search in the fall of 2008 for a father's group in the New York metro area turned up nothing, as did his informal attempts to connect with other fathers of young children in his community. He said, "Really what I wanted was to avoid isolation, to network and socialize with other guys in this mom-centric parenting world."[49]

Eventually he turned to technology and listed a get-together on Meetup.com to connect with other dads of young children who wanted to take advantage of all that New York City had to offer. The group started out slowly, and for the first several months a core group of four to six fathers would meet at playgrounds, museums, and other children-friendly places. Eventually Lance and Matt created an online presence. Through technology and word of mouth, many more dads learned about the network. The group started to grow exponentially, and by the beginning of 2011, over 400 men were members of the New York City Dads Group.

When I asked Lance what surprised him most when starting the group, he responded, "I went from trying to connect with a few dads once per week to something that has really grown. I have this core group of guy friends I communicate with often. It's so nice to be able to bounce ideas off of them. I never envisioned what it has built into. It has become a destination for so many fathers. It's a safe, comforting environment, sort of like a dad's fraternity. We do things with the kids, attend parenting workshops, and drink a few beers without the kids. It's great to have all those interactions."[50]

One of the ways that dads can help to dismantle gender barriers is by seeking out the companionship of other dads with whom they can share the many complexities and joys of combining their personal and professional roles. My hope is that fathers' groups become far more widely available so that dads have an opportunity to come together and define parenting on their own terms. Also, I hope they can be more forthright about both the joys and difficulties of parenting and of combining their many roles—as fathers, husbands, sons, brothers, friends, and professionals. The Libra model allows men to express both their nurturing capacities and their professional ambitions, without feeling like they have to make a stark choice between the two and knowing that they can have part (to my mind the best part) of both.

Common Things Both Women and Men Do to Sustain the Gender Cycle

1. Underestimating the impact of becoming a parent; failing to share hopes and concerns. The biggest way in which both women and men contribute to sustaining the gender status quo is by underestimating the impact that becoming a parent will have on their lives—as a couple, as individuals, as professionals. Many men and women do an insufficient amount of thinking, discussing, and planning regarding how they will combine their new roles as parents with their existing lives. Within three years of the birth of a child, two-thirds of couples perceive a decline in the quality of their relationship, according to research.[51] The very good news is that jointly planning for a child greatly mitigates the slippage into more traditional roles and the attendant downward spiral.

Having all the answers is not the goal of talking about your hopes and worries. No one knows how he or she will feel and react to becoming a new parent. Furthermore, there is much we learn along the way as we develop whole new parts of ourselves. But there are certain, basic questions couples should consider as they embark on becoming parents: How will becoming a parent impact my work in the short term (over the next year), the intermediate term (one to three years) and over the longer term (five-plus years)? What roles do we each individually hope to play as parents? How comfortable are we with child care? How much child care is optimal? How will we evaluate if whatever work-life model we initially decide on is working? What will we do if it is not working for one—or both—of us? How can we keep the channels of communication open as we move into this next stage of our relationship as a couple and family? These discussions lead to honest discussions and creative solutions that underpin strong, enduring marriages.

2. Underestimating the intensification of gender norms after having children. A Libra dad articulated the pull of gender for new parents:

> The truth is a lot of my friends—to some degree or another—are really trying to share parenting, but most people fall almost by default into the most standard ideas of how to parent. There is a societal ease with falling into roles. Every time a baby cries, there is a slight bit of greater ease with the mother going to the baby. There is not anything better about the mother getting the baby but it's what everyone expects. We have a lot of expectations that the care of children is covered by mom, even by people who are really open-minded about gender roles.

It is not uncommon for men and women who have seen themselves as peers—intellectually, professionally, and in all other ways—to be caught off guard by the persistence and power of gender norms once they become parents. Without planning, effort, and commitment to a different path, the default norm remains women prioritizing family and men prioritizing work. Unless men and women are aware of these forces and consciously make choices to combat them so they can write their own work-life scripts, it is very easy to get caught up in the tide. Becoming more conscious of the landscape allows you to make the best choices for yourself and your family, whatever those might be.

What Can You Do to Disrupt the Self-Reinforcing Gender Cycle?

Gender norms are deeply embedded and continue to profoundly influence how men and women define their work and life solutions after becoming parents. Solutions to managing work-life challenges are often treated as individual choices and trade-offs and do not consider the complex family-systems issues that more creative solutions require. Couples who discuss and work to define a joint work and life vision, both from the outset of thinking about having children and on an ongoing basis, are far better positioned to design flexible, evolving solutions that best fit their collective hopes, goals, and needs. My interviews with Libra couples underscored the transformative power of a shared work and life compass in helping them override typical gender patterns, evaluate decisions, reorient after changes both expected and unexpected, and move through the inevitable ups and downs of raising a family.

It is very helpful to consider several factors when thinking about possible work and life options. The mother's and father's work situations are primary in determining a family work and life solution. Key issues related to work include the degree of flexibility and support in their respective work environments (this is important but does not have to be the deciding factor), their personal skills and limitations in integrating work and home demands, their passion for and satisfaction with their work, and their relative contribution to the family income. Another critical variable is money management, encompassing the financial management skills of the mother and father and the perceived monetary requirements of the family. (Is this a family that tends to be fiscally conservative, or do they spend before saving? What is the level of agreement or disagreement between the couple about the best way to manage the financial resources of the family?) The roles that the mother and father hope to play as parents as well as their comfort with different types of child care, and the availability of child care options, are also factors. Finally, the temperament of the child or children, and the degree to which that temperament is a good match for the parents, plays a starring role in how parents ultimately devise their work and family solutions.

For couples contemplating a first or subsequent child, a good place to start to avoid devolving into typical gender roles is to think about the important issues that will need to be managed for your expanded family and how you envision sharing the load. Major work and personal areas of focus and responsibility include:

- Earning and managing money;
- Care of your child or children (this category is broad, including planning for child care as well as providing the day-to-day care);
- Care of the marital partnership;
- Self care, to keep each of you strong and resilient;
- Home economics, including feeding the family, doing laundry, maintaining the house, yard, cars, etc.;
- Care of relationships beyond the nuclear family, including friends, relatives, neighbors, etc.;
- Involvement in additional communities such as school, church, or temple.

While much of the personal and home management tends to happen with minimal effort before children, bringing children into the mix raises the complexity considerably, and open, proactive discussion is critical. There is no right way to organize the many family responsibilities. These issues get worked out by default—someone needs to earn a living, to buy the presents, to plan the vacations, to do the laundry, and to take the children to the doctor. But not acknowledging the role we play in perpetuating these default responsibilities may lead to resentment and hard feelings.

Discussing what is necessary to care for your family in this big-picture way reinforces the notion of working together as a team. It helps both men and women feel much more appreciated—however they are contributing to the welfare of the family—and the process alone serves to minimize falling into well-worn gendered roles. It encourages mothers and fathers to consider the trade-offs of time and money and to be more intentional in their choices. When men and women are aware of the continued power of gender norms, it empowers them to be far more in charge of architecting work-life solutions that are best suited for their families. With couples on the same page about solving the work-life puzzle, the sky is the limit.

CHAPTER 4

HOW WE WORK: DELUSIONS OF PRODUCTIVITY

We are becoming the servants in thought, as in action, of the machine we have created to serve us.

---John Kenneth Galbraith

I've often joked that being an organizational development consultant is akin to being a professional voyeur. Over nearly two decades I've had the good fortune to work with dozens of the most successful companies in the world, as measured by both their financial success as well as their progressive attitudes. Many of my clients have been leaders in their industries, as well as organizations that regularly appear on all the lists of the "best places to work" for employees. I have gathered a treasure trove of knowledge about how people work, what gets in their way, and what helps. I have also been witness—with a front row seat—to how the work world has changed. It continues to do so. Most organizations see themselves as highly unique, and this is true to some extent, but while each organization has its own footprint, the issues relative to how people work—what they struggle with and what enables them to work more effectively—remain surprisingly universal.

Work is being transformed all around us, and the pain of this transformation runs wide and deep. Similar to the transition from an agricultural to an industrial economy in the eighteenth and nineteenth centuries, we are in the throes of moving from an industrial to an information age. In this modern age, we are facing new problems about how we spend our time at work, and at home. Finding solutions today requires different approaches. For much of human history, accessing information and connecting with others have been key challenges to overcome; over a dramatically short window of time, this is no longer the case. No longer do colleagues working on opposite sides of the globe need to send the findings of their research through the mail, which would take days or weeks to arrive. Now a quick email with the report attached electronically will do the trick within minutes—and because it is so easy to share, communication may include several work-in-progress versions. No longer does a professional have to keep up with new developments through yearly conferences and reports in monthly or quarterly industry publications. Now, countless online sources jam their email boxes with the latest and greatest information. No longer do we turn off from work when we get home because all the files are in the office. Now, at the touch of a keyboard, we can access nearly everything we might need to keep working—anytime and anywhere.

Organizations and how they operate are evolving, but we are living day to day in the transition where vestiges of the old and new work norms combine. All the while, each of us is faced with the very practical challenges of caring for our families as well as finding—and/or creating—work that we care about *and* pays the bills. We are continually pushed out of our comfort zones as we learn the new rules, and often it feels like a struggle.

In order to work differently—and better—we need to understand how we are working currently and the very real impacts of our current approach on individuals and on organizations. This chapter highlights real-life examples of work teams and individuals who are positively transforming their work approaches, and they serve as inspiration for what you can do—as an individual, a colleague, a manager, a leader—to move us collectively in the right direction as our work lives continue to evolve.

The forces of technology, globalization, changing demographics, and the shifting employee-employer value proposition have altered how, when, and where we work, who we work with, and even what we classify as work. Job security—in the traditional sense of trading loyalty and good work for a steadily increasing paycheck, reliable health insurance, and a comfortable retirement—is a thing of the past. Professional competition is seen as boundless. No longer do we see the other people in our organization or in our industry (or profession) as the competition; instead anyone across the world with the requisite skills to do the job is the competition—and yes, we are constantly reminded that many are willing to do the job for a lot less. The impact of technology on how we communicate and on our experience of time cannot be overstated. Technology has redefined many aspects of our lives, particularly our work lives.

Similar to my perspective on how both men *and* women contribute to the gender cycle without really seeing what role they play in maintaining the status quo, I seek to bring a more holistic perspective to the problems with how we work. Organizational cultures and norms create many struggles in the workplace, but each of us also plays a central role in creating and maintaining destructive and ineffective work norms. Seeing the role you may be playing can help you create a better reality, no matter the specifics of your particular work situation.

As with my ideas around gender issues, my perspective on the sources of the problems at work has substantially evolved through time and observation. In the early stages of my career, it was far easier for me to see all the obstacles created by organizations, and to fully attribute employee struggles to integrate their work and home lives to these organizational challenges. Downsizing meant that the remaining employees faced increased workloads, bad managers engendered stress, frequently changing priorities caused wasted effort and confusion, and unrealistic deadlines drove employees to work all the time. These issues are real and clearly do impact how we work. But, through time, I also gained an important perspective as to how individuals contributed directly to their own work struggles.

The typical work experience of professional employees in the twenty-first century goes something like this: they feel acute pressure to do more with less (a favorite corporate slogan); they encounter a constant stream of emails and other forms of communication; they are working with colleagues and clients, not only across the office, but increasingly across the world; and they lack the time and space to think strategically, remaining fully immersed in responding to the parade of situations that cross their transom daily. Their list of priorities expands, and more time spent working at the office—or anywhere else—doesn't seem to compensate for the increasing demands. They work harder to keep up, yet feel farther behind. The pace of change feels overwhelming, and they struggle to create space in their lives for anything but work. Even the language we use to describe our relationship to work in the U.S.—work-family or work-life as opposed to family-work or life-work—suggests our priorities.

Work Overload Is Real

In all my years of conducting work-life research, the most prevalent finding has been the acute sense of overload that people experience at work. U.S. workers consistently log among the highest number of hours of any in the industrialized world,[1] and the U.S. holds the dubious distinction of being the only industrialized country where workers are not obligated by law to receive paid vacation time.[2] In addition to the U.S., the only countries across the world lacking paid parental leave are Lesotho, Papua New Guinea, and Swaziland,[3] and in the U.S., the Family and Medical Leave Act enabling unpaid parental leave covers only about 60 percent of the workforce. The number of hours spent working has risen through time for the professional class. While in 1980, approximately one in five college-educated men worked fifty or more hours per week, nearly a third have done so more recently.[4] In research, work hours were found to be one of the most important predictors of work-life conflict for men and a more important predictor of conflict than time spent on family care and home management.[5]

In my employee research, primarily with large multinational companies, exempt employees—those not paid for overtime and working in professional and management roles—averaged over forty-five hours per week, and those in management roles logged more than fifty.

In addition to working long hours, we are also not taking vacations, and if we do so, for many of us, work comes along. In 2008, the Conference Board found that the number of Americans reporting vacation plans within the coming six months was at a thirty-year low,[6] and more than a third of American workers do not take their full vacations. One in five employees reported working while on vacation to at least some degree, while one in ten reported working often or very often.[7]

It is not just the sheer number of hours we work, but also the way in which we work that adds to the struggle. Multitasking reigns supreme, and ads for smart phones—the must-have work tool of the twenty-first century professional—tout one's ability to run several "apps" simultaneously. Along with technological advancements that enable constant connection and access, our ability and need to communicate has skyrocketed. We both pride ourselves—and groan—at the number of emails we field on a regular basis and the number of meetings that fill our calendars to capacity. According to a study of nearly 8,000 managers, one in four described their communication load, including emails and meetings, as nearly or completely unmanageable.[8] A nationally representative study of American workers reported that men's perceptions of having to work very fast and very hard have risen substantially in recent decades.[9]

In interviews and focus group discussions, employees' struggles to combine work and home are vividly brought to light. I clearly recall a single young woman working in the information technology department of a growing health care company recounting how, when she arrived home from work, typically at eight p.m. or later, all she could manage was to plop herself in front of her television to eat takeout before falling asleep. Her story epitomized the notion of being completely drained by work. This young woman said she couldn't fathom how people at the company managed additional responsibilities such as raising a child. A dad in a focus group at a bank spoke emphatically about the stress introduced into his life by trying to get his toddler out the door in the morning to day care. He described becoming highly agitated with this daily struggle, and eventually his wife stopped working outside the home, eliminating this before-work gauntlet. Among the greatest challenges of this continued sense of overload was the degree to which it stripped people of their confidence. Men and women spoke about how escalating demands—and their sense of not being able to keep up—left them feeling incompetent. They described lacking any buffer should anything go wrong or a new priority get added to the list which created an ongoing source of stress and anxiety. In addition, they struggled with guilt over letting their colleagues or coworkers down, as well as perceived pressure from managers and those coworkers who set few limits on their work time or energy. They described feeling unable to leave or disconnect. These employees persisted in the face of frequent changes and ongoing shifts in priorities, yet their clarity and sense of forward momentum took a big toll.

Productivity and Confusion

We are very fond of the word "productivity" in economics and in business. Productivity is associated with output—or yield—and we have various ways in which we seek to measure it. For instance, a factory might measure productivity as the number of hours it takes to produce a certain amount of product, such as a tube of toothpaste, while in a service business, productivity might be based on the revenue generated by an employee divided by his or her salary (or cost). Like many things in life, productivity is a complex concept that cannot be fully captured with measurement. As Einstein so accurately observed, "Not everything that can be counted counts, and not everything that counts can be counted."

Higher gross domestic product (or GDP) is associated with a higher standard of living and a better quality of life. But there is much to debate in that perception. U.S. productivity gains in recent decades have been attributed to longer work hours, so that while productivity has risen, the experience of many workers has been a reduction in their quality of life on many fronts—more stress, less time for life outside of work, and declining health. While across nations rising GDP tends to equate with greater reported happiness and well-being, nearly all the differential can be explained not by income but by factors such as democratic governments that respect human rights, a just legal system, an effectively functioning government, and adequate health care. Furthermore, while the GDP per capita has risen dramatically in the U.S. since World War II, measures of life satisfaction have changed very little. This trend of rising GDP, coupled with stagnancy in reported happiness and well-being, has been similar in other wealthy nations such as Japan and those in Western Europe.[10]

Economic data also challenge the connection between long hours and productivity. Based on data by the OECD (the Organization for Economic Co-operation and Development), which tracks statistics such as average hours worked and labor productivity by country, the countries which log the highest hours at work (Korea, Russia, Mexico, and Greece among them) report very low relative productivity rates.[11] Michael Breen, author of *The Koreans,* aptly described why hours and productivity don't go hand in hand: "This is an authoritarian corporate culture. It's very bad form to leave the office before the boss does, so people will hang around doing nothing, and then when the boss leaves, they feel free to leave ... Because of all that, people don't have much of a life."[12] Across Europe, those countries with the most generous family-friendly policies reported the highest level of national productivity, and U.S. hourly productivity was lower than in several European countries that guarantee far more time off for family reasons.[13]

To add insult to injury, our ability to measure the productivity of knowledge workers is moderate at best. As an economics major in college, and having spent my early career in the investment field analyzing capital markets, I've long wrestled in my own mind with the concept of productivity. Is the value of a consultant or a lawyer or an accountant the amount of revenue generated by their work?

How do we measure the quality of their guidance? Is a research scientist that generates the idea for an eventual blockbuster drug more productive than one whose work helps to identify treatments for several rare diseases? Is a software engineer who develops an enormous amount of code but greatly interferes with the ability of colleagues to move ahead more productive than one who is not as prolific but doesn't derail the rest of the team? What is the true productivity of someone who contributes significantly to the bottom line, but does so in such a way that results in a constant churn of professionals that impairs client service?

There are no simple, straightforward answers here, and economists and business consultants do the best they can with the measurement tools they have. But too often, we act as though we've got this productivity equation all figured out, when in fact major pieces of the equation are missing. From my experience as a consultant, I know that there are many realities we can't fully measure, and so they are not reflected as costs: the loss of intellectual capital when experienced people leave, the cost of rigid managers who impede rather than facilitate the work of their subordinates, the problems caused by employees whose poor planning results in constant crises for many others, and the price we pay when employees lose confidence in their abilities and feel paralyzed because they can't maintain the pace. Some humility about the limitations of our ability to measure productivity—in addition to the need for a more holistic perspective—is clearly in order.

Problems with the Way We Work

Many of our current work norms are highly problematic. Time is a proxy for commitment in many workplaces, and there is a deep, enduring bias that more time translates to greater output and value. Both individuals and organizations fear working less. Face time (the perceived need to be seen at work) remains critical, even as we work in a highly mobile, increasingly global work world. A pervasive—and often false—sense of urgency colors many workplaces, and the work heroes remain those who can log long hours or jump on an airplane with little interference from other aspects of their lives. We have adopted an ADHD approach to work, endlessly trying to respond to multiple priorities simultaneously. We ricochet from one stimulus to another, never fully attending, needing to constantly retrace our steps. We have a strong bias toward the need for immediate accessibility and connection, to a far greater extent than is warranted by true business demands. There is a deeply entrenched culture of meetings in many organizations, many of which are poorly planned and executed. Schedule management—arranging, canceling, rescheduling—can sometimes feel like an end in itself. Everything feels like a priority, and while things get added, nothing seems to come off the list. We remain excessively busy, but too infrequently ask the strategic questions, or even question where we are adding value. Work is never done, and keeping our heads down and working harder seems the only answer. A focus on work-life balance, or purposefully working less, is seen as anathema to productivity and meeting business needs.

Several pervasive work practices defy what we do understand about being productive and effective. Based on performance research, we know that working at continuously high speeds, seeking to attend to several stimuli at once, and working harder and longer without planned breaks to regenerate is both unsustainable and unproductive.[14] A far better approach is to focus intensely for select periods of time, clearly identifying the types of activities to be attended to during those periods—whether deep-thought work, interactive time for meetings and conversations, or time for fielding email. In addition, building in breaks to refocus our minds and energies, even for brief periods, is important to retaining focus and attention. There's no doubt there is something satisfying about rising to the occasion and giving it our all in the face of a tight deadline, creative challenge, or a particularly vexing situation. The problem is that this kind of constant urgency has become the norm in many workplaces, and we enable this state of affairs by our own denial of the physiological rhythms of the human body. Most of us respond to rising work demands with longer hours, but our ability to be effective in those extended hours drops precipitously. We spend far too much time in the territory of diminishing marginal returns, where the additional time does not reap sufficient additional benefits. Yet the personal costs are quite high.

In my role as an organizational development consultant, one of my ongoing functions was to help employees and organizations to distinguish between work norms that added value and those that did not. As an outsider charged with listening and learning to get a picture of the work culture, I was able to see macro patterns across the organization as well as micro patterns defining subcultures at the department level. I could write a book solely devoted to the many unproductive, even toxic norms we've created in our modern work world, all in the name of what I would call the "delusion of productivity," but for the sake of brevity, let me share a few examples that illustrate how we work in the twenty-first century, and how it too often defies common sense:

The burden of "face time." In more than one company with intense pressure for face time, employees admitted to leaving a symbol—usually a piece of clothing such as a jacket or sweater—on the back of their chair, or keeping the lights on in their office or cubicle, so that it appeared they were still at work even after they had left for the day.

Meeting overload. At one highly successful health care company, the problems with the organization's perceived consensual decision-making process became increasingly apparent. The company prided itself on its collaborative approach, and people would regularly schedule meetings with many others present to ensure their involvement. Lurking within the consensus norm, however, was a hidden hierarchical structure. While many employees would attend a meeting, if the key people were not in attendance, the participants could not come to closure and move forward. Instead of canceling the meeting (which would amount to admitting that someone was in charge), the meeting would happen as planned, many people would attend, but in order to make a final decision, another meeting would need to occur at which the key people were present.

Employees felt very proud to work for this company, which most regarded as caring deeply about their employees and their customers, or members. But the intense meeting culture, predicated on the need to have everyone involved, was one of the core contributors to employee burnout. The multiple meetings used up so much time during the traditional work day that employees worked long hours at other times to manage the rest of their work responsibilities. People became fearful of falling behind and were losing their confidence in their professional competence. There was much to celebrate at this company, but because people felt so squeezed, one deadline flowed directly into another, leaving no opportunity to recognize all that had been accomplished. Among the key takeaways from our consulting intervention was the need to link consensus with accountability, and to punctuate their successes as a way to fuel up for the next challenge.

The catch-22 of billable hours. The billable-hours economic model of corporate law firms particularly illuminates problems of efficiency and effectiveness. When times are good, and there is more than enough work to do, associates feel the need to work hard and they struggle with long, often unpredictable hours. The strong upside is that they are billing lots of hours, the main currency in most corporate law firms. One might think a reduction in the workload would allow attorneys to slow the pace for a bit, but instead, insufficient work can translate to even longer work hours. As described to me by law firm associates, when the work slows, more senior attorneys often delegate less work, preferring to keep their billable hours high, but in the late afternoon or early evening, when they realize they can't get it all done, they will go searching for associates to help ease the load. Suddenly, the associate who has spent several hours doing not much more than trying to "look busy" has a legitimate deadline that is going to keep her at the office late that night. Alternatively, if the work pipeline remains dry and the associate leaves work, she does so with the knowledge that she will inevitably have to put in even longer hours in the future to compensate for the lack of billable hours on any particular day. It seems not only a toxic mix for associates, but also an ineffective way to run a business.

The billable-hours system also means redundant time—such as internal meetings on a case or client meetings with the full team present—is costly because not everyone can bill for all the time spent, especially more junior attorneys who attend but are primarily in a listening or learning mode. While it may be more efficient to send an electronic communication in lieu of active participation, for associates learning their trade, being able to see how their work contributes to the whole while they work on discrete assignments with limited scope makes the work far more interesting and gratifying. The end result of this combination—long hours, intense work-life conflict, and unsatisfying work (lacking a vision of the full landscape which helps to make the building years feel far more worthwhile)—is high turnover among law firm associates, with the attendant costs buried in an economic equation disproportionately focused on revenue and missing key variables.

A crippling lack of backup. Finally, consider the high-tech company, known for its efficiency, where activity was synonymous with productivity. In this organization, very lean staffing meant there was little duplication of effort. Very efficient? One might think so. But too often if one worker was unavailable or late delivering her work, or if any critical link was missing, everyone's ability to make progress was substantially impeded. Because of the lean staffing model, many employees had the role of being this critical link, with the related stress fueled by the need to always be available. This organization had also created a widely accepted norm that people managed email while sitting in meetings (even in meetings with the top leadership of the company), so people were constantly looking down at their laptops or smart phones, not participating, and then disrupting the flow when they reconnected to the meeting content and wanted to reengage in the conversation. At this company, efficiency trumped effectiveness, with high personal costs for employees and many unmeasured costs for the business.

In collaboration with colleagues at Catalyst, I wrote two pieces in a series on work efficacy. In *Beyond Flexibility*, the voices of employees we heard in our consulting work through the years give firsthand accounts of their experience of modern work norms:[15]

> I work smart, I focus, coordinate with others, get my work done and leave; but I am seen as less committed than the people who work more hours. It doesn't make sense for the company. And, I am worried about career consequences.
>
> In my practice group there is immense pressure and lots of stress. It comes from someone walking the floor and seeing if you are still around, asking if you are busy and if you are, they ask how late you stayed last night.
>
> It's almost like a competition of who works the most ... It's like efficiency's almost frowned upon. "Oh, if you got it done in 40 hours, you don't have enough work to do." Or if you're really fast at something or really good at it, it almost seems like you're slacking.

Our Personal Contributions to Work-Life Conflict

Our personal work styles, habits, and beliefs are key pieces of the work-life puzzle. Creating a different reality requires getting clarity on how you are contributing to the overwork and overload dynamic. No matter how supportive your manager, your coworkers, and your organization are, unless you take ownership for your impact on the workplace and strengthen your personal skills at putting up boundaries at work, you will not experience the kind of fundamental change that redefines your work-life productivity.

While consulting to one of the stalwarts of the "Best Companies to Work For" crowd, I kept trying to figure out what else this company could be doing to help mitigate work-life struggles. It was clear from conversations with senior leaders at the organization that not only did they deeply understand the importance of a work-life fit for organizational success, but they also had long made available a robust menu of work-life supports—including rampant flexibility—that was the envy of many organizations. Leadership was on board, most of the managers were on board, employees felt supported and lucky to work for this company, and yet, work-life conflict remained a pressing issue for many. There was clearly a piece missing here.

Reviewing the transcripts from focus group discussions and interviews brought out a clear theme of people referencing their own contributions to the work-life stress equation. They would say things like, "I push so hard because I am a type-A personality," or, "I work such long hours because I don't want to let my manager or my coworkers down," or, "I keep working because I feel the pressure and I don't know what else to do," or, "I push so hard because everyone else here is so smart and driven and if I don't, I won't be able to keep up." From an outside observer's vantage point, it was clear that this company had an abundance of smart and hard-working employees who were innovative, ambitious, and accountable. Yet many individuals admitted to a level of personal drive that was ushering them down a path of burnout, despite all the things the organization was doing right in seeking to help employees address their work-life challenges.

Across the American workforce, the people with the highest levels of education and in the highest status jobs—managers and professionals—have the greatest access to flexibility and the greatest control over their work schedules. They are also the ones who report higher levels of spillover from work to home.[16] In research about professionals in extreme jobs—characterized by long hours, high pressure, and high income—a key finding was the extent to which these individuals saw their intense work as fully their choice. These professionals did not consider themselves victims, but rather felt exalted and intensely turned on by the pace, the responsibility, and the rewards of their extreme jobs.[17]

Among several hundred professional men (60 percent in managerial roles) working at large companies, the vast majority indicated that their work environments were supportive of work-life issues. Two-thirds of the men, all fathers raising children, described work as only a small part of who they were, yet they were willing to expend the lion's share of their time and energy at work. Eighty-four percent reported they were willing to put in a great deal of effort beyond that normally expected to help their organizations succeed, and more than three-quarters of the men wanted to advance to a position of greater responsibility.[18] Over several decades, while men have reported increasing job demands through time, they also increasingly indicate having enough time to complete tasks. The researchers posited, "This change is likely due to the fact that technology has blurred the boundaries between work and family life, thus making it easier to complete tasks after the workday is supposed to be over."[19]

In an article titled "If You Need to Work Better, Maybe Try Working Less," Sue Shellenbarger, the long-time work and family columnist for the *Wall Street Journal,* shared her own experiments—and struggles—with working less. She wrote, "After years of working on and off throughout most weekends, I was trying a new approach by taking off at least one entire day every weekend this month, away from reporting, writing, and all other work. Early on, I hated it. As simple as it seemed, sticking to a time-off plan stressed me out at first. What I didn't see right away was that my little test was forcing me to improve the way I work."[20]

In addition to the pull of work because it never feels done, both adrenaline and ego play a starring role in our struggles with overwork. The primary reason professionals were drawn to extreme jobs was for the adrenaline rush (90 percent of men and 82 percent of women). The trouble is this reactionary mode robs us of the reflective thinking that is necessary to solve complex, multifaceted problems. Our overly developed sense of self-importance and perceived indispensability makes us lose perspective about where it is truly important that we be involved. Our insecurities about work push us to view our contributions—and the amount of time necessary to achieve them—as inflexible and nonnegotiable. For many of us, the "on switch" is stuck and we don't know how to shut it off. The highly addictive quality of responding to constant stimuli means that simple hard work and accountability have crossed the line into something much more uncontrolled and ego-driven. I am not suggesting all the struggles with overwork are in our heads and self-created. Many external factors are at play, but personal norms are also a core contributor to the problem and thus a critical part of the solution.

The Costs of the Way We Work

"Lean and mean," "Do more with less." These are the watchwords of our economy, and while there are endless conversations about improving productivity, there remains insufficient understanding of the costs of our prevalent work norms for individuals and for organizations.

The way we are currently working has costs for our relationships, our families, and our health. In an annual survey of attitudes in the American workplace, nearly two of three respondents indicated that job pressures interfered with their family or personal lives, and over half were stressed to the point of feeling extremely fatigued and out of control.[21] The Families and Work Institute characterized American workers as experiencing a "time famine" based on results from their national study of the workforce. Approximately 60 percent of those who were married or partnered did not feel they had enough time for their significant other, while three in four parents indicted having too little time to spend with their children.

In my employee research, the majority of employees indicated feeling completely drained at the end of the working day, and the reported impact of work stress on home was always greater than the impact of home stress on work. In addition, the incidence of reported burnout rose substantially as work hours rose. Professionals in extreme jobs—those characterized by at least sixty-hour workweeks, high salaries, and other characteristics such as 24/7 accessibility to clients or a large amount of travel—indicated highly negative impacts of their work in their home lives. Nearly two in three men—and one in three women—reported their jobs interfered with having strong relationships with their children. For about half of those in extreme jobs, their work interfered with their ability to have a satisfying sex life and a strong relationship with their partner or spouse.[22]

Our work norms show up in our collective declining health. According to national research, the overall health of the American workforce declined over the six years between 2002 and 2008, with men experiencing a more significant drop than women. A startling third of respondents registered signs of clinical depression, over 25 percent reported sleep problems, and 62 percent were overweight or obese. In addition, over 40 percent reported multiple indicators of stress based on a stress index (with statements such as "I'm unable to control the important things in my life" and "The difficulties are piling up so high that I can't overcome them"). Underscoring the critical importance of overwork in our lives, the most frequent predictor of health and well-being was work-life fit (followed by autonomy and economic security).[23]

Not only does the way we're working have steep costs for us as employees, it also has substantial costs for organizations—many of which are not well understood. In a knowledge economy, creativity is vital, yet research indicates many assumptions about what fuels creativity are dead wrong. Based on more than 12,000 diary entries tracking the day-to-day experiences of more than 200 professionals (across several organizations in multiple industries), an analysis by a professor at the Harvard Business school whose research is devoted to the study of creativity showed that people were least creative when they were fighting the clock and did not have time to engage fully and completely in complex issues.[24] Creativity requires both focus to reflect deeply and an incubation time for ideas to gestate. Furthermore, the analysis showed that acute time pressure impaired creativity, not just for the day the participants were feeling the time stress, but also the next day and into the next.[25]

How we feel about our work also greatly impacts how effectively we work. The researchers found that more positive feelings about work translated to greater creativity and productivity while negative emotions had just the opposite effect. The researchers learned that the anger and fear brought on by impending layoffs had a far more negative impact on both creativity and productivity than they had anticipated and the effects lingered more than five months later.[26]

Through my research, survey data across several companies similarly provided evidence of the organizational costs of modern work norms. Work-life conflict exerted a substantial toll on employees' ability to focus at work, to produce high-quality work, and to assume greater responsibility because they were already at capacity. Work-life stress was a driver of employee turnover, especially for professional women, which was costly for organizations in ways that were—and were not—measurable.

Despite a large body of data developed over the last twenty-plus years that documents the organizational benefits of supporting the work-life issues of employees, those who manage and lead organizations persist in sending highly contradictory messages. A global study found more than 80 percent of leaders and managers identified work-life supports as important to employee productivity and retaining talent. However, over half also reported the ideal employee was available to meet business needs regardless of business hours, and 40 percent indicated the most productive employees in their organizations were those without a lot of personal commitments.[27]

The Myth of Multitasking

Despite our love affair with multitasking and our perceived sense of being incredibly productive while we do it all—all at once, that is—the truth remains that multitasking is anything but efficient. According to David Meyer at the University of Michigan, one of the foremost experts on multitasking, who has spent the last several decades studying this phenomenon, multitasking translates into redundancy and requires more time to achieve the same result. Each time we interrupt our mental processes to focus on another thing, even for a mere few seconds, our brains lose the thread of what we were previously doing and need to effectively retrace the steps to get back up to speed. This reorientation requires mental energy and time. The cost of switching from task to task escalates as the complexity of the task increases, so that trying to do something that requires mental firepower—such as having a challenging conversation with a coworker or composing a thoughtful paragraph—means that much more time getting back up to speed after an interruption. Essentially, the more we multitask, the more we train our brains to only partially focus.

Our brains can do some things simultaneously, like listening to music and writing, or driving and talking (although based on my experience with Boston drivers, some of us are clearly better at that than others). However, the notion that we can participate intelligently in a business meeting while managing our email, or continually stop to respond to our smart phones while thinking through a challenging problem, doesn't make much sense based on what we know about how the brain works.

My own thoughts about multitasking have changed—a lot—through time. Given my somewhat pathological drive toward being efficient and productive, the thought of doing it all at once is highly appealing for me. I remember shortly after college standing in a bank line (remember we used to do that, actually stand in line and talk to someone at a bank?) while reviewing a spreadsheet for work and thinking how incredibly productive I was. For several years, while I commuted into downtown Boston through Cambridge, Massachusetts, with its seemingly endless red lights and lots of time spent waiting in bumper-to-bumper traffic, I would read the *Wall Street Journal* in short bursts. On what I considered a good day, I could read a feature story that started on the front page and took nearly all of an interior page of the paper. It used to drive my husband nuts when I would tell him this. While I stopped reading before putting my foot to the accelerator, I'd be lying if I didn't admit there were times when the story was just too interesting and I drove a short way, letting my foot off the brake, head partially down, while I finished the paragraph. I'm not proud of this, by the way. I also know that it has become commonplace for people to scan just one more line of a text as they start to drive away from a traffic light.

What changed my mind about multitasking and helped me to change my behavior was both professional and personal. As a consultant, I would be at a client site, retained to help the organization better address the work-life issues of employees, and I would hear about and see directly the problems with multitasking. I had one client who was the epitome of multitasking gone awry. He was like a pinball in a pinball machine: shooting this way and that, responding to the most recent stimuli with no sense of order or completion. Instead of spending a focused twenty to thirty minutes going through the material we needed to review, he interrupted the meeting multiple times to pick up the phone, answer emails that needed one-or two-line responses at just that moment, and jump up to look for something among the stacks of information strewn about the office. This was a brilliant person, with impeccable credentials, who was working in a way that was anything but intelligent. Our meeting about work-life challenges at the organization took well over two hours as I—and the other people in attendance—spent a whole lot of unproductive time waiting while he attended to this and that. The irony was palpable.

I also disliked the way being so efficient made me feel sped up all the time. I found it very difficult to dwell in that multitasking mode most of the time and then to be able to really stop and listen, whether to my child telling me a story about school in his typical childlike, wandering way, or to my spouse giving me lots of details about fantasy football or sharing the complexities of the people he manages at work. Ultimately, I stopped believing multitasking was the be-all and end-all. I make my best effort to focus and do one thing at a time, at some times more successfully than at others, and I wonder, as I see our collective drive to multitask accelerating, if and when people will start to question the costs.

Is There a Better Way?

The clear and unequivocal answer is yes. There are *many* better ways. There is not one perfect recipe, but there are many more satisfying, effective ways to work. They are better both for individuals and for organizations than those widely practiced in modern American workplaces today. Lotte Bailyn from the Sloan School at MIT was a pioneer in exploring the concept of dual agenda work redesign—a fancy way to describe creating workplaces that work for both employees and the organization. Several others in the work-life field have expanded upon her work and have demonstrated how we can work differently, more constructively, in ways that don't take such a toll on each of us personally and yet have positive impacts on meeting organizational goals.

My first introduction to what consultants in the work-life field commonly call "work redesign" was as a member of a team consulting to Marriott. Eventually our work was highlighted in the *Harvard Business Review*. The article "Changing a Culture of Face Time" describes Marriott's experience with a six-month work redesign pilot at three hotels in the northeast region. The goal of the project was to help Marriott managers improve their work-life balance while maintaining financial and customer service metrics. My consulting team conducted focus groups with managers—from the front line to the very top—who worked at the three hotels, as well as specialized working groups such as food and beverage, front desk operations, and sales and marketing.

Our consulting process uncovered structural issues such as inadequate technology support and insufficient bench strength among front desk managers. The process also uncovered a whole host of behavioral norms that greatly contributed to overwork, such as endless fine-tuning, lack of clarity on who was responsible and accountable for resolving particular issues, and frequent snarky comments about people leaving work early. The primary goal of the redesign process was to identify action steps and to prioritize solutions, letting each manager and/or work group determine which improvements they could implement immediately, as opposed to those more complex, involved issues that required more time, greater coordination, and higher-level authority.

Instead of endless emails flying back and forth to provide updates, as a result of the work redesign consultation, Marriott created an electronic communications board showing the latest information across the hotel and supplying the most up to date status on problems or changes. Another critical and highly symbolic change was the cessation of departmental and monthly financial meetings— long and tedious sessions that were considered a sacred cow but represented a poor use of time for many attendees. In addition, there was explicit communication from hotel leadership about ceasing the "banker's hours" comments.[28]

During one of the Marriott work group discussions, several sales and marketing employees talked about how they needed to work in the evenings to attend events and entertain clients, yet still felt obligated to maintain traditional office hours. As a result, they would spend the last few hours of their workdays trying to manage email, surfing the Internet, and attempting to catch up on mundane paperwork—all the while feeling highly ineffective. They felt unable to leave and do something more productive, like exercising or tackling their home to-do list. Working in the late afternoon and early evening was an exercise in frustration for many of the sales and marketing professionals. By the end of the pilot phase, managers in the sales and marketing department reported an average reduction of seven work hours per week, the most of any group of managers across the hotels.

Marriott documented some extraordinary improvements between the pre- and post-pilot results. Managers reporting that the emphasis was on hours worked versus work accomplished declined from 43 percent to 15 percent, and managers reporting their jobs were so demanding that they couldn't take care of their personal and family responsibilities was more than cut in half, from 77 percent to 36 percent. The time managers spent on low-value work—things they were required to do that added little value to Marriott's business—declined from twelve to seven hours per week, while Marriott observed no slippage in customer service metrics or financial impact.[29] Marriott found—something work-life professionals and those following the Libra approach have long known—that people were just as productive, or more productive, when working fewer hours yet more strategically and effectively. Employees with greater control over their work—those who will reap the benefits of working more efficiently—are highly motivated to do what needs to be done and to not waste time. Work redesign helps to unleash employees' best contributions.

A work redesign intervention with a strategic management consulting firm—the Boston Consulting Group, or BCG—provides another example of how thoughtful and strategic changes to how employees work benefits both organizations and individuals. The perceived norm in this work environment was the need to be highly accessible in order to provide top-notch customer service (for instance, the expectation that any email would be answered within an hour). In partnership with a business school professor, several consulting teams conducted experiments to explore the impact of planned time off. One of the first experiments required each member of a team to take a full day off a week.[30] Despite strong initial reservations from the consultants on the team, they went forward with the experiment both because the specific consulting engagement was focused on improving work processes and because their client was receptive. Living through the experiment helped the BCG consultants realize that excellent client service did not necessitate 24/7 accessibility.

Further experiments required consultants to *not* work or be connected to work in any way at least one night per week after six p.m. Consultants chose their designated night off ahead of time, versus in the moment, so as to minimize the tendency to work longer as a reflex just because there was too much to do. Again, there was substantial push-back by the members of the consulting team, even though they were being asked to disconnect after traditional business hours (after six p.m.). Representing the "extreme ethos" that characterizes many professions, several of the consultants were fearful that severing their electronic tethers would hurt their careers, even though the project was being supported by leadership at the firm. They also were concerned that they would somehow be letting down their colleagues or their clients. Over time and with direct experience, their anxiety decreased as the consultants started to look forward to this planned time for themselves. The "time off" experiments expanded subsequently to include ten additional consulting teams.

Data collected comparing feedback from consultants who took the time off and those who did not documented many benefits of time away from work. Those consultants experimenting with predictable time off were more satisfied with their jobs, more likely to imagine a long-term career at the firm, and more satisfied with their work-life balance, and they felt more able to deliver value for their clients. All the consultants participating in the experiments, and three-quarters of those not involved, indicated wanting their next assignment to be on one of the experimental teams.[31] The "time off" experiments were a powerful catalyst in starting to dismantle the unquestioned devotion to 24/7 access at BCG.

A third example of work redesign was focused at the individual as opposed to the group level. Working with approximately a hundred employees across twelve regional banks (all part of Wachovia Bank), the consulting team—led by Tony Schwartz president of The Energy Project—helped employees identify personal behaviors that were "energy-depleting" and tested strategies to strengthen their stamina and resilience.[32] Each participant—which included everyone from senior to front-line managers—was paired with a colleague who would act as an external support in between training sessions. The suggested strategies were far-reaching and encompassed the body, emotions, mind, and spirit, and they all had the common goal of increasing capacity and sustainability.

Participants completed an energy audit that gave them a snapshot of their typical norms and helped them understand where their behaviors were misaligned with what is known about peak performance from scientific research. The audit included statements such as:

- I don't regularly get at least seven or eight hours of sleep and I often wake up feeling tired.
- I have too little time for the activities that I most deeply enjoy.
- I spend much of my day reacting to immediate crises and demands rather than focusing on activities with longer-term value and high leverage.
- There are significant gaps in what I say is most important to me in my life and how I actually allocate my time and energy.

Wachovia employees then tried changes such as identifying and sticking to a designated bedtime, moving from two large meals—typically overeating at night—to eating every few hours with smaller meals and snacks throughout the day, to taking brief breaks to help stay focused. Managers scheduled lunch breaks with direct reports to recognize their accomplishments and to create an opportunity to connect on a deeper level, beyond just the monthly status reports. Multitasking was discouraged by techniques such as going into a conference room to write reports, not taking calls during meetings in employees' offices, and identifying specific times of the day to check email rather than responding all day long. One of the managers who began to check email only at designated times let others know that urgent matters should be dealt with by phone. He found that over a nine-month period he did not receive a single "urgent" call. Another manager committed to creating a window of time on his commute home when he would stop working—and try to decompress—so that he could greet his family with his full attention. Others committed to switching completely off from work for several hours every night to fully be together with their families rather than squeezing it in between intrusive work distractions.

As with the other work redesign interventions, data comparing those who made changes to how they worked and those who did not highlighted the business value of working in ways that support rather than challenge our natural bodily rhythms. Those participating in the training and experimentation brought in more money for the bank, through both increased deposits and loans, than colleagues who did not. They reported improvements to productivity and performance and improved interactions with clients and customers.[33]

In the work-life training I helped to develop and conduct while at Catalyst, we sought to have executives and managers reflect on what role they played in setting the tone and in managing work-life integration in their own lives. In an exercise where participants completed various statements related to work and flexibility—such as "I work best when ..." or "Flexibility in this organization means ..."—participants came to see the disconnect between their own use of flexibility to work most effectively and their reluctance to extend greater flexibility to those who worked for them.

An extremely valuable aspect of the training was what managers learned from each other as they grappled with their individual fears and reservations about flexibility and helping employees manage their work-life conflicts and challenges. During a work-life training session I conducted for a financial services company, a junior manager shared his strong opinion—it was black

CHAPTER 4: HOW WE WORK: DELUSIONS OF PRODUCTIVITY

and white to him—that there was *no way* a manager working on a critical, time-sensitive project could possibly work on a reduced schedule. One of the far more seasoned managers shared his perspective that retaining talent was among the most critical responsibilities of a manager and losing someone over a schedule change was short sighted. The senior manager went on to say that there were multiple ways in which the problem could be solved, enabling the manager in the case study to work on a reduced schedule as well as ensuring the project was well managed. The department head of the team being trained for this client gave me what I considered a huge compliment when he said that the training helped his employees to think differently about how they worked and managed others, and that it was going to lead to new conversations that would help the group figure out how to work better.

Toward the end of our work-life training sessions participants completed a short self assessment with statements such as "I encourage people that I manage to challenge work practices that may no longer make sense" or "I consider how my approach to work can send a message about what is expected or required." The post-assessment discussions further cemented the critical role these managers played in helping those they led and managed to work more effectively and in ways that provided the best work-life fit.

Research—both mine and many others—indicates that managers are a vital link, providing the translation of the work culture for people who report to them. Employees who feel supported by their managers and have the flexibility they need at work report higher job engagement, are more satisfied with their work, are less likely to look for another job, and report better mental health.[34] They are also less burned out and more inclined to go the extra mile at work. Managers really matter and can make a huge difference, but also remember that even the most supportive and flexible managers cannot protect you from yourself. What you do and how you work is and will always be a combination of the environment and the individual.

Why Is This So Hard?

If there is so much evidence about how to work smarter and better, then why are we struggling so much? Where is the disconnect? In addition to the many external factors discussed previously, our unquestioned assumptions and knee-jerk reactions are primary contributing factors to our pervasive sense of overwork and lack of balance in our lives. Organizations and individuals alike need to start asking some difficult questions:

- Does good client service really mean responding anytime, anyplace, anywhere, or does it mean responding thoughtfully when you can focus on the issue at hand? Does everything really need an immediate response, or do we create a crisis atmosphere by perpetuating so much false urgency?
- Can you truthfully have twenty priorities, or is anything below five or six by definition second tier? Would we be better off to admit the real limitations and enable a sense of accomplishment for progress on the top priorities rather than a sense of perpetual failure for never getting to the bottom of the list?
- Are the work heroes really those people who engender crises due to their poor planning and work habits yet swoop in to clean up the mess because they've prioritized work above everything else? Or are they those who plan, execute, and reliably deliver without all the drama?
- What work products need to be an A and in what cases might a B or even a C suffice?
- Do we need to have so many meetings that are poorly planned and poorly run, or would it be better to just cancel some until we can expend the energy to ensure they are more worthwhile?

- Can you really get much out of a meeting when you're on your Blackberry checking the latest emails that have come in? Or would it be better to make the hard choice and either engage or decline the invitation?
- Can you really be productive on your tenth hour in the office without a break, or would insisting on a reprieve be far more productive in the big picture?
- Can you really focus on that seventh meeting of the day, especially when you've barely had a moment to breathe or get some food? Or would creating a new norm, such as no more than a certain number of hours in meetings per day, or a required block of unscheduled time after a certain amount of time spent in meetings, be a better strategy?

Many of our present work norms are rooted in very childlike behaviors—never being able to wait for a response, being distracted and pulled off task by the latest stimuli, needing to act on whatever thought comes into our mind at that moment. I fear that much of our time at work is spent solving the wrong problems. Some companies still worry that telecommuters will take advantage of their flexibility and not work enough, rather than considering the more likely problem of workers finding it difficult to turn off. People multitask incessantly because of the perception that it is efficient, when in fact it wastes a lot of time for both the individual and many others. Our work culture has taught us to deeply believe that we can get it all done if we work harder, faster, and more efficiently instead of freeing us to ask first and foremost what must come off the list in order to add a new priority.

We greatly underestimate the toll frequently changing priorities take on both our effectiveness and our emotions. Lacking a sense of completion, we are robbed of the energy surge that comes from the feeling of a job well done. Demonstrating our tendency to underestimate the full complexity and perhaps unmeasured costs of so many change efforts in our organizations, a study tracking the impact of change efforts among Fortune 100 companies between 1980 and 1995 found that seven in ten did not improve the bottom line.[35] While physiologically our bodies have rhythms in which our energy ebbs and flows, we seem to think we can override the default setting and set the switch permanently to flow. New medical research is discovering that our circadian rhythms—the internal clock that dictates our cycles of sleeping and waking—are more influential than previously believed. Being out of rhythm over time can contribute to weight gain and depression, two major and growing health issues in the U.S.[36]

This is why work redesign is so powerful. It allows employees to openly discuss the white elephants and sacred cows that not only take up so much time, but also sap their vitality. Work redesign actively engages people in discussions about how they can collectively work better and, yes—in some cases—less. And changes leading to a far better work-life balance are much less dramatic than I suspect people fear. For instance, in a nationally representative study in which men identified themselves with one of three groups—work-centric (prioritizing work over family/personal life), family-centric (prioritizing family/personal life over work), or dual-centric (equal prioritization)—the level of reported work-life conflict varied greatly. Of the self-identified work-centric men, 62 percent reported work-life conflict in comparison to 42 percent of dual-centric and 36 percent of family-centric participants.[37] Yet the difference in their average weekly reported work hours was relatively small, with work-centric men reporting forty-nine, dual-centric forty-six, and family-centric forty-three hours, a difference of just six hours per week. Furthermore, the study found that the amount of time men spent working was more important in predicting work and life conflict than the time spent on other activities, including caring for their children, home management, or leisure.[38] Perhaps making some different choices and trying to work just one hour less a day could result in a profound shift in the work-life equation for many of us.

The greatest value of work redesign is that the benefits accrue to the employees as well as to the organization. If being more efficient just means more work getting piled on, it is easy to understand why people cultivate the art of being busy. The reengineering movement—highly popular in the 1990s—was all about improving work processes but left out the human part of the equation. Work redesign uses employee needs, desires, and constraints as a powerful catalyst for improving how work gets done.

What Can You Do to Make a Difference?

There are many actions you can take to work smarter and better. A first step is to reflect on how it is that you are working currently and to identify what is and is not working with your approach. You can identify the external realities that impact how you work, as well as seek to understand what you are contributing to your experience—assumptions, work habits, and norms—of feeling overworked and overtaxed. There are, and will always be, elements outside of your control, but there are also many elements within your control, or at least your ability to influence.

As an individual:

- Use your expert knowledge of your job and work to identify the best ways to meet your responsibilities; think about what it means to be effective in your job.
- Understand where you add value—particularly unique value—at work and seek to focus your energies there.
- Be accountable and do great work, including putting up limits, knowing that focused energy leads to better results.
- Understand your personal work style, your work skills and lack of skills; be honest about how you work best.
- Communicate your availability and your limitations and provide a mechanism to reach you on an exception basis.

As a colleague:

- Help identify what would improve your work and the work of your team/work group, and make suggestions to improve the efficacy of the group.

- Support the flexibility of your colleagues; help to eradicate the comments on banker's hours so as to create new work heroes.

- Seek to stay constructive and in a problem-solving mode when discussing workload challenges.

- Seek to be a strong performer and a reliable colleague.

As a leader and manager:

- Realize the impact the way you work has on defining the work norms and work culture; share your own personal struggles and strategies for managing work and life integration.

- Clearly articulate priorities and good performance for your team; provide a compass to assist those you manage with weighing competing demands.

- Consider preventing ongoing overload and burnout as a management priority in order to help employees sustain strong long-term performance.

- Empower employees to question work practices that no longer make sense; support and implement changes that improve work efficacy and employee health and well-being.

- Seek to understand the work-life priorities of those who work for you; incorporate work-life discussions into career planning.

Learning to work more sustainably and more effectively is not just the best way forward, it is the only way forward. Working ever harder and longer cannot be the solution. Doing more in a more distracted, fragmented way cannot be the solution. Having so many talented people feeling unable to sustain the pace cannot be the solution. Having to squeeze our lives outside of work into the margins cannot be the solution. We are at an inflection point where considering how to work differently, in a way that does not pit work contribution against our lives as an engaged parent, son or daughter, friend, or community member, is vital.

People are already working differently. Our global knowledge economy requires it, but organizations are slow to fully understand this change. In a research project to study flexibility across several companies, those organizations participating in the research were asked to identify employees working on normal schedules and not flexing in any way. To their surprise, the researchers found that a significant number of those employees explicitly identified as working on "traditional schedules" were, in fact, working on all different kinds of schedules, yet they were doing so under the radar. Individuals and organizations are far better served by lifting the shroud of secrecy about how employees really work so that people can share their experiences—what worked, what didn't work, and how it can be improved. The road forward is redesigning work in ways that reflect the challenges and opportunities of our modern era.

The Libra work and life model, anchored by intentionality, experimentation, evaluation, and improvement, is just the kind of approach that leads to better and more creative solutions, at home and at work. Women and men practicing the Libra approach are deeply motivated to work effectively so that they ensure time and space for the other critical priorities in their lives. They have much they can share about working in a way that enables room for both.

CHAPTER 5

WOMEN AND WORK: BEYOND WORK-LIFE CONFLICT

If women were portrayed as the smart, creative and visionary leaders they really are, I think more girls would aspire toward leadership and fewer men would fear women in their ranks.

---Ilene Lang

There is a strong bias that the challenges women face at work are all about the work-life struggle, and while that is an important contributing factor, it is far from the whole story. Most of the discussion about women leaving organizations and the workforce is focused on the work-life piece; the rest of the story is omitted. This chapter explores that "rest of the story," the pieces about systemic barriers and workplace norms—as well as the thoughts and actions of working women themselves—that stymie their professional development and advancement.

Women face a unique set of barriers to professional success, and the inability of organizational leaders (still primarily a homogeneous group of white men) to see and understand these issues is a key part of the problem. This lack of perspective is not born of malice, but of a lack of knowledge and experience. It is very difficult for those at the helm—for whom and by whom the system has been constructed—to understand the experience of outsiders for whom these privileges do not flow easily or naturally. Among the recommendations of a group of 200 leaders in business, government, and academia convened to shed light on what is holding women back in the workplace, one was holding the CEO accountable for hiring women into top level positions and, if women were not present among the leadership ranks, determining why they were not.[1] The prevailing assumption has long been that it is just a matter of time before women ascend to the highest levels of power and influence, explaining inequities by rationalizing that women have simply not been in the pipeline long enough. Perhaps twenty years ago that argument might have held water, but a decade into the twenty-first century, it is clear that time alone is not the answer.

In profession after profession, even those in which they have been part of the rank and file for many years, women remain poorly represented among the leadership ranks. Women have long accounted for approximately half of the professional and managerial labor force in the U.S., but they account for just 15 percent of corporate officers and 2 percent of chief executive officers among the Fortune 500 ranks.[2] While women have represented approximately 40 percent of law school graduates since the mid 1980s, they represent less than 20 percent of the partnership.[3] In medicine, women have comprised 40 percent of graduates since the mid 1990s (49 percent in 2008), yet less than 30 percent of physicians are female; in academic medicine, women account for one-third of the faculty yet just 17 percent of full professors and 12 percent of department chairs.[4] In 2010, women in government represented 17 percent of the members of the Senate and the House of Representatives and approximately one in four members among state senators and legislators.[5] In other words, women are present in all workplaces, but not in large numbers among those who set the strategy, provide the organizational vision, and profoundly influence the work culture.

There is no denying the existence of a huge reserve of talented women who are waiting in the wings, yet their incredible skill is not being fully tapped and their potential is largely unrealized. In fact, there is "growing evidence that the progress of women in America's workplace has stalled—and is now actually going backward."[6]

Organizational Barriers to Women's Development and Advancement

There are several organizational barriers that challenge the ability of women to develop and advance in their careers. Subjective interpretations of potential, an impossible standard for female leadership style, and insufficient mentoring and sponsorship all act as obstacles, as does the lack of access to important organizational networks. In addition, preconceived notions about what mothers want and rigidity in career paths—preventing women (and men) from modulating their work efforts during the intense years of caring for young children—contribute to the problem.

The performance versus potential dilemma. We had a saying at Catalyst: "Women get promoted for their performance, men for their potential." This observation was born of extensive research. In one client project for a major financial services organization, we conducted a study of nominations for advancement for a group of high-potential men and women. This group was the crème de la crème to begin with, and was generally very highly regarded, so we suspected we might find nothing of significance in our analysis. To our surprise, we uncovered a gender difference when it came to the characterization of leadership potential. Comments related to female candidates spoke to their skill and proficiency, while many more descriptors of the men explicitly mentioned leadership abilities, with statements such as "he's a natural leader" as opposed to "she's fantastic with clients." Men were positioned as though they already possessed the necessary leadership skills, whereas women were positioned as a work in progress, with qualifying language attached to praise for their great competence.

According to research, women attain promotions more slowly than their male colleagues. A national study covering a twelve-year period found that white men were more likely to ascend to the managerial ranks than men of color, or white or black women—even when all possessed similar qualifications. Even after controlling for variables such as hours worked and education level, men were found to have an advantage in attaining managerial positions.[7] A National Public Radio spot titled "Is Sex Discrimination at Work Still a Problem?" referenced a legal case where women middle managers at a telecommunications company asserted they were not being promoted to middle management positions at the same rate as their male colleagues. While these women were scoring as well as men on the objective, performance-based tests, they were consistently underperforming on the subjective, *whole person test*.[8]

Even in professions dominated by women, such as social work and nursing, men move up more quickly than their female colleagues.[9] Gender biases are also apparent in hypothetical studies emphasizing the depth and complexity of the issue. In an experiment first conducted several decades ago—and repeated more recently—participants were asked to evaluate an essay written by supposed candidates for a managerial position. Hypothetical male applicants were rated more favorably than female candidates based on the *exact same* essays, except when the essays addressed topics deemed feminine in nature.[10] Women are generally seen as less qualified and more risky despite much evidence to the contrary.

The importance of style. Women struggle mightily with finding an acceptable and comfortable leadership style at work. Despite progress, there remains much ambivalence about women and leadership as well as women and power. Catalyst has conducted seminal research demonstrating the complexities women face in cultivating their managerial and leadership styles. Women consistently identify that developing a style with which men are comfortable is a critical success factor for women leaders. If women are more assertive in their approach, they are perceived as effective leaders, but lacking interpersonal skills. If they are more collaborative in their approach (the expected feminine style), then they are considered too soft and not exhibiting leadership behaviors.[11] Another Catalyst study, conducted across several countries, assessed the degree to which men and women demonstrated ten distinct leadership behaviors, further illuminating the challenges of gender stereotyping.

In multiple instances, men were seen as more effective at whatever leadership behaviors were deemed most important in that cultural context.[12] Men have a far wider leadership palette from which to draw and can behave in more dominant or more friendly ways without being negatively judged. For women leaders, it is substantially more complex.

In addition to finding a leadership style that is seen as effective, women also struggle with finding one that feels natural. It is very important, particularly in American business settings, to talk about your accomplishments and to take credit, though your contribution may have been limited. There is a whole lot of posturing, particularly in certain professions and in large organizations where amassing resources of people and money is key. In these environments, making your point more emphatically and with conviction is associated with being a leader. Vulnerability is seen as weakness and acting as if you understand and are in control is rewarded—even when you don't and you're not. Many, perhaps most, women are socialized to be humble about taking credit and to share their ideas deferentially (for instance, prefacing comments with softening introductions like "I think" as opposed to stating their ideas as fact). Then they are thrust into work environments in which they are expected to do just the opposite. For many women, this assertive style feels uncomfortable. To further complicate matters, women who self-promote tend to be judged harshly and seen as boastful. Modesty is expected of women, no matter their talent or position.

The values mismatch. Women want their work to reflect their values. Many women don't feel hyped by the rush of playing and winning *the game*. They go to work so that they can earn a living, make a difference, solve problems, as well as grow and learn. They don't want to play a game. While women have become the majority of graduates in areas such as law and medicine, the number of women business school graduates has remained stagnant at slightly more than a third.

For the many women who do work in business settings (and other settings as well), the major inflection point comes once they have children. As the demands in their lives outside of work profoundly accelerate, they begin to perceive overly-competitive workplaces as a game of who can boast more while building the biggest empire, rather than a vehicle for solving problems. Many women decide they just don't want to spend their far more limited time and energy that way. They want work to feel more about them and what they care about; they want their professional lives to better reflect why they go to work in the first place. Perhaps not surprisingly, the leak in the pipeline of talented women is most severe during mid-career.[13] It is at this juncture when organizational norms that remain misaligned with women's aspirations, needs, and goals become that much starker against a backdrop of rising demands at home.

At a leadership conference I attended, I spoke with a woman who had a PhD in cell biology from an Ivy League school, an MBA, and many years of work experience. She told me that she left a big pharmaceutical company to start her own company because, as a woman, she just got tired of being among the lone voices, of seeing the picture differently, of fighting the uphill battles—all while trying to raise her children. Her work just didn't reflect the way she saw herself or her values.

Research among middle school and high school girls helps to explain the enduring gender gap. Researchers from the Simmons School of Management surveyed more than 4,000 teen girls and boys on their attitudes toward business careers. They found that while both girls and boys anticipated supporting their families financially, girls placed greater emphasis on helping others and on making a difference. Girls characterized business careers more negatively than boys and were more likely to perceive a business career at odds with their values and goals. However, they did not perceive starting their own business in this negative way.[14]

The way to engage girls and women in business is by helping them to see the incredible power of business to make a difference in the world, to solve complex problems they care about, and to be a forum for growth and change. The Simmons research suggests a future course of action, "demonstrating to girls, and others, that business plays a pivotal role in economic and social well-being." The report went on to say, "Girls need exposure to people and information that helps them realize that making a profit does not have to be inconsistent with doing good."[15] Despite its limitations and problems, the market economy is a powerful vehicle to make the world a better place if we harness it to do so. It is vital for women to bring their perspectives to the table of our organizations.

The problem of limited access and few role models. In addition to issues related to gender stereotyping, other major barriers to women's advancement include exclusion from informal networks, lack of mentoring and sponsorship, and a dearth of role models.[16] Women have less access to people and experiences that will help position them for leadership roles. These barriers tend to materialize in subtle and incremental ways. For example, a younger man might be invited to a baseball game with clients because of his involvement in a fantasy baseball group at work. Another young man might get invited to lunch because he reminds a senior colleague of himself at that age and stage in his career. These casual interactions lead to the development of mentoring relationships in which the mentors share their professional experiences and perspectives. Women have far fewer opportunities for these connections. They may not play golf, or it is assumed that they would not want to participate in a sports outing. Because of fears that an older man socializing with a younger woman could be misconstrued as personal rather than professional, many men feel reluctant to initiate such relationships. The end result is women have far fewer chances to develop mentoring relationships that would benefit them professionally.

While mentoring can greatly facilitate professional development, a very specific type of mentoring—sponsorship—is critical for advancement, particularly to the highest level of organizational leadership. What distinguishes mentoring and sponsorship is power. Sponsorship means someone going to bat for you and proactively facilitating your development and advancement, for instance, suggesting you for a promotion or advocating for your inclusion in a leadership development program. Sponsors are influential mentors who assist their protégés in gaining visibility and developing the necessary skills to advance. Sponsors play a crucial role in helping their protégés to stand out among multiple qualified candidates for leadership roles. They are particularly critical for women as an antidote to overcome the multiple barriers that stymie their career success.[17] Women need both mentors and sponsors in equal measure with their male counterparts. But since the leadership ranks remain highly skewed by gender, without specific interventions women typically lack the critical support needed to move up the career ladder.

Given the gender demographics of many organizations, women lack role models among the leadership ranks. Role models provide concrete and powerful evidence that it is possible for "someone like me" to succeed in any particular organization. When more women are running the show, and represent a critical mass at the top of organizations—not 10 percent or 20 percent, but 40 percent or 50 percent—their presence will change the dialogue and the norms. Women will have ample role models for success—not just the one or two women who seem to have made it, but many women with a range of styles, approaches, strengths, and perspectives.

Assumptions about what mothers want. There are rampant assumptions about women's preferences and desires relative to work once they become mothers. A pervasive assumption is that once a woman becomes a mother, her professional work will no longer be a priority. People assume a woman with small children will not want a promotion, will not want to travel or relocate, and will not want to take on a stretch assignment. They don't assume this about men when they become fathers, and the truth is that while some women may not want to expand their work responsibilities after having a child, this is not the case for the majority of women. According to a McKinsey study of women professionals, 82 percent of women with no children, 80 percent of women with one child, and 73 percent of women with more than one child reported a desire to move to the next level. There was a small decline as child care responsibilities escalated, but the great majority of women with children *did* want to continue to advance.[18] Well-meaning managers make assumptions without ever asking, trying to protect mothers from these hard choices. This approach is paternalistic. Women need first to be asked, and then allowed to decide, how they wish to prioritize their lives.

In many cases, mothers absolutely do want continued professional development and challenging work, but they (and any person deeply involved in raising children) typically need a longer time horizon to plan for work-related changes. Relocating on a few months' notice is much more of a challenge when it involves changing schools, revamping child care situations, and managing all the other complexities that go with raising children. Taking a big promotion when a child has just one year left of middle school or high school may not make sense, but twelve months later, the window could be wide open.

Organizations and individuals collectively struggle to envision how jobs can be restructured and adapted. Rampant rigidity in job design is unnecessary—and in many instances counterproductive—for organizational success. We have not applied strategic focus and sufficient effort to adapting jobs to suit the workforce that now inhabits them. Obviously organizations face decisions that are urgent, and there are some positions that are very challenging to reconceptualize, but too often decisions are made in haste, motivated by short-term benefits and implemented without sufficient analysis of long-term costs. A more creative and thoughtful approach would better serve both employers and employees. Job redesign provides an opportunity to recast jobs, many of which have become untenable as they have expanded in scope, and to adopt a more fluid design that better fits the needs of the organization and the evolving workforce.

The hours game. While women don't have an issue with working hard and excelling, they can't—and often won't—play the hours game. Many women continue to assume the dominant caretaker role in their families, and because they have strong feelings about their use of time, they are far more reluctant than men to accept long hours, especially long hours that they perceive add little value. In the research on extreme jobs (studying men and women in lucrative, high profile positions), the researchers documented that, even among this group of highly motivated workers logging long hours in jobs with big demands, women worked fewer hours than their male counterparts. Furthermore, women were far less likely to tolerate long hours in jobs they did not perceive as translating into the opportunity for substantial impact for their organizations. The researchers wrote, "The data suggest that women are not afraid of the pressure or responsibility of extreme jobs—they just can't pony up the hours."[19]

Women—especially mothers raising children—feel strongly that their time commitment at work needs to mesh with the reality and complexity of their lives. In the McKinsey research, 55 percent of women with no children, 63 percent with one child, and 67 percent with two children reported: *I will only pursue a job if it allows me to have a good work-life balance.*[20] Even the brightest girls, scoring in the top 1 percent of a standardized test in math during their elementary school years, reported the desire for part-time careers when interviewed several decades later as adults. Conversely, the brightest boys, as grown men, were more likely to identify full-time careers as their preference.[21] Across many focus groups with men and women professionals, I found that women were more attuned to the time requirements of jobs and to creative ways of adapting hours and job responsibilities, while men tended to see jobs as fixed in terms of both time and responsibilities. The desire for more contained work hours is not a matter of talent or lack of ambition for women; it is a matter of the desire to manage—and the reality of managing—a fuller palette of responsibilities in their lives.

Inflexible career paths. For both men and women, the historic and still dominant career path is linear and rigid. It is predicated on the industrial model of starting a career after completing one's education, working without interruption for one (or perhaps several) organizations through the years, rising through the ranks over time, and retiring with financial stability and reliable health insurance. Of course, we know it doesn't quite work like that for most of us anymore, yet the career paths in many organizations and professions remain based on this antiquated model.

Today, what we get out of the system is far more dependent on what we, and not an employer, put into it. For example, based on a national study of employers, employees are being asked to shoulder a greater proportion of the cost of their health insurance and retirement savings.[22] Yet because jobs feel so insecure, we cling like barnacles to an old model that identifies a primary career person (even if both parents work outside the home) and requires them to give their all to their jobs. This expectation leaves the primary career person afraid to put up boundaries or make waves.

This linear, time-constrained career path is especially at odds with the realities of professional women's lives. These women are often completing their graduate education in their late twenties or early thirties and starting their careers in earnest at the same time they feel pressure to begin raising their families. Despite our incredible medical advances, having a child at forty is a whole lot harder than having one at thirty. The up-or-out career model—which has been common in fields like consulting and academia—means that unless you continue to move up, reaching the leadership level within a certain timeframe, for instance becoming a firm partner or tenured professor, you are asked to leave the organization. In these rigid models, there is limited opportunity for those who want—and need—to establish boundaries around their work and aspire to define their own advancement clock.

These rigid career paths also do not align with the desires and needs of women during the later phase of their careers. Many mature women in their forties, fifties, and sixties have reached the stage when they want, and may financially need, to focus on their professional lives. In the traditional model, men who are at this stage, having spent decades focused on professional achievement, are looking to refocus their time and energy on other priorities, with work playing a less central role. In some professions, the word is that it's a young person's game (typically a young man's game) because the jobs require so much time and effort and exact such a toll that people lose their stamina even as young as their forties. The hope in these professions is to amass sufficient wealth to retire early. However, because we are a nation of spenders rather than savers, many have used those earnings to support lifestyles beyond their means and they must continue to work to continue affording what they have come to see as necessary. For other workers, health problems kick in that prevent them from continuing to work at an extreme pace, or at all, or their stock doesn't go up as much as they had hoped or planned for. Even in high-paying careers and situations, many are stuck working in a way that feels draining and unsustainable.

Work norms and career paths are evolving, but remarkably slowly, given the preponderance of highly educated and trained women and the changes in our family structures. The neotraditional family model of the father with the primary career and the mother working in the secondary career is the most common model among American families today.[23] People who seek to be very involved in raising their children—both women and men—are going to need more flexible career paths with longer time horizons. The rising tide of women and men wanting to work in retirement, both for financial reasons and to pursue work that engages them, also need new career models. Research shows that three in four workers aged fifty and older anticipate working during their retirement years.[24] Rigid career paths that require linear, upward movement, maximum effort during the child-raising years, and ramping down in the more mature years do not provide women or men who are dual- or family- rather than work-centric—or those facing a whole host of circumstances such as health problems, financial market chaos, elder-care responsibilities, job loss, or the need for professional retraining—the flexibility they need to adapt their work through the decades of their lives.

Rigid career models don't serve the *majority* of people in the current workforce. Yet this huge disconnect, between inflexible career paths and the changing needs of the workforce, persists in part because the people leading our organizations do represent the very small minority for whom the incredibly intense, full-tilt career model with outsized rewards actually does work. While our lives are far more fluid and very different from the ones our parents and grandparents lived, we continue to encounter career models that seem so clearly designed for another era.

Women Undervaluing Themselves

There are several organizational issues that stymie women's career development and advancement, but women themselves contribute to the struggle as well. In my consulting work, there was a clear pattern of women employees being far less aware than their male colleagues of the need to advocate for themselves professionally. Women perceived the route to success as working very hard, doing a fantastic job, keeping their heads down trying to do more than required, and waiting to get noticed.

Younger women perceive there are fewer gender issues at work because, at more junior levels, competency is easier to measure, more concrete, and a far more significant variable in the success equation. However, with advancement, competency is assumed, becoming the baseline rather than a differentiator, and subjective criteria become more important. The further you ascend in the organizational hierarchy, the more critical interpersonal connections become. Differences by gender in access to networks of mentors and sponsors start to build at more junior levels but become more apparent and critical through time.

Take for example the common scenario of a young man being included in a golf outing with a key client. The young golfer is not only building his relationships with more senior colleagues in his organization, he is also building a foundation with the client. By spending time socially, he starts to be viewed as a resource for solving business problems. The younger man may also call on his golf companions to facilitate decision-making and problem-solving. It becomes a virtuous cycle—the younger man becomes more visible and better positioned and through time is perceived as an emerging leader. Conversely, a woman professional invited to attend a Friday golf outing declines both because she doesn't play golf and she feels like she has so much work to do that she can't forfeit that day in the office. She knows that, with her daughter's birthday party that weekend, she will have no time to work. Women need to consider that a better approach might be to accept the invitation and then renegotiate the work deadline, or to decline, while sharing her limitation on that day, yet being emphatic about her interest in being included in the future.

In one of my favorite consulting projects of all time, we analyzed data for a large bank to explore the career development experiences of men and women in the leadership pipeline—those directly below the executive level. The data crystallized gendered norms regarding self-perceptions of readiness and risk tolerance. Among the major findings from the research was a "gender confidence gap," with women being less likely to seek a promotion than their male colleagues, but more likely to seek continued skill development through a lateral change. Women were more likely to attribute not receiving opportunities to issues under their control (e.g., requisite skills and/or education), while men were more likely to attribute lost opportunities to issues outside of their control (e.g., budget shortfalls or favoritism). Men were more likely to apply multiple times for jobs—whether or not they had the qualifications—while women tended to apply only when they were very well or even overqualified. It was noteworthy that the lack of confidence stood in stark contrast to objective performance data. Survey participants were asked to indicate their most commonly received performance evaluation over several years at the bank, and at every level, women consistently outperformed their male counterparts.

A Self-Fulfilling Prophecy

Consider two smart young professionals who eagerly start their careers side by side: one a man, and the other a woman. They work hard, learn a great deal, and feel excited by their future prospects. Work is a major and important part of their lives. As their careers progress, the young woman starts to get assigned to the less high profile projects—in part because she doesn't ask for specific assignments and opportunities and her male colleague does. He seems to understand the need to advocate for himself. She typically eats lunch at her desk so as to get more work done, while her male colleague frequently goes to lunch with the group manager who shares his love of fishing and video games.

Over time, the woman's portfolio of work starts to look less compelling—comparatively speaking—even though she does very good work and receives excellent feedback. Four years into her career, she still spends a lot of her time writing reports and managing internal department projects while her male colleague has gotten involved with a cross-company task force, has been assigned as the liaison with another department for an important integration project, and, far more often, is in a presenting role at department meetings. Her professional path and her male colleague's start to diverge; he becomes a rising star while she becomes frustrated and disenchanted.

The issue of work-life balance adds further complexity to this picture. Despite her disillusionment with the increasing imbalance in career velocity, rather than leaving the organization, the young woman works harder, hoping her commitment will get noticed. When her male colleague gets promoted, for a position that she would not have dreamed of applying for because she did not see herself as fully qualified, she nevertheless feels cheated. At the same time she finds out she is pregnant with her first child and is quickly absorbed in the joy and drama of that experience.

Upon coming back from maternity leave, her life becomes all about the struggle to combine her professional work with the huge new role of being a parent. The difficulty of juggling is compounded by her growing frustration at seeing her male colleague continue to excel, even though he, too, is a new parent. While she is pushing herself to the limit at work to prove her commitment, she is unable to log the same number of hours as her male counterpart because her husband's job is less flexible and she manages the lion's share of the child care issues. Conversely, her colleague's wife is at home and he seems to be able to work whenever he wants and for as long as he needs. In the midst of all this, her manager tells her she isn't quite ready for a promotion to the level her male colleague has occupied for the last two years.

No matter how effectively the woman streamlines her work in order to manage both her work and home responsibilities, she cannot mitigate the perceptions of a work culture where efficiency is not rewarded and face time is a proxy for commitment. Without sufficient time and flexibility needed for the key relationship-building necessary for her career development, she struggles to prioritize this element of her professional work. Torn between the competing demands of work and home life, eventually she seriously contemplates leaving her job.

When she does leave, she reports her decision was based on wanting more time to be with her family—which is true *in part*—but in fact, her decision was based on much more than that. Upon her departure, the organizational story that women don't stay and are not worth investing in is reinforced and leaders are that much more reluctant to advocate for the next talented young woman that comes along. Ah, the complexity!

Against this backdrop, women continue to get paid, on average, 82 percent of what men make, and much of that discrepancy is *not* directly linked to choices under a woman's control (e.g., working part-time or choosing particular specialties). In an in-depth study of women and men alumni of prestigious business schools in the U.S., Canada, Europe, and Asia, the pay gap was evident from the very first job after business school—*based only on being a woman*—and widened through time.[25] The study controlled for factors such as parenthood status, geography, and function. Other research—

holding constant for factors that might explain the gender pay differential—similarly found that women were being penalized financially just for being women.[26] Despite progress, the gender pay gap remains alive and well.

The gender story at work depicts a self-reinforcing cycle. Women encounter work cultures that fit far less well with what they value, how they operate, and the part work plays in their lives. They get penalized and marginalized for trying to push against the system, seeking to work less than full-time or refusing to attend seven a.m. meetings. They struggle to redefine organizational norms such that refusing a relocation does not translate into a lessened desire for professional growth or that speaking less forcefully does not denote a lack of leadership. And if women do give up and leave, the folklore is reinforced that women are not ambitious, will always prioritize family, and don't have what it takes to succeed.

The First Step Is Understanding the Problem

Lest you throw up your hands in complete resignation, know that there are many things that can help disrupt the cycle of women facing obstacles they do—and do not—understand. Organizations, and women themselves, can work to avoid discouragement, disillusionment, and eventually departure. First and foremost, we must understand and accept that there is an issue to begin with. The word that is used over and over to dodge the issue of obstacles specific to women is meritocracy. Ever since my first research project in the early 1990s, meritocracy has been used to connote a work environment in which ability and opportunity go hand in hand. Organizational leaders deeply believe that everyone is getting the same shot and if employees work hard and perform, then they will be justly rewarded. As I've illustrated, however, things are far from that simple.

Deloitte Touche Tohmatsu Limited (Deloitte)—an organization that has received great recognition for its progress on women's advancement—began its diversity journey in the early 1990s with the recognition that, while women continued to join the firm in huge numbers at the entry level, very few women remained to even be considered for partnership. The then CEO of Deloitte put the issue of better understanding and responding to the exodus of talented women high on his priority list. One of his colleagues recounted the firm's experience through the first decade of Deloitte's women's initiative in a *Harvard Business Review* article titled "Winning the Talent War for Women: Sometimes It Takes a Revolution." He wrote:

> To be frank, many of the firm's senior partners, including myself, didn't actually see the exodus of women as a problem, or at least, it wasn't our problem. We assumed that women were leaving to have children and stay home. If there was a problem at all, it was society's problem or the women's, not Deloitte's. In fact, most senior partners firmly believed we were doing everything possible to retain women. We prided ourselves on our open, collegial, performance-based work environment. How wrong we were, and how far we've come.

Major resistance to women's initiatives—or diversity initiatives in general—rises from the supposition that singling out a group of employees for *special treatment* isn't fair. The question repeatedly raised is: *Isn't that just discrimination in reverse?* What people fail to recognize is that the default in most of our organizations is a *tipped playing field,* and the work that happens under the diversity umbrella is an effort to level the playing field—or at least make the pitch less steep. If we fail to acknowledge that there are systemic barriers to women (and those with other dimensions of diversity) and attribute the ongoing discrepancies to serendipity and choice, then the organization won't expend the necessary resources to counteract the powerful forces already at play.

Change begins with organizational leaders recognizing that women persistently lack representation at the highest levels, understanding the business cost of this underutilization of talent, and prioritizing focus on women's development and advancement as an important business issue (rather than just a nice thing to do). They must collect the data so that they can clearly see the current situation and understand why change is critical. Several research studies demonstrate that organizations with a preponderance of women in their leadership ranks perform better financially.[27] The hypothesis is not that women's mere presence causes this result, but that women's representation and financial performance are correlated because the organizations more attuned to issues around gender diversity—and that do not want to squander the contribution of half of the professional workforce—are likely better managed companies in all kinds of ways.

Organizational Interventions

Once the case has been made for why an organization needs to focus on diversity issues, there are many types of interventions that help to drive change. An important intervention is monitoring progress and holding managers and leaders accountable for improving women's representation through time. Questions to explore include:

- Are women getting promoted to the same extent as their male colleagues?
- Are women continuously overrepresented in some areas (e.g., human resources) and underrepresented in others (e.g., line management)?
- Are women leaving the organization overall and/or in particular areas of the company at disproportionate rates?

At a meeting of leaders in business, government, and academia, held to better understand the obstacles holding women back in the workplace, participants set out an action plan targeted at creating new opportunities for women. The recommendations included several organizational interventions to drive results: establishing programs to train and encourage women to assume positions requiring profit-and-loss responsibility, developing company-wide (and industry-wide) mentoring and sponsorship programs, recruiting women outside of the normal channels, and creating rotation programs for high-potential women to ensure they receive broad leadership experience. The journal report, titled *A Blueprint for Change,* provided recommendations by both industry and career levels.[28]

Organizational Interventions in Practice

Several years ago I spoke at an event where women attorneys, both senior and junior level, met with their women clients at a lovely spa. As we sat waiting for our various appointments, with towels wrapped around our heads, chatting over lemon water, I was struck by how comfortable I felt. It was in sharp contrast to my early experiences in the investment field. I could see the kinds of connections women early in their legal careers were making with clients they admired and looked up to as they talked about their work, their children, and the luxury of having this time to relax. This small event symbolized women's ways of developing important professional connections, the way golf games have represented for men through generations.

Reciprocal mentoring has great power to facilitate growth and change. An expansion of the typical mentoring concept, where someone more senior in their career shares experiences and guides those more junior, reciprocal mentoring reinforces that both parties can learn from one another. This kind of mentoring approach has been employed particularly regarding the use of technology. Younger employees who have grown up as technology natives act as mentors to educate senior executives who grew up in a different technological era. Reciprocal mentoring as applied specifically to gender issues is a pairing of women in early- or mid-career with (typically) male leaders and senior managers in order to share their world views and experiences of the organization. Through authentic professional relationships that develop away from the glare of political correctness, organizational leaders come to understand, in nuanced ways, the differential challenges—including and in addition to work-life balance—that women encounter in their professional journeys. Meanwhile, these women become visible to the leadership while learning about the challenges of managing and leading in today's complex business climate.

Another key area of intervention to support women's career development is workplace flexibility. As I described in the chapter on our modern approach to work, a flexible workplace supports working differently and strives to create new *work heroes* practicing a dual-centric approach. Workplace flexibility broadens and reenvisions career paths that aren't working for women's lives—or for most people's lives. This is critical because right now, at the beginning of the twenty-first century, less than one in five American families represent the traditional model, with the father earning income and the mother working at home to care for the family.[29]

There *are* new models being created, and many organizations are experimenting with new approaches. The Catalyst Awards process, begun in the late 1980s, is a means to study and profile model approaches to women's career development and advancement. Each year, organizations submit comprehensive applications providing detailed information about workplace women's initiatives and the resultant impacts. From the full group of applicants, a smaller group of finalists is identified, and a Catalyst team conducts in-depth site visits to assess the extent to which the written information reflects actual organizational practices. As part of that process, the Catalyst team meets with the leader of the organization—usually the chief executive officer—as well as others from the leadership team. They meet with women and men at multiple levels, ranging from mid- and senior-level managers to those just starting out in their careers. I had the good fortune to serve on the Catalyst Awards team one year and found that the site visit brought to life the degree to which what was on paper was actually happening on a day-to-day basis, and in ways that were enabling women to thrive.

For instance, at Safeway, a major supermarket chain, the store manager role was the gateway for senior leadership positions at the company. In its efforts to expand the representation of women store managers, Safeway made a seemingly small change that had a major impact. Former company practice dictated that store managers work in the store on all holidays—some of the busiest days for grocery stores. Safeway changed the expectation to be that store managers could decide whether to be on premise, or to entrust that responsibility to someone else at the store. As a result, store managers became far more focused on developing their assistant managers, enabling them to assume the top leadership role on important holidays. This, of course, made it possible for the store manager to limit the number of holidays they spent away from their families.

Another important change at Safeway was allowing job sharing for store manager positions. This enabled women (or anyone wanting or needing to limit their work time) to assume a leadership role while simultaneously placing limits on work. Importantly, those on reduced schedules at Safeway had the same access to mentoring, leadership networks, and participation in leadership development programs as those on full-time schedules. This is not the case at many organizations. As a result of these changes, Safeway greatly increased the representation of women among their critical feeder pool for top talent.[30]

Perhaps not surprisingly—given that they have been in the vanguard since the early 1990s in encouraging women's leadership—Deloitte also introduced a new model that greatly expanded the framework for creative career design. Deloitte found that, despite a long history of supporting the work-life issues of employees, and a proliferation of flexibility-related programs, many employees, especially women, continued to struggle to meet their work and life priorities. As part of an effort to revamp the vision and agenda of their Women's Initiative in 2004, the firm began to build a new model of career design, named Mass Career Customization, or

MCC™. Using the concept of a lattice (a way of making choices based on multiple options and pathways) to replace the more rigid notion of a career ladder (which directed choices in a fashion that was primarily linear and upward), Deloitte conceived a framework for evaluating personal career trajectories.[31]

Deloitte's new career framework identified several key shifts in how employees perceived their jobs and how organizations perceived workforce planning: Work is a place you go versus work is what you do. Career paths are linear and vertical versus career paths are multi-directional. And perhaps most importantly, many workers are similar versus many workers are different. The framework encompassed four key dimensions—pace (speed of advancement), workload (ranging from part- to full-time), location and schedule (ranging from highly restricted to highly flexible), and role (ranging from individual contributor to leader)—which provided a foundation for designing a wider variety of career paths.[32]

Every employee at Deloitte, including the most senior leaders at the company, completed an MCC profile based on the four dimensions. Plotting the career histories of company leaders through time, using the four dimensions, reinforced that there was more than one way to get to the same destination.

Deloitte's model allows far more fluidity as employees think about and seek to design the career trajectory that is right for them. Deloitte found the introduction of MCC resulted in substantially more robust career conversations between employees and their managers, leading to major improvements in employees' perception that they have the support they need to manage their work-life issues. Anne Weisberg, a former Catalyst colleague and former senior advisor to Deloitte's Women's Initiative, partnered with Cathleen Benko, Deloitte's managing principal of talent, to publish the book *Mass Career Customization: Aligning the Workplace with Today's Nontraditional Workforce* in 2007 to capture Deloitte's journey in creating and implementing this new approach to career management at the firm.[33]

What Can Women Do?

Women have a definite and important role to play in ensuring their own career development and success *and* in the success of professional women more broadly. There are several strategies that will help women to improve their personal career outcomes in addition to strategies that will help their organizations continue adapting to the needs of a twenty-first century workforce.

Career management. Women can—and need to be—more strategic about managing their careers by creating a vision for their future career development. The goal is not to have all the answers, but to make thinking about these issues part of an ongoing process. For example, if a woman plans to stop working for a period of time while raising young children, she should consider how to maintain professional connections and stay current (at least somewhat) with the issues in her field or profession in order to facilitate reentry. If a woman works remotely or reduces her work hours, she should determine how she will maintain a presence so that she is not forgotten when new opportunities arise. If she is offered a promotion but refuses, she should be clear that while the timing is not right, she is interested in future growth opportunities. In many ways, women can improve their professional success by more proactively managing their careers.

Advocacy. In addition to getting clearer regarding future career goals, it is critical that women become more skilled at asking for what they want at work. In the modern workplace, where career self-management is far more the norm (for good or bad), all of us need to develop greater comfort with advocating for ourselves. Women need to let others know if they are ready for a stretch assignment or if they are interested in developing a particular area of expertise. They need to indicate the desire for a promotion or a willingness to relocate for the right opportunity. They need to be forthright about what they need to excel professionally and about their professional goals.

With time and practice, women can become more comfortable with self-advocacy in several areas. One of the most important of these areas is salary negotiation. Asking for increased compensation is highly uncomfortable territory for most women. While I was conducting a mentoring workshop with the most senior women at a retail conglomerate, a woman leader shared her story of discovering that she was getting paid substantially less than her male colleague, despite receiving glowing feedback. She indicated that she'd never asked for more money but happily accepted what was offered. After finding out that her pay was substantially lower, she reported never again going into salary conversations without the expectation of actively negotiating. It is important to arm yourself with comparative salary information—to the best of your ability—which will likely increase your comfort and confidence in the salary negotiation process.

Collective action. Women should develop relationships with other women professionals in their organization and in their industries. For example, they can start or join an existing women's professional network. From sitting in my first focus groups with women investment bankers in the early 1990s, to managing the employee networks group at Catalyst, I have repeatedly seen the power of women coming together to share their experiences and to drive change in their organizations.

Women must play a vital role as mentors and sponsors to the women who are coming up behind them. Over my nearly two decades of consulting, I saw a major shift in the attitudes of senior women toward advocating for other women at work. Previously, women's networks were started by mid-career women with the most senior women—those who had fought hard to ascend to their leadership roles—preferring to distance themselves from anything that struck of women being different. In more recent years, however, it often has been the most senior women seeking to band together and drive change that improves the experiences of all women in their organizations.

At all stages along the career ladder, women can—and should—reach back to those coming up behind them. Most women benefit from speaking with other women, even those only a few years ahead of them in terms of career stage. You are very likely a potential mentor for many women, even if you are earlier in your career. You can harness that power to help improve the situation for women in your organization and your industry.

Finally, there are many men—most of them quiet supporters—who believe deeply in gender equality and fairness. Women need to cultivate their support as a means to expedite change.

Concluding Thoughts

Women in the U.S. first surpassed men in earning bachelor's degrees in 1996 and passed them in earning advanced college degrees in 2011.[34] To squander such an incredible asset of talent would be a colossal waste. Yet a vision for gender parity in leadership roles remains elusive. It is clear that significant changes in our work cultures and career models are needed. Some women will make the trade-offs—fighting against work cultures that feel foreign, at times even hostile, and to work environments that are at odds with their lives as mothers—but the vast majority will not.

Instead, women will leave organizations to start their own businesses (a positive development), stop working altogether because of their frustration (resulting in a loss of income and professional capital), or remain working, but in ways that underutilize their talents and squash their ambitions. In all of these scenarios, organizations lose and women lose. With more men making work-life balance a priority, if we allow our conception of leadership and advancement to remain predicated on time and accessibility, then we will have a narrower and narrower pool (of women and men) from which to draw. This approach is the antithesis of garnering the best thinking at the table—including varied perspectives—to solve the complex problems we face as a society and a world.

Based on my experience working with the United Nations, I am hopeful that this is not the direction we will travel, choosing to draw from an increasingly narrow slice of the potential workforce. I consulted to the UN to help them in developing a work-life strategy for an historic new United Nations entity, UN Women, an organization charged with bringing a global voice to issues for women and girls around the world. At the launch event for UN Women, Secretary General Ban Ki-moon spoke about how the full engagement of women is required for the UN to continue making progress on its key priorities, issues such as improving global health, reducing poverty, and maintaining peace. We need women leaders at the table of all our organizations. The extent to which we can have women fully represented at leadership levels, creating organizations that reflect what is important to them, the better it will be for all of us.

Chapter 6

Extreme Parenting and the New Family Norms

The most important thing she'd learned over the years was that there was no way to be a perfect mother and a million ways to be a good one.

---Jill Churchill

Parenting can feel extremely challenging for modern parents. The bar is high, and ever rising, for what is necessary to successfully raise children in the twenty-first century. We've adopted many norms outside of work that contribute to the unceasing intensity of our family lives. Even when we are not at work, we are motivated by a false sense of urgency, over-scheduling, fear-driven decisions, and an accompanying lack of belief that we can stem the tide or do things differently. We all have an enormous amount of information coming at us, and it is challenging as parents to sort out the headline and sound bite from the more complex and nuanced picture. Conditioned to be in fight-or-flight mode, we feel pressed to stay on the move, if only just to try to keep up, try to get by, try to meet all our obligations.

Society has made women the default point person on parenting in the twenty-first century. This was not always so, and it's a reminder of how social context—which we all experience as reality in our time—does change and evolve. Before the Industrial Revolution, women had few parental rights and fathers were seen as ultimately responsible for ensuring the character of their children.[1] Yet in the 1960s (when I was born), men were perceived as the tangential parent and required permission even to be in the delivery room during the birth of their child. Leading experts of the day believed that babies could develop that "special bond" with only one person, ideally the mother, so the dad's job was to get out of the way.[2] Culturally we've swung from one extreme, with fathers as the lead parent, to another, with mothers being on the hook for creating (and I use that word intentionally) great children. We need to find our way toward a more shared approach where both parents are relevant and deeply involved. Medical research is helping us out. Recent research at Tufts University, focused on studying the parental brain, found that expectant fathers had physiological changes, such as increased levels of cortisol and prolactin and decreased levels of testosterone—all of which are associated with promoting attachment and nurturing.[3]

Women, typically in the forefront, and men, often in the background, struggling to define their roles as equal and primary parents, are bombarded with information about what it means to be a good parent. Amidst all the noise, it is challenging to get clarity and to stake a claim in creating norms that are right for our children and families and reflect our values. In a job where there truly is no manual, in a job that is emotionally compelling, many of us struggle to find our way.

The Twenty-First Century Model: Parenting on Steroids

In the new millennium, parenting feels like an extreme sport. While children used to be seen as generally resilient, and life experiences—both good and bad—were considered helpful to prepare them for the inevitable ups and downs and unpredictability of adulthood, the modern perception is that children are fragile and require intensive focus.[4] We worry that a single decision, such as a child not starting a sport early enough or not taking enough advanced placement courses to get into a top college, could have serious negative consequences. Even our language embodies our intensely child-focused approach. We describe ourselves as stay-at-home mothers and fathers rather than homemakers because so much of our focus is spent managing our children's lives, almost as if parents were their children's agents. Our home lives, like our work lives, have been dramatically altered by technology, which is speeding life up and expanding the world of possibilities. All this has resulted in heightened anxiety, a sense of acute busyness in our lives outside of work (as well as at work), and a feeling that home is not the respite it used to be. The stakes feel high all the way around, and far too many parents feel stressed, overwhelmed, and exhausted.

We are further burdened by an idyllic picture of the way it used to be. Mothering and guilt have become close bedfellows, with modern mothers, particularly those working outside the home, wondering and worrying if they are spending enough time with their children. Francie Latour, the author of the article "The Bad Mother Complex: Why are so many working mothers haunted by constant guilt?" shared her personal experience of feeling guilty about not being able to play a game with her six-year-old because she needed to work, even though she had traded the long commute and rigid world of a newspaper reporter for the far more flexible world of a freelance writer and editor working from home.[5]

It turns out that the guilt women feel while juggling is a much bigger issue than their competence at doing the actual juggling.[6] Yet modern mothers—working outside the home or not—spend more time with their children than mothers did forty years ago. In addition, fathers spend more than twice as much time with their children as fathers in the 1960s, 1970s, or 1980s.[7] Our kids are getting a lot of our time! This was a surprise even to the researchers who studied the historical time data, as illustrated in the passage below from an article highlighting the study results.

> It seems reasonable to expect that parental investment in child rearing would have declined since 1965, when 60 percent of all children lived in families with a breadwinner father and a stay-at-home mother… The researchers found, to their surprise, that married and single parents spent more

time teaching, playing with and caring for their children than parents did 40 years ago.[8]

Where has this extra time come from? Well, our houses are perhaps not as clean, since women have significantly cut back the time spent on housework. Men do more, but not enough to cover the loss. We also do a lot of multitasking and spend less time on ourselves, recharging our parental batteries. Despite an enormous body of evidence that the bonds between children with working (versus stay-at-home) mothers are similarly strong,[9] and despite the empirical data that we spend not less but *more* time with our children than mothers in previous decades, mothers (and increasingly fathers) guiltily worry they are not doing enough for their children.

Multiple factors contribute to the intensity we experience as twenty-first century parents: a proliferation of media and electronic devices, heightened security concerns for our children, outsized expectations of our kids' enrichment needs, and a high-pressure and test-focused approach to public education. In addition, rampant expert advice reinforces the notion of a "right" way to parent and has contributed to the erosion of our parental confidence. The good news is that the Libra work and life model helps parents confront and manage the reality of these external forces so as to create a more relaxed and saner approach to family management. The Libra approach helps keep parents focused on what they can influence and on the well-being of the whole family, children and parents alike.

My husband Bryan has an idea (okay, a fantasy) for a new product, the *parent energy meter*. This device would provide real-time, visual feedback, perhaps like a thermometer, helping children to understand what behaviors cause their parents' energy to plummet—like getting into it with your brother about who got a micron more of dessert—and what behaviors add to the parental energy reservoir—like helping to set the table without complaining. Children would be able to see the connection between energy-inducing behaviors and positive results, such as playing a card game or some pick-up basketball, and energy-depleting behaviors and negative results, such as grumpy parents or no family time for fun activities. The Libra work and life approach helps parents to recharge their batteries so ultimately they have more to give and to share with their children, more energy, more focused attention, more joy.

Plugged In Yet Checked Out

The precipitous rise in connectivity and the inescapable pull of our screen worlds exert considerable stress on modern-day parents. Our children are inundated with messages from their electronic worlds as we, their parents, strive to share our values, to protect them, and to create strong relationships.

The time children spend on their various media devices begins in their very earliest years and is growing. Forty percent of three-month-old babies are regular viewers of screen media[10], and the average preschool child spends thirty-plus hours per week in front of screens[11]—more time than outdoors. Of real concern is that screen time can be habit-forming; research has found that the more time young children spend engaging with their various media devices, the greater challenges they face turning them off as they get older.[12] Daily media use among school-age children has grown dramatically in recent years, with school-age children spending seven and a half hours per day, every day including weekends, on recreational media (not related to school), or over fifty hours per week. If you count all the media multitasking that goes on (e.g., watching television and texting), the *daily* average jumps to ten and three-quarters hours![13]

Similar to our children, we adults spend a great deal of time on media. Television viewing accounts for more than 50 percent of adults' discretionary time and represents the greatest use of time after working and sleeping.[14] The time adults spent watching TV rose in response to the 2008 recession, when time experts suspected Americans might use former work time on pursuits such as education, exercise, home repair, or volunteering.[15] Instead they watched more TV (and slept more).

In addition to the problem of kids' screen time crowding out other activities—resulting in big declines in the amount of time children spend outdoors and engaged in physical activity[16]—much of the information that children receive through their electronic worlds is highly problematic. Consider that the average American child has witnessed over 8,000 murders and 100,000 other acts of violence by the time they finish elementary school[17] and the average preschooler sees nearly 25,000 commercials.[18] Music videos, ever popular with teens, contain on average over ninety sexual situations per hour, eleven of them hardcore ones such as oral sex and intercourse.[19]

Media imagery heightens gendered thinking and perceived limitations. Based on the largest study ever conducted on movies and television shows for children under age eleven, researchers found that the more television girls watched, the fewer possibilities they saw for themselves in their lives, and the more boys watched, the more gender-biased their outlooks became.[20] While the key aspiration of female characters was romance, virtually no male characters shared this aim. Furthermore, the majority of female characters in G-rated movies had body proportions that could not exist in real life and were dressed similarly to females in R-rated movies.[21] The media provides a steady diet of strong imagery, for girls and boys, from their very earliest years, about what they should look like, who they should emulate, and what they should care about.

The pervasiveness of violence in the media is another big stressor for modern parents. In an analysis of more than 200 studies on children's media viewing, the effect of television violence on aggressive behavior was described as *only slightly smaller than the documented effect of smoking on lung cancer.* A growing body of work also establishes a connection between aggression and violent video games. Among several hundred third- through fifth-graders, higher usage of violent video games was correlated with significantly increased aggression, both in the short term and several months later, even after controlling for factors such as gender and baseline levels of aggression.[22]

Media use is also linked to materialistic values and family stress. Children's exposure to advertising increases their purchase requests, leading to greater parental conflict.[23] A landmark market research study in the late 1980s sought to help retailers increase sales by highlighting ways to exploit children's nagging. With the deregulation of children's television in 1984, placing virtually no limits on how marketers could reach children, kids' consumer spending rose by more than 800 percent through 2008, from $4.2 billion to $40 billion.[24] Our children are being bathed in advertising from their youngest years right through to their cell-phone and iPod days. Sadly, nearly two in three parents report their children define their worth by what media-designated "status items" they own.[25]

Perhaps the greatest challenge of parenting in our media-saturated world is that it leaves us disconnected from our children, ironically even while sitting in the same room. After finding her husband and two children immersed in their individual screens each evening, often eating dinner in front of them, one mother insisted the family spend a week without any computerized entertainment. Her family was horrified but succumbed, and on the first night of the freeze she made the family's favorite dinner and dessert. Being completely out of practice with making conversation together, they found the meal so uncomfortable that everyone fled before dessert was even served.[26]

Danger Is Rampant

Another contributing factor to our intensive parenting model is our safety concerns for our children. The very definition of being a good parent is protecting your child and keeping him or her safe from harm. In the twenty-first century, there is a deep sense of pride that *good parents* always know where their children are and have a constant electronic connection if they are not with them physically. "Good" parents generally keep very close tabs on their children and don't let them do things perceived as potentially unsafe, such as crossing a busy street to walk to elementary school or going to a friend's house as a teenager if the parents are not home. In the past, children reached these milestones typically at far earlier ages. But today, hyper-vigilance is the watchword, whether parenting a two-year-old or a sixteen-year-old.

The sense that danger is lurking around every corner is pervasive, fueled by high-profile, sensational stories of children being kidnapped, hurt, even killed—all the very worst things any parent could imagine. Despite statistics documenting a declining tide of violent crime over the past three decades, our collective perception of danger has gone in the completely opposite direction.[27] The U.S. Department of Justice started a report series in 1988 titled NISMART (National Incidence Studies of Missing, Abducted, Runaway and Throwaway Children). The most recent report was published in 2002 and shows *the problem of missing children is far more complex than the headlines suggest.* Stereotypical kidnappings—those terrifying headlines that we hear over and over again whereby kids are kidnapped by a stranger or slight acquaintance, transported and held for ransom or with the intent to kill or harm, accounted for 115 incidents in one year—out of 75 million children under eighteen in the U.S.[28]

A quick web search for "child kidnapping" helps further explain why parents experience such anxiety about safety for their children. According to a website that came up on the first page of a Google search, a child is reported missing or abducted every forty seconds in the U.S., which translates to over 2,000 children per day, or 800,000 children per year. (Conveniently, the organization will sell you an e-book and bonus DVD for just $29.95 to help you prevent this horror.) Well over half a million children missing or abducted each year is admittedly an incredibly scary figure and makes these horrors sound nearly common, yet further analysis reveals this statistic to be greatly exaggerated. It appears that the 800,000 annual figure quoted represents child maltreatment,[29] a much broader category than child abduction, encompassing both abuse (30 percent of the cases) and neglect (70 percent). Furthermore, the perpetrator in the vast majority of the cases is a parent, not an acquaintance or stranger.[30]

The story we continually tell ourselves, and that is taken as a given without question or examination, is that our children cannot enjoy the greater freedom and autonomy most of us experienced as children because the world is simply too dangerous today. But despite our heightened fears, the data makes the case for relaxing our safety concerns. The 2008 child maltreatment rate (including all forms of abuse and neglect) has fallen through time and in 2008 was 23 percent below the rate in 1990.[31] Violent crime against youths ages twelve to seventeen similarly reflects a declining trend, with the victimization rate generally trending downward through the mid-1980s, increasing slightly through the early 1990s, and then dropping precipitously over the next fifteen years.[32]

Our hyper-vigilance as parents compels us to want our children under an adult's constant supervision. This perceived need to be monitoring our children at every moment contributes to parental stress both because there is far more to coordinate and navigate and because there is little perceived buffer. Instead of older elementary and middle school children learning, with guidance, how to navigate their way home from school, parents have added management of this task to their daily chores. Parents must plan for someone else to pick up their children from school or they experience firsthand the frequent mid-afternoon traffic clogs and the pressure to make it to school in time to secure a parking spot. No longer do we feel content that if we are running late to pick up a teenager from sports practice as it starts to get dark that all will be fine; instead, we frantically try to text or call en route and feel stressed about the potential danger.

My strong feelings about safety misperceptions have, admittedly, been greatly influenced by my mother's nervous temperament. As a child, I could see and sense that my mother had many fears, especially about danger and safety issues. Informed by a steady diet of television and radio programming, which comprised her primary source of data, she would call me, once I became an adult, to share her fears—about contamination of our food supply, about weather disasters, about day care scandals and child abductions. I always wanted to say, "But Mom, what's the data?" My goal in these conversations became to respectfully listen rather than to debate. The greatest irony for me was that, while my mom was immersed in all the latest dangers, she didn't wear a seat belt because she didn't like that it wrinkled her clothes. It felt to me like a dramatic example of spending mental energy on the wrong problems.

Despite our fixation on our children's safety, we don't question the psychological costs of the messages our children receive, overtly and subtly, that the world isn't safe. Their internalization of fears may have far greater repercussions than the actual safety risk. Research shows that more frequent viewers of television, adults and children alike, are more concerned about being the victim of violence and generally perceive the world as a more dangerous place.[33] In our new, wired world, the adult imagery that children regularly encounter is a far greater concern than stranger danger, yet collectively as parents we spend little energy protecting against media influences.

Enrichment Requirements Are High—and Growing

As parents, we struggle with an inflated sense of what children need to develop and thrive. The fear that our kids won't get ahead, may not get into the best colleges, or won't be able to compete in the global economy, color our thinking. One mother articulates the dilemma:

> Every year when college admissions season rolls around, I read articles about how the applicant pool is bigger and stronger than ever before. But are we really seeing better kids,

or just slicker packaging? ... Are we creating Frankenstudents—artificial monsters, impossible composites of skills and achievements that rarely coexist in real life? I look around at the adults I know, and I don't see anybody who resembles this glossy hyperachiever.[34]

She goes on to say, "This climate of parental anxiety is nuts. The way kids are being packaged for college is cynical and fake ... But opting out of it is nerve-wracking, too. If everyone else is playing the game, can your child afford not to?"[35]

This angst and fear is not dissimilar from the way many parents felt during the Industrial Revolution, when they worried if their children would be able to function effectively in their rapidly changing world, moving from working as farmers and craftsmen to working in factories.[36] In the evolution to a knowledge economy, where the rules of success are ever evolving, we have created a baseline of enrichment for our children that is incredibly high—and often misguided. An article touting online family management systems as one means to ease the stress characterized the gauntlet of the typical middle-class American family: parents working long hours in their jobs as a sales representative and a technician for a big high-tech company, while their two children, ages six and fifteen, participated in three sports teams, driver's education classes, and a scout troop.[37] I have no problem with an online calendar system and think these tools can be extremely helpful, but I wonder if this family (and many others like them) would be better served by stepping back and asking, "Does all this activity make sense? Is it working for my children? Is it working for me and my spouse? Where might we cut back?"

During the preschool years, "mommy and me" classes, swimming lessons, music and movement classes, and playgroups have become common, but full-throttle activity typically hits in the elementary school years. Most kids participate in at least one sport, perhaps an art or drama class (or playing an instrument), an additional activity such as scouts, and potentially involvement in a religious community. And this is typically considered a "light load." Parents spend a whole lot of time coordinating and transporting their children to these activities, as well as supervising their involvement. Multiply the typical American child's extracurricular load by two or more kids and you've got an unpaid part-time activities coordinator job on your hands.

We rush to get our children involved in extracurricular activities from a very young age, fearing that they will be unable to compete if we do not, but in many ways we are receiving signals that this early and intense immersion is not serving our children. Injuries, burnout and exhaustion, and declining creativity are among the problems that have surfaced.

For instance, no longer do youth sports function primarily as a fun way for children to be active, participate and make friends. In many communities youth sports have transformed into a caste system of elite teams, with kids picking *their sport* as early as age ten, often practicing year-round and attending specialized clinics. But up to half of pediatric sports injuries are linked to overuse, formerly a rare health issue for children.[38] In addition, children's abilities and bodies can change dramatically from year to year, and their preadolescent talent often bears little resemblance to their abilities once they hit puberty, especially for boys.[39]

The sports frenzy coincides with the majority of children becoming discouraged or losing interest before they even hit their teen years. According to the Institute for the Study of Youth Sports, by age thirteen approximately 70 percent of children stopped being involved.[40] Among the most common reasons kids gave for stopping a sport were complaints that it wasn't fun anymore, that they were tired of playing, and that it felt like too much pressure.[41] The co-director of the Sport Psychology Program at Massachusetts General Hospital reported that the pressurized culture of youth sports "creates a frenzy and what is lost is the perspective about what is actually good for the child."[42] Rather than fostering a lifelong interest in physical fitness, our intense sports focus for young children seems to be doing just the opposite, making sports feel like an obligation instead of a joy.

The meteoric rise in children's extracurricular activities is also linked to declining creativity. Children need unstructured time to ponder, to daydream, and to imagine. Similar to adults whose creativity at work is negatively impacted by constant time pressure, children's lack of unstructured time is taking a toll on their creativity. From 1990 through 2008, American children's scores declined steadily on an assessment measuring creativity, particularly for children during the elementary years.[43]

An article on raising gifted children highlighted the downside of our intense approach and the importance of following your child's lead. Based on a study of 700 famous people, researchers indicated kids don't excel for long unless they are driven to achieve by their own internal motivation (in addition to their parents' encouragement).[44] One child highlighted in the article was playing guitar with adults by the time he was two. He switched to violin at age eight and performed so beautifully that his parents dreamed of him playing on major stages one day. Based on advice from a neighbor, the boy's mother switched her son's violin teacher from a local folk musician, whom he loved, to a classical teacher focused on technique. Within a year, the boy lost interest and stopped playing. Among the obstacles cited for gifted children were adults' high expectations, fear of failure, and pressure from peers. The advice of a father whose son at age seventeen was leading a stem cell research team before entering a doctoral program was, "The key is for the parent to find out what the child's interest is." When the child is encouraged to pursue something that truly interests him, "that talent will never disappear."[45]

Education = Achievement (Perhaps Learning)

In the educational realm, an early academic focus, beginning in preschool and culminating in what feels like a high-stakes college admissions gamble, greatly contributes to parental stress and the experience of unceasing demands. Parents feel the need to ensure their children receive an excellent education. At the turn of the twenty-first century, that belief translates to deep parental involvement. Parents commonly help their children with homework—which is greater in quantity and starts at a younger age than in generations past—and tap into resources such as tutors to assist their children with shoring up weaker skills. Parents manage, schedule, and coordinate outside enrichment activities like music or foreign languages—deemed "extras" in cash-strapped public school systems. Finally, parents feel the need to work ever harder to pay for all these resources and to help guarantee their children have the best shot at success.

The very early school experience has become highly intellectualized, with reading readiness at the top of the list. The problem is, we are asking young children to accomplish tasks for which many of them lack the developmental skills, particularly young boys. Young children learn primarily through play and experience, yet they spend four to six times as much of their day being drilled in math and literacy concepts as playing.[46] The amount of homework for children aged six to nine increased three-fold during the 1990s, despite the fact that research indicates there is little to no value from homework for children at this young age.[47]

Scholastic pursuit is increasingly displacing recess and play for our young children. While in 1989, 96 percent of elementary school systems (including kindergarten) had at least one recess period daily, a decade later that had dropped to 70 percent of schools.[48] The reported incidence of ADHD has risen, as standardized testing has increased, and boys, more likely to need a physical outlet, were more than four times as likely as girls to be expelled from school.[49] The focus on academics earlier in the school years is robbing children of the time to play and learn to self-regulate. At the same time, ADHD (often described as a lack of focus and self-management) is the primary diagnosis for kids struggling in school.[50]

With anxious parents wanting to do everything they can to help their children be prepared, the advent of educational toys—the Baby Einstein phenomenon—has skyrocketed, despite evidence that almost all of these purchased tools are totally unnecessary. In a National Benchmark survey, parents were asked to rate the value of various activities in helping children become better learners. Top examples of activities described as very effective were: a twelve-month-old rolling a ball back and forth with her parent, a four-year-old collecting and sorting leaves in the yard, and a six-year-old playing cards with his dad. Two items from the list—identified as least effective in helping children become good learners—were a four-year-old memorizing flash cards and a two-year-old playing a computer activity.[51] It seems what we have always done instinctually as parents, with no specialized equipment or method, is right on target.

Struggles with our educational approach are evident well past the early school years. The documentary *Race to Nowhere* has swept across the country, particularly in affluent communities where student and parental stress is rampant.[52] The film's director, a corporate attorney living in an affluent suburb in California, reports in her "Letter from the Director":

> Three years ago my only knowledge of film came from buying tickets at the box office and going to see a movie with my kids. *Race to Nowhere* was inspired by a series of wake-up calls that made me look closely at the relentless pressure to perform that children face today. I saw the strain in my children as they navigated days filled with school, homework, tutoring and extracurricular activities. But it wasn't until the crisis of my 12-year-old daughter being diagnosed with a

stress induced illness that I was determined to do something.[53]

The movie depicts how educators, parents, and students collectively feel caught in a system that induces acute stress and is antithetical to developing a lifelong love of learning. The movie highlights parents and students experiencing a single test or a single grade as determinant of the child's future. Students in the film talk about filling their heads with facts to ace the exam, only to forget them soon thereafter. The repercussions of the testing and assessment focus, according to teachers, are that children are drowning in content, preoccupied with performance, learning only what's going to be on the test, and using cheating as a way to cope.

Teachers credit the No Child Left Behind legislation with creating intense pressure to deliver improved standardized test scores since underperformance translates directly to reduced school funding. While the No Child Left Behind legislation was intended to ensure every child was proficient in a baseline set of skills, the film characterizes it, in practice, as teaching to the top 2 percent of students and forgetting the bell curve. As a result, some students experience acute stress to perform; others, who feel unable to keep up with the academic load, become apathetic and simply give up trying. What gets emphasized for students is how to succeed academically, without enough focus on figuring out what is important to them as people. Most importantly, those in the film indicate that such heavy focus on evaluation and assessment in school engenders a lack of critical thinking and discernment—the very skills that are vital in a knowledge economy.

In my town, a suburb outside of Boston known to have a strong school system, where educational achievement is paramount, 62 percent of high school students report experiencing extreme stress due to academics, and three-fourths of kids believe the town itself encourages unhealthy competition, according to a 2009 Youth Risk

Behavior Survey. A senior at the high school in my town shared his thoughts on the problem of an overly stressful school culture:

> I am not advocating for a stress-free school. In many ways, stress is formative. Stress, and the occasional failure, can teach resiliency, the ability to recover and plow onward. It can teach you that you're a lot stronger than you think you are. But chronic stress inhibits learning, risk taking and curiosity. There's nothing that makes a student feel more hopeless and discouraged than piles of relentless work. Nothing is more self-alienating than the sinking dread that all you are is the facts you've crammed, and now you're just a shell. There is no fire in you anymore, no true hunger.[54]

According to research, students continue to experience intense stress at the college level, with 61 percent of college students indicating feelings of hopelessness and 45 percent reporting having trouble functioning.[55]

The irony is that while we spend a tremendous amount of time and a whole lot of energy worrying about how to support our children's intellectual development, research suggests that in more affluent families, these parenting details have little influence on children's intelligence. A research study with a large sample of identical and fraternal twins speaks to the age-old nature versus nurture debate. Researchers from the University of Texas at Austin and from the University of Virginia studied 750 pairs of American twins over a period of several years.[56] When the children were tested as infants, the home environment accounted for the great majority of the variability in mental abilities at every socioeconomic level, but when the children were tested as toddlers, the results portrayed a very different picture. Among those in lower-income homes, the environment continued to play a major role in explaining variability in mental abilities—thus those parents at lower rungs of the socioeconomic ladder that read to their children, made those special trips to the zoo or museum, and spent time building block towers and having tea parties had a critical impact. But among children at higher socioeconomic levels, the environment played a negligible role in explaining the variability in intelligence while genetics was a primary factor.[57] At a certain economic level, the baseline is so high—for experiences, access to information, positive interactions—that genetic predisposition becomes the key driver of mental abilities.

Other studies have explored the variety of factors that might help explain why class differences do impact children's mental abilities. By age three, children in wealthier families hear about 500,000 encouragements (compared with 80,000 discouragements). For children in households on welfare, the ratio is reversed.[58] Ironically, in many of the middle- to upper-income communities, where parents expend a huge amount of energy worrying about so many decisions for their children, the nuances likely matter very little. On the other hand, for lower-income parents who struggle with inflexible workplaces, far less access to high-quality child care, and weak schools, the support we provide as a society does make a huge difference.

The Difficulty of Finding Your Own Parenting Style

The book *Battle Hymn of the Tiger Mother*, by Amy Chua, sparked energetic discussion about parenting standards all along the strict-to-lenient continuum. For those who may have missed the uproar, the *Wall Street Journal* provided an excerpt from the book in a January 2011 article titled "Why Chinese Mothers Are Superior," which portrayed a strict parenting approach to inculcating excellence in your children. The article described the author as never allowing her daughters to attend a sleepover, be in a school play, or get any grade less than an A, among other requirements. The author shared a dramatic story of working with (one might say forcing) her eight-year-old daughter to master a complex piano piece. The session involved the daughter ripping up the score (which her mother taped back together) and her mother denying the child food and the opportunity to go to the bathroom while they continued the practice session. Eventually the daughter mastered the piece and all had a "happy" ending.

Scanning the paper one Sunday afternoon, I saw the provocative headline "Why Chinese Mothers Are Superior." After reading the story myself, I shared parts of it with my teenage son. He had a pained look on his face as I read the paragraphs about the piano practice, and we had a brief discussion about the story afterward because unhealthy student stress has been a prominent issue in our town. Having had an initially strong reaction to the article, I obtained a much broader perspective on the Tiger Mom phenomenon through my research for this book. It was another powerful lesson in getting *the rest of the story* and underscored how the framing of these issues adds oxygen to the fire, polarizes our discussions, and challenges our ability as parents to find a more moderate parenting road.

It turns out the excerpt in the *Wall Street Journal* was from the beginning of the memoir and represented a starting point in the evolution of Amy Chua's parenting style. In fact, the rest of the book illustrated how, through time, Ms. Chua softened her approach, particularly in response to her older daughter strongly rebelling during her early teen years. Additionally, the book was marketed as a self-help resource, giving the impression of espousing a parenting philosophy, when in fact it is a memoir. The author described it as her "parental coming of age book." In a follow-up article in the *Journal* a week after the original piece ran, the author described her far less sensationalized thoughts about parenting:

> There is no easy formula for parenting, no right approach (I don't believe, by the way, that Chinese parenting is superior—a splashy headline but I didn't choose it). The best rule of thumb I can think of is that love, compassion and knowing your child have to come first, whatever culture you're from. It doesn't come through in the excerpt, but my

actual book is not a how to guide; it's a memoir, the story of our family's journey in two cultures, and my own eventual transformation as a mother.[59]

The response to the original excerpt was like a tidal wave, generating more comments from an article than the *Journal* had ever received before. To my mind, the intense response serves to illustrate just how strongly most of us feel about parenting, belying how vulnerable we feel in this incredibly important role, and how much we struggle with our choices, whatever those may be. After attending a talk at Smith College on the Tiger Mom book, I felt highly discouraged that the positioning of the book had fed into the polarized discussions that make a more balanced, pragmatic approach to raising children so difficult. I left the discussion knowing that the book, while misrepresented as supporting a parenting philosophy, was instead a quintessential memoir of the immigrant experience in which parents see education and accomplishment as the road to prosperity and a better life.

I strongly identify with the immigrant experience. Having grown up in a family of seven children with a "Tiger Father," who would question why an A- wasn't an A+ and stressed excellence in all pursuits, I know firsthand that an "excellence is the only way" approach has mixed results. For some, it encouraged striving to greater heights, while for others, the pressure was crushing. In the end there is no simple recipe or foolproof method that is the parenting end-all and be-all.

Research underscores my personal experience that there is not just one road to excellence. As Americans, we are warned that our children are falling behind, particularly in comparison to many Asian nations, and may not be able to compete in future job markets. This information heightens the already widespread unease we collectively feel about job security and professional options (e.g., that American jobs continue to go overseas, leaving fewer options and greater competition at home). We hear references to American children scoring poorly (relative to our size and wealth on the world stage) in international tests measuring academic proficiency.

According to the Program for International Student Assessment, on tests measuring abilities in reading, math, and science, several Asian countries—including South Korea, Japan, Hong Kong, and Singapore—did score very highly. But this is only part of the story. Several other countries with different educational approaches, including Canada, Australia, New Zealand, Switzerland, and Finland, scored very highly as well.[60] In Finland (scoring second in science, third in reading, and sixth in math in the international student assessments), high school students regularly get less than one hour of homework and children don't even start school until age seven, a year later than in the U.S. There are no valedictorians or classes for gifted children in Finland; instead, the kids for whom academics come more easily help their classmates who are struggling. Finnish children encounter little standardized testing throughout their school years and Finnish parents don't fret about college.[61]

When I did some consulting in Iceland, having been retained to speak about women in leadership and on corporate boards, I similarly found that education was seen simply as preparation for one's future professional work rather than a high-stakes, Ivy League-or-bust mentality. We spend a tremendous amount of energy in our struggle with the idea that there is a right—or only—way to parent and help our children be successful, when in fact there are many ways.

Erosion of Parental Confidence

One of the biggest challenges for modern parents is an erosion of confidence in their parenting reflexes and skills. The rise of the parenting "expert" in the twentieth century—emphasizing the notion that there is a right way, and thus a wrong way, to parent—coincides with a decline in our collective parenting confidence.[62] But there is no one parenting model that is going to work for every child or family. We become the experts on our children by spending time with them, observing them, and coming to understand how to best support them. And while it is very important to keep an open mind and continue learning, as our children grow we become more skilled with, and comfortable in, determining how parenting advice applies to our unique family situation.

Children differ so much in their innate temperaments, strengths, and struggles that what works for one child may require a very different approach for another. Children's needs are very diverse, and while some need intensive parenting, others require much less. Because our families are smaller, without a broader generational perspective, we have less experience with seeing that each challenging stage, too, shall pass. It all feels so critical, so vital, and so urgent when we are in the middle of it. But wisdom is born of experience and sometimes you will learn by wishing you had made another decision.

When our older son Skylar was in an after-school kindergarten program, the teacher insisted that he do without his favorite stuffed animal during nap times. Skylar had bonded with his special yellow stuffed bear as an infant. By kindergarten, that bear was tattered and dingy gray, deeply loved in that Velveteen Rabbit way, and an enormous source of comfort, especially while falling asleep. When it came to nap time, we deferred to the teacher, who said that children would play with their stuffed animals rather than sleep. In retrospect, I don't consider this a good decision for any of us. Skylar was understandably very sad and didn't like to go to after-school that year, while Bryan and I felt terribly worried and guilty—caught between the system's norms and what felt right to us. But I also don't worry that the decision caused undue harm. What I do think, reflecting on that incident, is that I wish we had been stronger—and more confident—in our parenting instincts.

Parenting can be a very isolating job, particularly when your child requires intensive parenting, is outside the norm, or doesn't fit well with the systems and activities that comprise your everyday life. There is a lot of pressure to put on a good face and minimize the challenges. We feel the need to be able to do it all ourselves as parents, even when our approach doesn't seem to be working, or we are burned out. We would all be better served by trying to redefine the role of the good-enough parent, especially the good-enough mother, knowing that there are too many facets of parenting to believe we could possibly get them all right all of the time.

As parents, we have a major and important influence, but there are also many variables outside our control. It is the alchemy of the child's temperament, the parent's individual skill and temperament, the strength of the parental relationship, and a whole host of external factors—many of which we as parents have limited or no influence over—that come together in the parenting equation. We have developed a false perception that parenting is an input and output scenario, like creating a blueprint or programming a computer, such that if you fine-tune all the details, your end product will be precisely as you had envisioned, or in the case of parenting, your child will turn out happy and successful. The truth is you can do everything right and still your child may struggle mightily, or you can do a whole lot wrong and inevitably your children will learn from those experiences, some of which may build their character and resilience. The key is to keep an open mind as a parent, to learn to trust your instincts, and to be as kind as you can to yourself and your child (or children) as you struggle together to grow through this deep, life-defining experience.

What Do Children Really Need and Want?

The Libra approach—characterized by staying focused on what is right for your child and family, identifying where you can have influence, and putting energy into what you can control—serves modern parents very well as they struggle to get clear on what their children really need and want to thrive. It is true that technology plays a far bigger role in all of our lives than it did in decades past, but instead of giving up and assuming we can have no impact, we can help our children to become savvy media consumers. It is true that current education policy has resulted in rising homework loads and less time for play, but instead of feeling resigned, we can work to ensure that our children do have unstructured time when their bodies and brains can refuel. It is true that many messages in our culture emphasize a highly competitive, win-all mentality, but instead of letting ourselves get caught up in the hysteria, we can step back and determine the amount of effort and competition that is appropriate for our child's age and temperament.

I suspect so much of what children really need and want is far simpler, and easier for parents to deliver, than we've made it out to be. For instance, with small children, things that parents have always instinctively done—rolling a ball, reading books aloud, keeping them near while you do all the day-to-day stuff required to care for a family and manage a household—are the best things you can do to help them learn. As children move through their teen years into young adulthood, simply being with their families is what they enjoy and want. A survey conducted by the Associated Press and MTV found that among people aged thirteen to twenty-four, the most common response to the question "What makes you most happy?" was spending time with my family, followed by spending time with my friends.[63]

A key part of finding your parenting compass is understanding your child—their strengths and weaknesses, how they learn, what energizes them, and what depletes them. Armed with this knowledge, it becomes easier to navigate the various systems and norms you face as a parent and to feel more confident in your decisions, whatever they might be. Below are several ideas of what children really need and want in the twenty-first century.

Kids need a place that helps anchor them. As children cope with the modern reality of full and busy lives, they need home to be a place that helps to ground them. Home should represent a place where they can let down their guard, feel safe, and process all the stimuli they too face in their daily lives. What children internalize from a very young age is the quality of their home environment (busy or quiet, animated or low affect, high energy or sedate). Research among more than a thousand twins discovered that those raised together (fraternal and identical) were far more likely to describe their parents similarly than those raised separately.[64] It seems the gestalt of the home environment—the big-picture feel—is what kids soak up.

Dr. Stephen Durant, a faculty member at the Harvard Medical School and co-director of the Massachusetts General Hospital Sports Psychology Program, who works closely with child athletes, suggests creating a family mission statement that helps to articulate what is important to you as a family and what your family is all about.[65] Creating a forum to discuss situations that family members face daily—work challenges, issues at school, problems with friends—gives parents an opportunity to share their values.

One such value that helps children is appreciation. Approximately half of our temperaments can be attributed to genetics while the other half comes from experience, so there is abundant opportunity to help children develop a sense of gratitude.[66] Kids who feel and act grateful experience many positive outcomes, as the following studies illustrate. Fourth graders, particularly children with low moods, felt better about themselves immediately after expressing their thanks in person and taking a "gratitude visit," as well as a few months afterward. Middle-school students in an affluent northeast community who wrote down things they were grateful for were more satisfied and optimistic than those who were instructed to list things that annoyed them. Among more than 1,000 high school students, those who indicated the most gratitude were better students and had more friends, while those who were most materialistic reported grater envy and less satisfaction in their lives.[67]

At the conference "Current Issues in Youth Sports: Raising Healthy Children in a Competitive World," Dr. Durant of Mass General talked about the value of parents helping their children think about how to respond when they are struggling. He described the golden rule of emotional health as understanding that we should not suffer alone, and emphasized that parents play a key role in their child's lives by helping them identify their go-to people and the go-to behaviors that help them move past adversity. Go-to people (in addition to parents) might include teammates, siblings, coaches, teachers, friends, spiritual advisors, or mentors of any sort. Go-to behaviors are restorative, provide concrete ideas for focusing energy, and represent an alternative to destructive behaviors and thinking. For instance, doing something for others was described by Dr. Durant as helping you "get out of your own business" and focus elsewhere. He characterized activities such as music and art, nature, and prayer or meditation as providing an opportunity for children to "listen for that inner light."

Children need a refuge from the complicated and demanding world they face, and we as parents can help to create a place in our homes, and a space in our lives, that anchors them with a perspective that is broad and deep, a foundation that helps them deal with the situations and complexities they face daily.

Kids need opportunities to stretch their imaginations. Children need a steady diet of unstructured time to create their own play. Increasingly, research has found that what masks as simple child's play is in fact the foundation for developing critical skills such as self-regulation and problem-solving. For most of human history, children's play was unstructured, unsupervised, and based on using what they could find around. That changed dramatically in the second half of the twentieth century, when toy companies started advertising year-round rather than just during the few weeks before Christmas. As a result, children's play became focused on specific toys rather than on activities.[68] But imaginative play, during which children have an opportunity to create their make-believe worlds, is an important vehicle for strengthening their self-regulation and executive functioning skills. Structured play decreases the private speech that children (as well as adults) use to practice controlling themselves.[69]

Boredom has become a rarity now that children are typically never far from a screen that can entertain them. I don't believe you can even buy a minivan today without a built-in DVD player in the back seat. Yet a little boredom can be a good thing. While it taxes us as parents—who hasn't appreciated that a video or an iPod can be a lifesaver when you need some quiet time?—when kids are forced to entertain themselves, they will find a way to do so. When kids are in charge of their play, they learn critical problem-solving skills and have a chance to stretch their imaginations. What do you do when pretending to be Robin Hood and you don't have a bow and arrow? What do you do with the little kid who is not very skilled at the game but still wants to be a part of the group? What do you do when everyone wants to do something different and you have to find a way to compromise? And perhaps most important in this wired day and age, what do you do when you're bored and can't rely on a screen to fill the void?

Teens, as well as younger children, benefit from open space in their lives. A mother of three teenage children instituted a technology fast for her family, which she describes in her forthcoming book, *The Winter of Our Disconnect*. She said, "It got to the point where we would inhabit the same room, but we weren't connecting." For six months they unplugged everything with a screen and she promised her kids proceeds from the book as incentive. In addition to the family spending time on board games and family dinners, which formerly felt out of reach, her son started playing his saxophone again and her two daughters wrote a novel together.[70]

Many children's lives are as scheduled as any adult, with not a night during the week or a weekend afternoon with nowhere they have to be or nothing they have to do. Just building in some windows for free, unstructured time provides some needed balance.

Kids need limits. With the goal of creating home environments that allow children to decompress and recharge, we need to set limits that will allow this to happen. Creating limits regarding media can make a big difference: reducing their exposure to violence and unhelpful images of beauty, curbing incessant advertising, providing opportunities to process what they are seeing, creating more family time and more space for non-media activities.

Given that two-thirds of school-age children say the television is usually on during dinner, and nearly half report it is on *nearly all the time*[71], simply turning it off provides more quiet and an opportunity for connection. Given that only about three in ten school-age children have rules about the amount of time they spend playing video games, using the computer, or watching television, and that those children with any rules about media usage spend about *three hours less per day* using media than those with no rules, there is a huge opportunity to give our children the gift of more time by making them turn it all off.[72] A specialist on cyber-bullying contrasted the bully of old, from whom you were safe when you walked through your front door, with the modern-day electronic bully who follows you into your home. She suggested parents require teenagers, those being bullied or not, to dock their electronic devices when at home and be allowed to use them only for a set duration of time or with parental permission.

In addition to limiting media time, in many households parents have an opportunity to create parameters around media content as well. Fewer than half of school-age children have any limits on what they can watch on television and less than a third on what video games they can play.[73] As important as limiting content, parents can share their children's media experiences and use this opportunity as a forum for conversation, sharing family values, and listening to what their children take away from their media interactions.

According to a comprehensive analysis of the impacts of media usage on children, "Electronic media can have both positive and negative effects on children's development and it is thus overly simplistic to argue that the media are detrimental or valuable to children." Instead, research concludes that content really matters and can heighten problematic behaviors such as anxiety and aggression in children, or conversely, can enhance positive behaviors such as cooperation, altruism, and acceptance of others. The author, who conducted a comprehensive review of research exploring the impact of media experiences on children, goes on to say in her report that the influence of media is affected by a child's age, developmental stage, gender, and temperament, making a strong case for the important role parents play in determining appropriate media exposure.[74]

Bryan and I bring very different media experiences to parenting. I grew up in an environment where there were few, if any, limits regarding television. In my house the TV seemed always to be on, while Bryan's parents were quite strict. Consequently he went to his friends' houses to indulge, until their parents made them go outside and play. As an adult, I watch little television, support media limits for children, and am a light recreational media user. While Bryan and I are generally on the same page regarding media boundaries for our sons, he is clearly drawn to media far more strongly than I for its entertainment value and could be described as a moderate user. I sometimes watch sports events with Bryan and my sons as a family bonding experience, and I have tried to develop some tolerance for the silly YouTube videos my sons love to share. Bryan and I purposefully rent movies or watch programs on television that reinforce our family values. We also use the media as a catalyst, when the opportunity arises, to discuss challenging topics.

The stratospheric rise of the media is reality. As Libra parents, we play a vital role in helping children to manage the powerful role of media in their lives: sharing it, limiting it, interpreting it, and helping them to make sense of it.

Kids need help developing life skills. While a disproportionate amount of time is focused on academic skills, it is the broader life skills that will serve the test of time for our children. Ellen Galinsky, the president of the Families and Work Institute and author of *Mind in the Making*, describes such life skills as focus and self-control, communicating and making connections, critical thinking and self-directed learning, and being able to see another person's perspective.[75] These skills allow us to work with and relate to others, to make sense of the world we live in, to manage and filter the vast amount of information coming at us, and to remain focused and effective in the midst of many competing priorities.

Galinsky highlights focus and self-control—or the ability to pay attention while filtering distractions—as especially critical for navigating our high stimulation and fast-paced modern world. She defines critical thinking as the ongoing search for reliable information to guide our thinking and actions, another vital twenty-first century skill, as the importance of discerning what is meaningful from a seemingly endless supply of information has risen dramatically. Perspective-taking fosters empathy, or seeing the world from another's vantage point; in doing so, we are able to consider another person's perspective alongside our own. She emphasizes that these life skills are equally as important for adults as for children and we promote them in our children by modeling them ourselves. She tells parents that we don't need expensive programs, materials, or equipment to instill these critical skills in our children, but can promote them every day through the practical and fun things we do with them.[76]

Life skills also include experience with the practical day-to-day activities that are necessary to care for a family and manage a home. Because our children's lives seem so busy and intense, it feels natural to want to shield them from having more to do, especially mundane chores. But involving children more (as is age appropriate) in the many tasks of home and family management helps to balance the intensity in other parts of their lives. In families with male children, involving boys (and men) in this way reinforces gender equality and the importance of caretaking for all family members.

Like many parents, Bryan and I struggle to be consistent about ensuring our sons help at home—doing the laundry, walking the dog, doing a general pickup on Sunday night before the start of a new week. We are no poster children here, and it feels so much easier just to do it ourselves sometimes, especially when our sons were younger or newer to a task. But over and over again we see how much more capable they are of managing home responsibilities than we've given them credit for. We've also found our efforts to involve our sons have helped them to become far more knowledgeable about what goes into caring for a home and family. It has made them more appreciative, so that when food is overcooked, or their favorite piece of clothing is dirty and in the laundry pile, they are more thoughtful and respectful in their response. After an evening (rare, I admit) when our sons were completely in charge of making dinner for the family, Bryan and I could see how proud they felt of their accomplishment, and we felt incredibly energized by their contributing in this meaningful way.

Kids need the opportunity to be with and learn from both parents. A central benefit of the Libra approach is a broader array of skills to draw from because both mothers and fathers are highly engaged in their children's lives. Each parent brings unique strengths to parenting, and ensuring children have active involvement with their mother and father independently benefits them greatly. In our family, Bryan's tendency toward routines and rituals helps provide comforting rhythms in our sons' lives, while my drive for newness leads to exploration and new discoveries. While Bryan far better understands procrastination and is the go-to guy when emotions run high because a homework assignment turns out to be more difficult than expected, I, with my strong planning bent, help the kids think about how to break up big projects into smaller pieces.

Based on research, fathers are less likely to jump in when children are frustrated with a toy that is not doing what they want, while mothers are more likely to intervene so that their children can succeed. Both approaches build skills, the ability to persevere through frustration as well as the opportunity to overcome a problem with help. Fathers tend to wrestle and play more actively with their children while mothers tend to prefer snuggling. Active play helps build confidence and self-regulatory skills while close, gentle contact reinforces intimacy. When children are having a tantrum, fathers often seek to distract them, while mothers tend toward helping them express their feelings about what is happening. The result is that children learn both to be more resilient and to develop problem-solving skills through talking.[77] Either mothers or fathers can provide what children need to develop and thrive, but children benefit that much more when they have the involvement of both.

What children most need—and want—are parents who have a high regard for one another and are generally fulfilled in their own lives. I am not talking about some sort of nirvana here, but rather a plain, basic comfort with your situation and choices. Children want their parents to be happy; it provides them with a deep sense of security. When school-age children were asked if they had one wish about the way their mother's or father's work affected their lives, the most common response was they wished their parents were less stressed.[78] All our efforts to be perfect parents will never be as valuable to children in the long run as parents who enjoy their lives as individuals as well as part of a couple and family.

According to Josh Coleman, author of *When Parents Hurt*, as well as several other books on parenting and marriage, the challenge for modern parents is this: "We have an intensive parenting model that is problematic for parents today. What I see is great parents and this misguided notion that children require so much from their parents and if they don't get it, the consequences will be dire. This creates an intense amount of anxiety at home ... It's a bar that is constantly being raised, but part of being a good parent is taking time for yourself. Children will always want more. You cannot calibrate whether you are doing enough for your kids."[79]

As children get older and become more conscious of the world around them, they look to the adults in their lives to see different ways to live and be in the world. Children seeing parents who always seem stressed, unfulfilled in their lives, and resentful of their spouses get the picture that being an adult is not such a great thing and that becoming a spouse or parent is not very appealing. I'm not suggesting that kids need to view adult life as a constant good time, without challenges and disappointments. Life can be hard, extremely so at times, and I don't think the goal is to give kids an unrealistic picture of that. Sharing honestly about what we value, our challenges and successes, and what energizes us as adults and as parents really matters to our kids.

Our children see what is important to us whether we want them to or not. Some women feel that they should be home with their kids because that is what society tells them they should want, but their need for accomplishment comes out in other ways. One of the Libra dads I interviewed relayed the story of a female relative who was by temperament very driven yet felt the expectation to be an at-home mother. She was going borderline crazy at home, so she became very involved with her church as a means to focus all that energy. This Libra father shared his confusion over the choices made by these parents. He said had she not given up her business after becoming a mother (she was an entrepreneur), the children could have gotten the same level of parental attention—from both parents combined. Furthermore, she could have kept working while creating more time for the kids to spend with their dad, who himself felt great pressure as the sole career-parent to be highly successful at work, when a more moderate approach is what he truly desired. The Libra life is about breaking these gender shackles to determine what is right for you as an individual and for your family. Doing so is a gift that you give to your kids.

Our children may be a whole lot more forgiving of us than we are of ourselves. Nearly three in four respondents among children aged thirteen to twenty-four said their relationship with their parents made them happy.[80] Women evaluated by their spouses and children were surprised to find that their family members gave them much higher marks than they gave themselves. A large technology company seeking to support a group of high-potential women in the organization worked with an outside firm to conduct a "360" family performance evaluation. The women's spouses and children (over about age eight) provided feedback on how mom was doing as a partner and parent. While in several instances the women struggled with guilt about not being able to do enough or not being with their kids as often as they would like, in fact their kids felt fine about the arrangement.

An Alternative Approach: Downsizing Parenting for Happier Kids and Calmer Families

It is imperative to start by asking whether your current approach to family management is working. Is it working for your children? Is it working for you as adults? What is the balance between enjoyment and drudgery? If it is not working, where might you be able to make some changes? Some individuals and families thrive by being constantly on the go, but many long for a slower-paced alternative to the modern norm. If you find yourself perpetually overwhelmed and exhausted, if you find your children seemingly always tired, often out of sorts, and frequently pushing back about going to the next event (e.g., practice, rehearsal, class), I invite you to consider the Libra alternative to family management.

An important goal of the Libra life model is to purposefully bring the intensity down and to be judicious in the use of time and money, seeking to ensure that family priorities and practices are aligned. The Libra approach seeks to create a buffer in the family system, allowing the parents and children to more easily bend and flex as situations arise. In the Libra model, parents strive to consider, and respond to, the needs of the whole family—children and adults alike. In so doing, they create both more of what they need and at the same time more of what their children need. It is a virtuous cycle.

For instance, by limiting the number of extracurricular activities, we save substantial wear and tear—for children and parents alike—by reducing the driving around on school nights and the weekend time spent moving from one event to another. Fewer activities means more time for family dinners, finishing homework earlier, and for much needed sleep, helping to strengthen family connection and children's health. Some of the money saved can be used to pay for a caregiver so mom and dad can enjoy time alone as adults, helping to nurture their long-term relationship.

With the Libra mindset as our compass, we can stop feeling so much pressure about the need to raise a smart child or a talented one, knowing that our job is to provide a solid foundation. We can rest assured that teaching our kids those important life skills, which we do best by living our lives in a more intentional and thoughtful way and by sharing our experiences, is among the best things we can do to equip them for adulthood. We can remember that children learn from difficult experiences as well as from easy ones and that those sometimes can be the most powerful lessons. The Libra approach helps to reinforce that there is not one right way to parent, but there are some guiding principles that can inform what works for our individual family needs.

By treating screen time as a privilege for our children rather than an entitlement, and by creating screen parameters, we can limit the amount of time kids have access to their media world. A benefit of this managed media approach is new found time for other activities (such as helping out with chores, if you can negotiate that one). Another benefit for our children of fewer hours watching television or surfing the net is reduced exposure to marketing, helping to reduce the nag factor and resultant conflict. As adults, by managing our media use in a thoughtful and purposeful way, we both model this behavior for our children and create more discretionary time in our own lives.

With greater comfort about the real safety threats, the exaggeration of which has contributed to the precipitous drop in outdoor time, we can send our children outside to play, with the benefit of helping them to be active and appreciate the beauty of nature all around them. We can give our children greater freedom, including windows of unscheduled time when they can decompress and refuel.

The Libra work and life model helps us to stop feeling so much guilt, confident in the realization that we are spending a great deal of time with our children. It enables us to understand that taking care of ourselves and fostering our relationships with our spouses are hands-down among the greatest gifts we can give our children. Having fun as a family builds strong bonds, and it's hard to have fun when everyone is feeling continually pushed to their edge. The Libra approach creates wider buffers and leads to less pressure across the family system.

A benefit of the Libra approach is that the active involvement of fathers can help mitigate the intense pressure many women feel as mothers. One Libra mom explained how her husband helped her to keep a more balanced perspective regarding all the pressure for kids to achieve, while another said she became more relaxed with her kids after seeing her husband feel a much lesser need than she, when he was in charge, to be interacting with them at every moment. A Libra dad shared his perspective: "My wife is someone who will buy every book, read every article known to mankind. I am not that way. I think if there was one right way there would not be so many books. I think you have to go with the flow [in raising a child]. You can't break them and they are a lot more resilient than you think."

Bryan and I strive to operate in a way that is less chaotic and pressured. Certainly it does not always go as planned, but on many nights we eat dinner together as a family, put on quiet background music while the kids do their homework, and we read the paper, perhaps catch up on work, or do one of the many things required to keep the home fires burning. There is great comfort in this rhythm in our lives. We seek to create a space in our home, literally and figuratively, where we can put the demands of all our lives on the shelf so we can have time together to recharge and rejuvenate.

CHAPTER 7

THE LIBRA WORK AND LIFE MODEL IS THE SOLUTION

Two roads diverged in a wood, and
I took the one less traveled by,
And that has made all the difference.

---Robert Frost

Welcome to my world, circa 1997, when my older son Skylar was born: Bryan and I had arranged simultaneous parental leaves—his for two months and mine for four—while Skylar was a newborn. When Skylar was just a few weeks old, I read an article in a parenting magazine which started something like this: "Job description, new parent—24-hour shift, no compensation, no supervisory support, on-the-job training, feedback mostly negative."

I could really relate. Bryan and I felt strongly that we wanted to go through this on-the-job training together. We both felt like we didn't know much about parenting an infant and so spent a year saving and arranging particulars with work so that we could have this time together getting to know our son.

From early on we tried to develop a semblance of sleep shifts during the late evening until mid-morning so each of us could get some uninterrupted sleep. During Bryan's shift he would typically settle Skylar and then try to sleep himself, waking if Skylar needed something. On the other hand, I preferred to just stay up for my shift—even if it was from midnight to three in the morning, knowing that I could get some uninterrupted sleep with Bryan in charge. We both returned to our jobs—mine as a consultant and his as an application architect for a software company—on 80-percent schedules, working primarily four days per week and each having a day at home to be with Skylar. The other three days he went to a family day care provider in our neighborhood and then to a day care center nearby. For the first several years of Skylar's life, a typical week in the Levey household was Monday in care, Tuesday with Mom, Wednesday in care, Thursday with Dad, and Friday in care.

That first year of our life together as a family was one of the greatest on record for me and, I believe, for Bryan as well. During our parental leaves—while we were building up our confidence and skill as new parents—we would go to the park, the zoo, the mall, and for hikes with our dogs in the woods. Skylar was born in the spring, so the days were getting longer and warmer, which certainly helped. A special ritual we commenced early on was the "night to yourself," which meant on the day you were home with the child (or later, children), you had that night to yourself to do whatever you wanted. You might do an errand, catch up on work, go see a movie, or meet up with a friend for dinner. It didn't matter; there was something magical about having even one night that you knew was your own, even if you used it to finish up the bills that were calling to you from the pile. The norm was you had to be home by 5:30 sharp, because we both knew that after being home with a child (or children) all day, the other person was waiting for their few hours to control their own destiny.

With travel and job changes for both of us—and another baby—there were some adaptations through time, but the basic structure of both of us working 80-percent schedules with the kids in care for three days persisted until Skylar was eight and Forrest was nearly four. I worked for two different organizations over this period and Bryan for three. I advanced from a consultant to a senior director, while Bryan's trajectory took him from a software architect to the director of the engineering department. To the kids we were one entity—the parent—and they knew either of us could solve their problems or meet their needs. To each other, Bryan and I were co-pilots, partners, sharing the ups and downs of traversing these worlds and knowing we had a backup every step of the way.

The Core Elements of the Libra Model

Several distinct elements characterize the Libra model and distinguish it from other work and life models:

1) Men *and* women want *both* work and active family involvement in their lives.
2) They share a deep sense of partnership.
3) They share a drive for moderation.
4) There is an absence of preconceived notions that gender roles dictate work and family choices.

In a Libra marriage, women and men want both professional work and deep involvement with their families in their lives. These couples feel like they will not be fulfilled if they are unable to express these multiple parts of themselves. Many men in my interviews described their deep need to play an active role in their children's lives. They were eloquent about how not being involved would weigh heavily on their hearts. One dad shared feeling very concerned about the long hours expected at a new job, but hoped if he proved himself, he could influence his manager to be more flexible. Instead, he encountered a brick wall, and during the few years in that job, which kept him away from his young children far more than he was comfortable, he became highly depressed. For me, one of my greatest sources of satisfaction has been wearing different hats, and I have felt so privileged to have a window into these different worlds—the school yard and the board room, the homework juggle and the email shuffle, the music recitals and the women's conferences, the soccer game sidelines and the airport security lines. The women and men that I interviewed described a strong pull toward both professional and family life:

> We each really wanted both pieces; his wanting to stay home with the baby [for the first year] was not for me but because he wanted that relationship with the baby. He wanted to be

the nurturer. I wanted to work and be a breadwinner and have a deep stake in the professional world that was mine. Neither of us was doing it for the other. There was a debt-freeness to it.

It [this shared approach] is for people who want it all, who are multifaceted. You want to be nurturing, you want to have a career, you want to work on all those different facets.

A screenwriter shared the importance of both his work and his family:

I really want to write. I like to receive payment for what I am doing but I write because I like to write. It is one of the best things in my life. … Men also have these needs. I really need to be with my child. I love her so much. I would not be very involved if I had a regular job. I would not have the opportunity to spend most of this time with my baby.

Because the norm pulls women toward domesticity, those in Libra marriages typically have strong feelings about their need to nurture a professional identity that is distinct from their children and family. Men in Libra marriages feel a strong desire to be highly involved and engaged with their children, despite the norms that pull them toward paid employment and financial support of their family.

I felt like I was as much a parent as my wife. I wanted to be involved with the kids. I started in the very beginning. I was going with what felt comfortable.

The traditional model I see from a male perspective is, here's your window: from age thirty to fifty-five you make hay and work as hard as you can, move up the ladder and be responsible for making all the money. Once you are good financially, then you go back and look at the relationship, but by that time it may be too late ... The biggest thing is we both felt the same about what was important when it came to a family and raising kids. We both wanted to establish a relationship with the kids that was long-lasting. We wanted to build this foundation.

Even as both men and women had some kernel, some piece of themselves, that they wanted to develop professionally and as parents, this desire was not always clear or well articulated from the outset. For instance, in one family, the woman—who had been in graduate school but left after her first child was born to be home for several years—moved into the primary wage earner role while her husband earned his PhD. His desire to return to school was the catalyst for moving into a far more equally shared arrangement, both economically and in caring for the family. Another man, a long-term management consultant who started his own consulting firm several years before, was in his fifties when he and his wife had their first child. He said their friends saw them as the couple that would never have children. They traveled extensively and greatly enjoyed their work and their full lives together. Yet this dad, having become comfortable with caring for his newborn child while his wife was home on maternity leave, ultimately decided he wanted to simultaneously run his consulting practice and assume the role of primary caretaker for his daughter several days a week. His goal was to scale back—not eliminate—his workload in order to spend this precious and fleeting time with his baby.

Bryan has often told me that he expected to play a significant role as a father, but my need for an equal partner was a catalyst for him to make more significant changes to his work schedule—and as a result open up new possibilities in his life.

> You were saying, "I need an equal partner in this—in all ways." And if you had not said, "This is important," I don't think I would have gone to a four-day schedule—and I would

have missed a lot. I could have seen myself in a marriage with us both working five days and spending just weekends and nights with the kids. Spending that day alone as caregiver was significant for me in bonding with the kids and feeling capable. I don't think that happens very often for fathers, unfortunately. Or it could have been the other way; I could have been with a woman who thought she needed to be home with the kids all the time, and for me that would have been a huge trap. I would have got caught up in the work vortex.

The Libra model promotes a deep sense of partnership that permeates the relationship and everything you do. Both members of the couple become generalists rather than specialists and can readily substitute for one another. In the descriptions that Libra men and women give of a typical evening in their households, it sounds like a parental symphony. An architect with his own firm—whose wife works as a corporate attorney—described to me a typical evening routine at his house: When his wife arrives home from work, she will immediately play with their daughter. He will do "all the other stuff," such as starting dinner and picking up the house. They will then have dinner together as a family, and after their daughter is in bed, he and his wife will spend an hour or two together, catching up on the day and sharing each other's company. When his wife goes to bed, he will often work for a few more hours into the late evening. When he has client appointments in the city, he will take his young daughter on the train and meet his wife on the platform. His wife will take their daughter into her office where she will color quietly or perhaps watch a video. (He characterized his wife's office as having a ton of flexibility.) Then he will retrieve his daughter at his wife's office and head home with her on the train.

Another couple—both academics who share a tenure-track teaching position and are raising two young children—alternates who will assume the heavier teaching load (one versus two classes) each semester. The person not teaching on a given morning is with the children until their afternoon naps. The spouse who returns home from the morning teaching routine spends the kids' nap time writing (a major priority for both of them) and then takes over as the active parent when the kids wake up. Meanwhile, the parent who has been with the kids all morning gets a chance to focus on work from early afternoon until dinner time.

Men and women describe a feeling of being on the same team. One man said, "You are in this together, and will figure it out together, whatever comes your way." Libra couples come together as a family unit to respond to, and manage, all the potential obstacles of living this lifestyle. They work to balance the needs of both members of the couple—as well as the needs of the children—in a dynamic, evolving way. One man I interviewed described going through a period when he deeply disliked his job, feeling very unfulfilled professionally and working in what he characterized as a highly dysfunctional work environment. One weekend, when he seemed particularly lethargic and was lying on the couch, his wife approached him, saying, "We need to talk about this." He shared with her his intense conflict about not wanting to be impulsive and quit his job without having another option lined up, but at the same time he dreaded going into work every day. His wife told him that she would support him in quitting the next day if he wanted to, knowing that it would put some financial strain on the family during his transition to a new job, but recognizing that his mental and physical health was also critically important. He ultimately decided not to quit at that point but said that having his wife's blessing if he needed to do so made all the difference.

The deep sense of partnership—and of co-parenting children—is both an input to and a product of the Libra approach. One of the greatest challenges in describing this shared approach to parenting and financial caretaking is when the focus shifts to the complexity of the logistics. The June 2008 headline article in the *New York Times*, "When Mom and Dad Share It All," describes many elements of the Libra model, including experimentation, creativity, and avoiding defaulting to gender norms. I was thrilled to see a spotlight shone on this partnership approach. But as someone who has walked this road for more than a decade—and interviewed people who are both currently raising their children this way and have already raised their children this way—I was disappointed that the article did not capture the transformative experience of sharing it all and of having a partner who knows the full range of your joys and your struggles.

Logistics are indeed a key part of making the Libra approach work, as is the willingness to negotiate and work constructively to solve problems. But as most Libra couples will tell you, the conflict that may arise when managing the logistics recedes greatly through time. As illustrated in the comments below from my interviews with Libra women and men, you become seasoned as a couple at managing the logistics as a team and the complexities become dwarfed by the spirit of partnership you experience.

> This model allowed me to satisfy needs in many areas of my life—both having the kind of family situation that I wanted and also being involved professionally. Also, my husband could be the person that he wanted to be. I did not have any preconceived notions of what he should be as a man. Mutual respect in our relationship is core. We pay attention to each other's aspirations, hopes, and dreams. One person is not more important at the expense of the other. I respect him as a father, as a professional, as a person.

> My daughter is in graduate school and she is thinking about transferring. When I see my daughter calling in on another line and I see my husband picking it up, I know he can deal with it. He can handle it so that I can keep doing what I'm doing. Even now [with adult children who have been raised in the Libra model], I am still supported by his 50 percent and vice versa; I am that to him as well.

In 2002, the ThirdPath Institute shared *Reflections on Fatherhood from Shared Care Dads*. These fathers powerfully described what this approach meant for them and their families.[1]

> I love the time I spend with my daughter now but that's not all. I also like knowing that what I am doing today is laying the groundwork for tomorrow and for the rest of our lives together. Doing shared care has helped my wife and me because we understand each other better and appreciate each other more. I certainly thought she was doing a great job when I was working fulltime but now that I am working much less and doing half of the care, we have this tremendous depth to our relationship because we are both able to do this extremely important thing. She really has confidence in me, and I have the utmost confidence in her, as well as an awareness of, and appreciation for, everything that goes into being a parent.

> The more time I spend with my wife and daughter, the more time I want to spend with them. I love when we are all together. My daughter and I do so many things together. I play with her, put her to bed, bathe her, read to her - everything a typical mom would do, but there is no distinction between her mom and me. I have been there for her first tooth, her first walk, her first trip to the potty, and the day she figured out how to ride a bicycle.

The Libra model promotes a drive for moderation over the longer term. Embedded in this model is a feeling of sustainability and of creating time for what is most important to you. A Libra mother shared how her husband helped her find better balance in her mothering role: "That's something my husband has taught me. You can be a great parent and still have time for yourself." Money is an area where Libra families make conscious choices. The focus in Libra families is more on the quality of life rather than the standard of living. One dad characterized his choice to work less than full-time as "purchased freedom." In the comments below, two Libra parents highlighted the importance of moderation in their work and life solutions.

> What drives it is if both people really want to have it all, or as much of it as they can get. They want work in their lives, children in their lives, and they don't want to sacrifice. What they have to do to get that is have all these things but in some moderation. You have to be satisfied with some moderation but you will have the full menu.

> I have been promoted. What I get recognized for is what I am good at. I am not overly ambitious. I don't want to be head of the department. I want that work-life balance. I am very conscientious, I work hard, and I am good at what I do.

The use of child care is an area where Libra families desire greater moderation. Many couples (including Bryan and me) greatly value high-quality child care and expect it to be a critical piece of their work-life puzzle, but they also want to have some time during the typical workweek when they can be with their child or children. For one group of Libra couples, the catalyst for this shared work and life approach was an egalitarian relationship and the importance of the woman's career. As described by a Libra woman in one of my interviews, the support of husbands and partners was critical for enabling women to pursue their professional goals.

> In these [Libra] couples they tend to be very smart women—that is a variable—and they are men who appreciate smart women, who enjoy it [their wife's professional success]. The women are talented, smart, and ambitious and want to be a player. They want to get satisfaction out of their world outside of home.

In one family, a woman attorney and her husband, who was a real estate broker, hired a full-time nanny when their first child was born. While the husband had greater flexibility at work, his job could be very demanding and was often unpredictable. His wife, not wanting to leave behind a successful career, returned to work full-time with some ambivalence after the baby was born. The inflection point occurred when their son was about two and the wife had been working intensely on a case over a period of several months. Her husband happily "filled in the gaps," but she knew that she needed more time to be with her family. Eventually, with encouragement from a friend, she went to the chairman of her firm and was surprised that he granted her request for an 80-percent schedule with no reservations. With the birth of a second child, she eventually cut back to a three-day schedule and she and her husband began their long-term journey of sharing care, including the use of paid child care as a key part of their work and life solution. The wife described getting to that point this way: "I think a lot of it was necessity, a lot of it was desire, and a lot of it was evolution."[2]

In other Libra couples, a strong desire—an anchor, really—of their approach was the goal of not using outside child care. An information analyst for a pharmaceutical company and a project manager for an education company, working 60-percent and 80-percent schedules respectively, had tried several other work-family models before they came to the Libra approach. As children, both had witnessed firsthand the unpredictability of jobs, and even whole industries, as one grew up in a town that saw its steel industries fail and another grew up on a family farm. For this couple, family was at the epicenter and was what endured in the face of any hardship. He earned a doctorate in chemistry and she a master's in computer science, and they were able to leverage those skills to achieve their shared goal of having a parent home nearly all the time with their children.[3]

A Libra dad I interviewed, who works as a writer in television and the theater, shared that he and his wife considered a full-time job offer he received but ultimately decided it was not the right decision for their family. He said, "It is a priority for us to be her caretakers. We discussed that some months ago, relative to a professional opportunity for me. Someone offered me a job but it would have been full-time. We discussed the idea to hire a nanny during the day, but we decided it was not a great idea. It was not what I wanted and it was no convenience for the baby."

While moderation is a defining characteristic of Libra couples, it does not mean that parents must work a reduced schedule. It does, however, mean there is a strong drive to erect boundaries around work and to create flexibility so as to respond to the unexpected challenges that are part and parcel of raising children. For example, one couple I interviewed were both attorneys working full-time now that their children had reached school-age, yet they remained conscious of keeping their work hours in check so as to safeguard time for their children, each other, and themselves.

The Libra model instills a sense of shared independence whereby couples do not have preconceived notions about gender and roles. Each is far less likely to become the primary earner or the primary caretaker by default; those roles are decided through open, ongoing discussions of what makes sense for each member of the couple individually as well as for the family. Several Libra women I interviewed admitted not being sure about their desire to have children until they met their future husbands. They characterized themselves as being inspired to have children with *this particular man*. The comments that follow illustrate Libra women's and men's flexible thinking about gender roles.

> I was not interested in a woman who had rigid thoughts about how I should provide financially, just because the man provides for the family. I would have found that attitude too conservative and restricting. I'm not saying that's a bad thing, and it can be very effective, but I needed to see the shape of our life together as a couple first.

My husband is so patient and he has no problem investing that energy into our son. He is really into parenting. It has just kind of worked out. I never would have imagined it. We picked the right person for the right job. I get a lot of fulfillment in my work. It is allowing so much personal and professional growth. With his [professional] job he can do it at home.

I like people who are independent, not people who have no motivation to accomplish something for themselves. I did not want a life partner who was content to follow along on the sidelines of what I was doing.

Interestingly, whether the starting point was professional achievement for the woman, an egalitarian marriage, more time for life outside of work, or reduced child care—or multiple factors in some combination—the end points were often similar, and resulted in both members of the couple contributing significantly to financial resources *and* the day-to-day care of the family.

Characterized by the long-term goal of gender equality, the Libra model provides a compass that couples can refer back to, set, and reset as they move through time. On any journey, there are times when you get off course, when by choice or necessity you move away from your ideal distribution of sharing financial and caretaking responsibilities. Libra couples know that these are only temporary situations.

One Libra couple described a period when the wife was working full-time in a very intense job while her husband worked part-time as an adjunct professor and assumed the primary parent role. This arrangement was more by necessity than choice and did not fit their vision of an equitable work-life model. The wife longed for more time with her children, and the husband—who wanted to be very involved with raising his children—found the infant stage very taxing at times. The couple's long-term perspective and shared vision enabled them to weather this period. Having met in graduate school, they talked from their early days together about how they would jointly raise their children and what kinds of jobs would ideally suit them. The couple saw her overly demanding job situation, while not optimal in the short run, as an opportunity to strengthen her credentials and better position her to craft the job situation she desired. This time was an investment, getting them closer to their end goal. The couple also had a history of strong communication and prioritizing their relationship, which served them well during this time.

Choices, Trade-offs, Pragmatism, and Change

Libra families make choices while understanding that there are inherent trade-offs in all decisions. But these choices are not nearly as stark as they are typically portrayed—total career focus and no time for family versus always prioritizing family above work and consequently forsaking professional development and advancement. In the work and life discussion, the choices tend to be portrayed in very black-and-white terms that feel scary, extreme, and impossible. My research suggests the choices are more nuanced and play out much more on a continuum, with many couples and families finding a comfortable way to operate in the messy in-between, alternating between times of greater career focus (whether they are working full- or part-time) and greater family focus depending on their stage in life, external factors such as changes in their work lives, and the specific needs of their children, all of which can vary widely. The media has certainly done its part to heighten and reinforce the differences between working moms and stay-at-home moms, when in reality the vast majority of women move in and out of these roles, for a whole host of reasons, across the lifespan. While these artificial differences make for good headlines, they do not tell the full story.

One couple I interviewed for this book described theirs as a matter-of-fact story. Both hold advanced degrees and have worked in mental health for many years. The wife began her career doing clinical work and eventually moved into management roles in mental health clinics before shifting her focus and becoming a management consultant with a focus on diversity issues. Her husband is a psychologist and has run his own practice for decades, including the years when they were raising their children. She described their very practical thinking about managing work and family issues: "We both accepted the assumption that I would have a career that involved ambition. I got into management positions early on. My workweek was thirty-five to forty hours and combining work and family did not seem like a big insurmountable thing. It felt like we could just figure it out."

The husband from the matter-of-fact story explained in our conversation that he was more active with his children than most fathers he saw. He said that while he had altered his work schedule in order to care for his children, and most men had not, he saw himself as only incrementally more active—just 25 percent more. He remarked, "It was not like these other fathers were uninvolved." This is a situation where a small investment reaps amazing rewards. For a father to have that special space to be with his children that is all his own, and for a mother to feel total confidence that her children are well taken care of by their father so that she can focus her energies elsewhere, is very powerful. It helps set in motion a shift in power and responsibility that leads to a far more shared, egalitarian approach.

The Libra approach is a highly pragmatic one. Men and women remain focused on the possibilities rather than the obstacles and come together as a couple to jointly solve problems. The Libra solution is characterized by multiple inflection points where a couple steps back and takes stock, evaluates how their choices are working, and then identifies how they want to make changes and adapt as they move forward. The changes range from small to large and making adaptations is part of the process.

For example, at one point Bryan had ramped up to full-time because it made sense for his position, while I had cut back to a 60-percent schedule in part to manage major elder-care issues. It soon became clear to both of us that these schedule changes shifted our work-life equilibrium in ways we did not like. Bryan really missed the opportunity to be the parent in charge after school, and since I was home more, I was defaulting to always being the one getting dinner on the table. Bryan made a small change in his schedule that really helped. One day per week he went into work very early and left the office at three in the afternoon so he could be the parent in charge—picking up the kids after school, walking the dog, managing any after-school transportation needs, as well as making dinner. This afforded me the flexibility to stay focused and work later on that night. I eventually returned to a 90-percent schedule, closer to our long-term ideal, but that seemingly small change in Bryan's schedule made a surprisingly significant difference in the rhythm of our week.

An attorney, the father of two daughters, had spent some time after law school doing policy work. When his younger child was preschool age, he and his wife jointly decided that the increased income that came with working for a large law firm would be beneficial for the family at that point. (She was also working outside the home to support the family.) He began working at a large firm on a full-time schedule but sought to stay highly involved in caring for his children. Avoiding the pattern of working evenings and weekends, and making it a priority to be on the six o'clock bus home, he encountered push-back at the firm. At some point he approached the firm about working on a reduced schedule, but they would agree to do so only if he was taken off the partnership track. It is easy to see how this attorney could have lost faith, given up, and decided law firm life was simply incompatible with his vision of being a highly involved parent. Not willing to make the concession of partnership potential for a reduced schedule, he eventually left the large firm and moved to a mid-size firm, where he was able to negotiate what he was looking for and eventually became a partner.

How the Libra Family Looks and How It Is Unique

There are several research studies that capture characteristics and elements of Libra families. One such study was conducted by Catalyst, my former employer who is known for conducting seminal research on issues that impact working women. The study focused on the experience of dual-career couples, with both members of the couple being full-time salaried employees.[4] These couples were characterized as having two-income independence—an increased sense of freedom to customize their careers in ways that made sense for their lives and their families, such as stepping on or off the fast track, changing jobs or even professions, or striking out on their own. Like Libra women and men, these couples highly valued their ability to control the speed and trajectory of their career paths. A group among the study participants, labeled loyal high-achievers, who met several criteria such as having received a promotion or award within the last five years and often going above and beyond what was required, were even more likely than their colleagues to customize their careers. The majority of study participants indicated they would keep working, even without financial need, consistent with men and women in Libra families feeling driven to both work and nurture as part of who they are.[5] Their comments illustrate both the importance of conscious choices and the career flexibility engendered by a dual-career work-life solution.[6]

> I still want more challenging jobs, but I must live near my job and the kids' school. I used to work pretty long hours, and sometimes I didn't bother to come back home because my husband was out of town anyway. That's all different now. I'm still interested in getting more interesting assignments, but my family is the most important thing right now.
>
> It certainly has allowed me some flexibility. I've gotten into some businesses on my own. So it has allowed me that

> flexibility, knowing that she had the steady job and the paycheck.
>
> It probably takes pressure off of him to be the primary breadwinner. I think he knows that if things don't go the way he anticipates in his career, [my working] gives him the luxury to quit if he wants to, or take time to look around for another position.

The marriages were described as highly fluid and dynamic, with frequent reexamination—by both members of the couple individually as well as together as a unit—of their decisions and priorities. The majority indicated that having a working spouse was positive for their career, and there were no meaningful differences by gender in the reported challenges or difficulties of a two-career marriage. Couples described the benefits of their dual-career approach in terms of "intellectual equality and kinship."[7]

> It would be hard for me to not be married to a working person. We each are experiencing self-fulfillment from working. We each bring intellectual stimulation to the marriage, which is great.[8]
>
> A feeling of equality between the two spouses. Equality, in the sense of being peers with comparable types of jobs. In the relationship between my wife and me, there is not an issue of being dependent. To me that's a real benefit, because that removes some obstacles from the relationship.[9]

Perhaps predictably, the greatest challenge reported was a lack of time, and those couples who were raising children felt the pressure of blending these two roles more keenly than those who were not.[10]

> I would say that role overload is a big [difficulty]—just trying to get everything done, just trying to meet all the demands and not let anything slip through is really difficult.[11]

The Libra model, while sharing many of the benefits of dual-career couples, also helps to mitigate the intensity of time demands by ensuring that both members of the couple are highly motivated to boundary work so as to allow space for other priorities. The theme of making choices around work to support their egalitarian marriages was evident in the Catalyst study of dual-career couples.[12]

> I stay in certain types of positions and in this location due to us being in a dual-career marriage. I need to limit my travel. Both of our careers mattered. I played a big role in encouraging her to reach her potential: her goal of becoming a lawyer. We both like emphasizing our two careers.[13]

A study by the Cornell Careers Institute at Cornell University looked at the experiences of a large group of dual-earner couples, primarily middle class, who were employed as managers, professionals, and technical workers.[14] Among these dual-earner couples, in every family configuration ranging from non-parents to empty nesters, the ideal number of work hours for both men and women was less than their actual reported hours. Families in the various stages of raising children, from preschool to teenage, identified *ideal* weekly work hours as approximately thirty to forty, with women consistently reporting a lower number of desired hours than men.[15] This hours range is quite consistent with those reported by many Libra couples, where both partners together work in the seventy- to eight-five-hour range. Similar to the story of highly engaged fathers and husbands doing more at home, but only incrementally more, ratcheting down hours even 10 percent to 15 percent seems to represent a profound and desired change for families struggling to do it all.

Interviewers in the Cornell Careers study identified three primary strategies that dual-career couples use to "buffer" the family from work demands: 1) placing limits, 2) constructing a one-career/one-job structure in which the wife typically scales back her work commitments and aspirations, and 3) trading off, where the two parents essentially take turns emphasizing one or the other's career during different periods over the life stages. Libra couples and families would typically use placing limits and trading off among their strategies for striking the desired balance between work and family demands.

The author of a 1983 book on American couples—who explored the management of their work, relationship, and money—interviewed a subset of the couples originally profiled for a second time around. Those interviewed in the second phase shared many characteristics of Libra couples. "These couples were distinguished by their ability to build their relationships on fairness and collaboration and to avoid traditional gender roles."[16] These couples, many of them remarried, were described as intentionally creating a partnership and marriage very different than their first—far more egalitarian and far less traditional. The couples sought to make their relationship and friendship front and center, and in the process many made choices to forgo overly demanding job opportunities to put their relationship first. So as to avoid the problems they had experienced in their first marriages with their gendered approaches to parenting, on this second go-around they made joint parenting a priority. Overwhelmingly, these couples endorsed their partnership approach and created much stronger marriages based on sharing across multiple roles.[17]

Another study conducted by Catalyst followed the experiences of a group of twenty-four women over a ten-year period from 1989 to 1999.[18] The study provided an opportunity to understand the career paths of long-term users of flexible work arrangements—people who spent an average of nine and a half years working on a flexible schedule.[19] Like Libra women and men, these women painted a picture of feeling in control of their careers, being highly satisfied, and having made intentional choices—understanding the trade-offs—in their work and personal lives. They saw flexibility as a tool to maintain their career momentum and continued to progress professionally as described below. More than half had earned promotions while working on a reduced schedule.[20]

> I've been treated very well by [my company] and I've been very successful here. I have progressed with promotions, so [the telecommuting arrangement] hasn't hurt me in any way. I feel like I'm really connected at home and that's really important to me. It makes me feel like I can really combine it, and combine it well. I'm balancing everything the way I want to balance it.[21]

Those moving back to full-time schedules felt less satisfied with their ability to balance, and the longer hours created a major source of dissatisfaction for some. Nonetheless, these women reported clear responsibility and awareness surrounding their choices while deeply appreciating the time they spent working a reduced schedule.[22]

> Would I have extended the time I did the reduced schedule? Yeah, I definitely would have. But it was at that point that I took the director job, and there's no way that could have been done on a reduced week. So I made a conscious choice at that point. And I did it for career advancement.[23]

> Year by year as you step up to the next challenge at work, you put in that next hour that you didn't before. As I look back when I did that four-day workweek—it was just a beautiful arrangement. It gave me great balance.[24]

These women identified the flexibility of their husband's schedules as an important factor in determining their professional choices.[25]

> My husband was a partner in an engineering firm and left a year ago to start his own business. He works out of our home, and it's fabulous as far as the flexibility that he has. He's able to be there in the mornings to see our young son onto the school bus. I drop the older one off at middle school on my way to work. And then he can plan his day so that he's there by the time they get home from school, about 4:00 p.m.[26]

Strikingly, all but one woman among the group—which had a median age of forty-three, with the median age of the youngest child at ten—were in their first marriage.[27] Similar to Libra couples, this fact suggests an effort to prioritize the long-term health of the marital relationship.

Though the study was focused on the experiences only of women, their comments represent the full range of challenges and benefits consistent with the feedback of women and men in Libra families. Some struggled with others not seeing those on reduced schedules as committed and having to choose at times between expanding their hours or forgoing advancement. But they also reported many benefits, including *not having to choose* between hours and advancement, creating time for other important priorities such as community work, and having the opportunity to make major professional contributions. The women in the longitudinal study reflected the fluidity in their career paths, the weighing of the benefits and costs of career choices, and the comfort with defining their own way that similarly characterize Libra families. The primary difference in Libra families is that both members of the couple choose together how they will navigate the path of home and work and support one another in erecting boundaries in both spheres.

There Are Many Paths to a Libra Life

My personal story is just one path of many that eventually end up at approximately the same place: intimately sharing in the care of the family, economically and in every other way. Some start down this path from the outset, while others don't begin to explore this work and life solution until their children are preschoolers or school-age. For some, sharing in this way was purposeful and planned, while for others, it evolved through time. For some, positive childhood experiences informed their thinking and their goal of sharing work and home, while for others, challenging situations motivated them to want to find another way. The catalyst for couples moving into a Libra arrangement varies widely, from a parent dying, job loss, or a child's health issues, to planned career changes and a desire to dial down the frenetic pace of life. How you get there and when it happens are less important than knowing that if your goal is to live in a Libra family, there are many ways to get there, no matter where you find yourself at this moment.

Many assume that external factors dictate one's ability to create a Libra work and life solution, and while certain factors absolutely influence the ease or challenge of following the Libra model, the far more important point is that this approach does not require someone to work at a particular organization, in a particular profession, or in a particular job. The Libra approach lets you begin from wherever you are. There are no absolutes here, and my many years of consulting have taught me that for every situation there is an exception. There are lawyers and doctors, academics and business people, managers and individual contributors who do this. There are people who work for themselves and people who work for companies that do this. There are people who have moved from traditional family structures or reverse traditional family structures (in which the father is at home and the wife is in the workforce) who do this. Living a Libra life is about wanting this gender-flexible and more moderate work and life approach, about experimenting, adjusting and readjusting, and about making this your compass as a couple so that through time, you can together create this reality in your life.

I have spent most of my career working to change corporate systems to make them more family friendly and equitable so as to enable both women and men to thrive professionally and personally. There is no doubt that many systems in our country, such as the lack of affordable health care and the absence of paid parental leave, make the Libra approach far more challenging than it need be. We must continue to work on adapting the major systems that are so poorly aligned with the realities of families in the twenty-first century. Yet there is also much we can do in our own lives to wrest control and create the families and marriages and organizations that inspire us. My hope is to broaden your thinking about viable work and life solutions, to inspire you with the stories of many other couples that are walking this road, and to equip you with ideas and strategies to employ on your journey, all with the goal of making the Libra life a reality.

Chapter 8

The Benefits of the Libra Approach: One Plus One Equals More than Two

Thousands of candles can be lighted from a single candle, and the life of the candle will not be shortened.

---Buddha

The power of the Libra model lies in meeting head-on many of the issues we struggle with every day as twenty-first century families. Today we suffer health issues caused by toxic levels of stress, we ignore critical physical and emotional needs, and we endure marriages strained by intense working *and* parenting requirements and insufficient time and effort to devote to the relationship. We lack family time dedicated to relaxation and unscheduled activities, and we struggle with overwork caused by job insecurity, career fears, and lack of knowledge and skill about how to work more effectively in an information-saturated, constantly connected work world. It can feel as if we are losing control over our time—and our lives.

Families that follow the Libra approach, and the organizations that employ them, see benefits in three key areas:

Choice. The Libra model expands choices, offering opportunities for husbands and wives to develop multiple parts of themselves. Men can develop their nurturing capabilities, and women can pursue their professional goals. It provides choices for couples to prioritize their relationship and it allows children to see that, when they are adults, they can craft a work and life solution that is right for them. It creates choices for professionals who want to model new approaches to managing and leading, attracting and retaining younger generations of talent and the many engaged employees seeking a more balanced approach. Having options is critical to avoiding the energy-sapping sense of being "stuck" in a situation where you have little opportunity to spend time on what helps you recharge, where your needs seem irrelevant and your hopes unattainable, and where the opportunity to improve your situation seems remote. Many decisions in my life have been directly connected to my deep desire to maintain flexibility and choice, and in my many years of following this approach, I have found the Libra model directly supports that goal.

Fulfillment. The Libra model gives parents an opportunity to develop deep and fulfilling relationships with their children and to create space in their lives for personal pursuits that bring them joy. It engenders a strong marital partnership, a close bond forged by sharing the full range of joys and challenges of raising a family. Couples are able to walk in each other's shoes and act as a team to jointly navigate—at work and at home—all that is required so both can live full and balanced lives. The Libra approach offers fulfillment for children by providing a deep sense of security and the knowledge that either mom or dad can meet their needs. Organizations benefit (and thus fulfill their business needs) through employing people who are deeply motivated and strive to be highly effective at work so as to sustain a mutually beneficial work-life fit. Libra professionals bring skills developed from other life roles and a balanced perspective to managing work and people.

Flexibility. The Libra model supports greater flexibility at home and at work. Families are better able to roll with the punches if someone loses their job or if a child needs special support, because parents are already involved in all aspects of caring for the family, financially and otherwise. If promotions don't come as quickly as desired or parenting a toddler or teenager feels impossible, Libra women and men can focus on other life roles that are also of great importance to them. By creating buffers and designing backup into key parts of your life, the Libra model brings down the stress level both at work and at home. In the family, flexible roles benefit couples who support and learn from one another personally and professionally and children who have a broader parental toolkit from which to draw. At work, Libra professionals help embed more flexibility into the work system. They tend to plan well, ensure backup, develop others, and seek to prevent problems and crises. The strong drive for Libra professionals to create space for other priorities is a catalyst for improving how work is accomplished.

Amy Vachon, coauthor with her husband Marc of *Equally Shared Parenting*, describes how a focus on balance supports choices, fulfillment, and flexibility for women and men:

> We live in a 24/7 world. What shared care parents learn is to be more intentional about their use of time, [to put] more breathing room into [their] day-to-day lives. Scaling back my work has allowed me to have one day home with my son. Because I have a flexible schedule, it opens up the other realms of my life to do other things. Even if I'm in touch occasionally [with work on my day at home], my whole world seems to open up. ... You set up a lifestyle where you are not exhausted and don't need vacation to survive. You set up an everyday life that is satisfying and not overwhelming.[1]

As I said in the introduction to this book, bringing a systems perspective to the work-life balancing act allows you to see the connections between interrelated elements—how women and men each have a role to play in maintaining the status quo regarding gender norms, how exaggerated parenting expectations contribute to the problematic busyness in our lives, and how to identify and manage these obstacles by developing greater skill and comfort with putting up boundaries at home and at work. In addition to creating a framework for understanding the challenges, the systems perspective illuminates the benefits—choice, fulfillment, and flexibility—for each individual, for the couple, for the children, and for the workplace.

The table that follows summarizes the benefits of the Libra approach.

	Expanded Choices	Fulfillment/Efficacy	Flexibility
For Individuals	• Provides greater latitude in career choices • Provides the opportunity to develop multiple parts of oneself	• Provides an opportunity for each parent to develop their own relationship with their children and to develop their unique parenting style • Creates more time and space for personal pursuits and interests	• Builds resilience into the system; spouses provide backup for each other
For Couples	• Allows greater time and energy devoted to the couple's relationship	• Engenders a strong marital partnership by encouraging couples to *walk in each other's shoes*	• Enables couples to learn from and support one another in both their personal and professional roles
For Children	• Provides a model that, as adults, they can customize for their own work and life solution • Provides a model of balancing the needs of self and others	• Provides a deep sense of security and comfort knowing that either parent can meet their needs and that their parent's relationship is solid	• Creates a broader pool of parental resources from which children can draw
For Workplaces	• Models a new style of management and leadership that is better suited for the modern workforce	• Provides professionals who are motivated to work effectively and productively • Provides professionals who bring skills developed in other life roles • Provides professionals who bring a balanced perspective to the management of work and people	• Provides a catalyst for improving work processes and practices

Benefits for Each of the Individuals within the Couple

Choice

For mothers, fathers, and professionals, the Libra approach provides the backdrop for each member of the couple to develop multiple parts of their identities and to comfortably move between important roles. Women assuming the role of the primary parent, as often by default as by design, limit their professional choices, and the conflict drives many to feel unable to manage both work and home. As Pamela Stone describes in her book *Opting Out?: Why Women Really Quit Careers and Head Home*, husbands consumed by jobs that don't allow them to more equitably share in child-rearing constitute an important factor in the decisions of these talented women to stop working outside the home.[2] Multiple women in my interviews referenced watching their contemporaries struggle with professional aspirations that were never explored. Both men and women commented on their childhood perceptions of mothers who had much potential that remained unrealized.

The shared approach of the Libra model encourages thinking outside of traditional roles in regard to career and family. As a result, men and women in Libra couples are better able to navigate the inevitable complexities that arise when combining professional careers with raising children. One woman I interviewed left her job after a decade to go into business with a friend who was also a professional colleague. She described her husband's support in making this possible: "Soon after marrying my husband, I left my job and bought the business. I had started taking classes to make a career change and saw that as an avenue to have the flexibility I wanted when we were raising children. He was very encouraging through the whole process." A woman architect shared her story of ramping up from a reduced schedule to a full-time schedule, facilitated by her husband's flexible job situation as a software engineer and their highly shared approach to caring for their children.

A woman engineer in one couple left her job before having her first child because the job lacked the flexibility she was seeking. Coincidentally, a year or two later, her husband, who was also an engineer, got a new job with her former employer. In those intervening years the company had adopted several new policies, including a formal process for seeking a flexible work arrangement. While reviewing benefits literature for her husband's new position, she saw information about flexible work schedules and began to consider the potential for job sharing with her husband. After much research the couple submitted a well-designed proposal for their unorthodox approach. The company was willing to give it a try, and the couple began a job share that lasted more than five years. During their shared tenure, they moved into multiple positions, including a promotion, while raising their two young children along the way. The woman engineer—who always prided herself on being a little unconventional—was able to continue her professional development while both she and her husband were able to dedicate substantial time to raising their young children.

For men, a key benefit of the shared approach is having greater choice around career decisions, as well as being able to play a far more central and intimate role in the care of their children. A Libra man I interviewed was able to start his own business, and leave a firm where he felt at odds with the philosophical approach and business model for growth, because of his wife's financial support. In other families, men trained as attorneys parlayed their skills into new opportunities, becoming a consultant on business ethics in one instance and utilizing strong writing skills to become a communications specialist in another. The Libra approach frees fathers to choose to spend more time raising their children.

> I am always available to be involved at any level that I want to be in all aspects of my life. I can spend a week bearing down at work, or if there is a family or school event, I can make the time to do that instead. I choose to balance all those things out rather than fitting into a time-structured model.

A father running his own design business remarked in our interview:

> I am parked near my daughter's nursery school and I am looking at all these palatial homes. I know for a fact, because I talk with many of the moms, that their husbands are gone all the time from early in the morning to late at night. Some of them travel. The moms are alone with their kids. That is the life I would have to lead for my wife to be home all the time.

Research studies have found that women and men involved with multiple roles (up to a limit), such as work, parenting, and community service, were less stressed, had fewer stress-related health issues, and had higher overall levels of well-being than those who were more specialized and involved in fewer roles. Among over 200 middle-class women aged thirty-five to fifty-five, who varied in their employment, marital, and parental status, researchers found that the factor accounting for most of the variance in psychological well-being was employment status. Women working outside the home indicated greater well being than non-employed women regardless of their parental or marital status. Married women with children in high-prestige jobs reported the highest rating of well being among any group.[3] In a study of white women over a three-year period, those women who increased their workforce participation from homemaker to part-time or full-time work showed lower levels of depression, while those who decreased from full-time to working low—fewer than twenty—or no hours per week reported an increase in symptoms of depression.[4] Similarly, men in more egalitarian marriages, who do more housework and child care, are physically and psychologically healthier, and live longer, than men in less egalitarian relationships. They smoke and drink less, are more likely to stay in shape and to regularly see a doctor, and they have more sex. They also report higher levels of marital satisfaction.[5]

Fulfillment

Each parent is able to develop an independent relationship with their child or children, and to define his or her own unique style of parenting. This is particularly satisfying for men, who often lack the support to parent in the way that feels natural and comfortable for them. Many men are emphatic about how the Libra approach allows them to spend time with their children and build the confidence and competence to parent that they see many men lack. Libra fathers shared the joys—and challenges—of being a deeply involved parent:

> I had a chance to really parent my children in a way that most fathers don't get to—day to day—with all the tedium and frustration of that. I wanted to know what that experience was like. Most dads are involved in playing with their kids, with extracurricular life, but not in the day to day. It is a much fuller experience of truly being with my kids. Knowing them and nurturing them—that was extremely fulfilling for me.

> I am more invested in the family. I have strong relationships with my sons. They view me as a co-parent. If I look at my colleagues in a more traditional setup, they don't have that balance. They don't understand their place at home. They don't enjoy being home that much. The kids turn to the stay-at-home spouse for their nurturing.

> I really wanted to be a very involved father, to see my son go through his milestones. When he falls down he is just as happy to come to me as my wife. I found that fantastic. I get to just hang out with him two days per week.

Men with adult children, who were deeply involved during the child-rearing years, talked about how the foundation they built sustains their current-day relationships with their grown children:

> When they are little and you are around, then they keep you around. You have a relationship that you've built over time and if you had not built it over time, it wouldn't be there.
>
> I did not feel like I was the total support. My spouse was pulling her weight financially and I got to be close to my kids. I've done a lot of things with them that I might not otherwise have been able to do and I have a very close relationship now. It has lasted.
>
> My daughter gets a three-month [parental] leave and she wants me to come down and help with the baby. I think that is a consequence of how she saw me in my role as a father.

Many fathers described how it would have been easy to miss this sense of intimacy if they had not been involved with their children in such a direct way. It can be difficult to perceive what it feels like to be the primary nurturer for your children if you've never played that role. As such, men can underestimate the importance of the daily, small moments that are so central for young children—such as knowing their favorite books, listening to their conversations with their toys as they play, and understanding just how they like their grilled cheese sandwiches cooked. Libra dads shared their thoughts about those "small moments":

> My father was kind of like a weekend dad. I don't know how much my son will remember of this time, but I have created this bedrock of being tied to his well-being and his life. Both he and I are going to get the benefit of that. How wonderful it is to be there for all those tiny moments. It's not the big milestones, like learning to walk, but the little ones, like he fell off the slide. I get to be there for all those little things.

I have colleagues who are male who would never fall into this role. They see it as a benefit that they don't have to take care of all the busy work of being a parent. It's easy to see busy work but I would argue that the busy work is the emotional work and it is important. It is finally about deepening your relationship with your children. I also understand [their reactions]. It is a pain; it is tiring and often not fun. I can think of a colleague who said, "I wouldn't do that." He is pleased to have that more traditional experience of things. I don't feel especially judged by him but we look at each other a little curiously having such different lives.

A profound benefit for parents of the Libra approach is their greater ability to take care of themselves and to make time in their lives for what they enjoy and helps to strengthen them. My husband's middle-of-the-night snowstorm drive one winter underscores the importance of this special time. Bryan is someone who has always loved cards and games and he has played in a monthly poker group for over fifteen years. One night, several years ago, when our older son was a toddler, Bryan was scheduled to play poker about a half-hour drive from our home, and a huge snowstorm was predicted. He decided to participate and spent over two hours driving home from poker in dense snowfall. His decision to play reinforced just how important this monthly ritual was for him, and apparently for the other seven men in the group as well. Not one of them missed the game!

Libra men and women shared their stories of making time for themselves. As an antidote to his intense work culture, a Libra dad took up yoga. A mother became involved in environmental issues in her town, which was a real priority for her, while in another family the father was able to use his engineering skills to work with kids in a science club, which provided him with great satisfaction. Libra women and men carved out time to play musical instruments, write for pleasure, participate in exercise classes and sports, and take art classes, all with the goal of balancing the responsibilities in their lives with activities that brought them great pleasure. A woman engineer who shares the care of her baby daughter with her husband described how the Libra approach allows them time for themselves:

> Being shared-care parents helped us get through this year [with a baby] so we were not overly stressed out. We take turns allowing the other person to sleep in the morning. It makes a big difference. We help each other so we are fairly well rested. We take turns going out with friends. In the early months it was so nice to get out and feel like an adult again. I came back refreshed and recharged, feeling like a normal human being again. My husband got back into practicing guitar. We want to work on that [creating time for ourselves] a little more—it's not perfect but we keep ourselves sane.[6]

Raising children is intense in the youngest years, but it's also intense in different, less physical and more mental ways as the children enter elementary, middle, and high school. Without being intentional in safeguarding some time and space just for you, it will in all likelihood be swallowed up by the deluge of demands. I am acutely aware how difficult this is, particularly for most women. Sharon Meers, in a talk on her book *Getting to 50/50: How Working Couples Can Have It All By Sharing It All*, described the difficulty even very self-confident women feel in approaching their partners about wanting a highly shared approach to careers and children. She indicated women have been socialized to think that asking for something just for themselves is selfish or demanding. She went on to say, "Women have a low sense of entitlement. Sometimes they can't even identify what they want. The hardest thing to do can be to look in your soul and ask what would make you happy."[7]

For me, prioritizing time for self care makes intellectual sense, but I still struggle emotionally with the idea that taking care of myself makes me the best mother that I can be. My strong instinct is to respond to all the demands around me and to make sure that everything is in order before I get *my time*. Like many women, I struggle with the feeling that I'm being selfish by doing something just for me. I have learned to push myself—even when the long to-do list is screaming for attention—to go and take a walk, take myself out to dinner, sit and read the paper, or just breathe.

Through the years it has become ever clearer to me that when I feel more centered, my parenting skills are at their best. I can far better manage sibling flareups, the intense energy bursts of two sons, the sadness about a lost toy, or the frustration over a difficult homework assignment. When my sons were younger and we were in the time-out phase of discipline, Bryan and I would occasionally suggest mom or dad needed a time-out. We would joke with each other that we didn't mind this time-out business for parents. In fact we quite liked it, often asking one another, "Can I go first?"

Flexibility

Parents assuming multiple roles in meeting the needs of the family embed flexibility and resiliency into the system. This thinking may sound counterintuitive since many people still believe greater specialization of roles reduces the complexity of making the family engine run in the twenty-first century. However, men and women in Libra families report their fluid roles allow them to fill in for one another as needed, thus easing the stress of a busy family life:

> We make each other's lives easier. Everyone splits everything. It reduces that burden. It made our first year [as parents] much easier than expected. We are both equal parents. It gives us freedom knowing that we can both do it all.[8]

> It [sharing care of their school-age child] is huge in terms of the flexibility that it gives both of us. I think how easy it is to just live our lives, to have two people who can cover for each other. It makes it very easy and very stress free.

Our cultural bias is that the bread-winner in a single-earner family—or the person with the primary job, typically the man, even if both are working—deserves maximum flexibility because there is only one career to consider. In reality, the pressure associated with the primary career sharply reduces flexibility. Having two people employed allows each to be freer to articulate priorities. If one person must be ever mindful not to threaten the perceived primary source of income, that person will likely feel far less freedom to act in ways that make sense for his or her life.

In interviewing my husband Bryan, he said, "You do not have the full weight and the pressure as if your job was the only source of income. You don't have that pressure and you can advance at the right pace." Bryan recalled being asked on short notice to attend a conference that was occurring while one of our sons was in his school play, in one of the key roles. He declined the invitation and added that if he felt his job was the primary one, declining travel in this instance would have been a much more difficult choice to make. He likened it to walking along a ledge with a five-foot versus a fifty-foot drop. In the first case, the fall would be far less significant and the perceived risk worth taking, while in the second scenario, the potential harm from the fall would encourage far more risk-averse behavior.

A Libra dad recounted how having both parents in the workforce gave him the flexibility to restructure his work and enabled far greater sharing of the parental responsibility with his wife:

> Given that I was traveling a great deal when our first daughter was born, and my wife was making a good income without traveling, I restructured my life to work from home and be available for parenting as a major focus. While this meant letting go of aspects of my work that I enjoyed, it was clear that we had a "window of opportunity" to be fully engaged with the girls during their preschool years. We made this our priority and feel very good that we did.[9]

Benefits for the Marriage

Choice

The strength of the marital partnership is critical in Libra families; it forms the bedrock that supports the whole system. It is typical in our culture for couples to shortchange time and energy for their relationship once they have children. Like carving out time for yourself, creating time for you and your partner to stay close requires you to be intentional. Parents often carry guilt about not spending enough time with their children, particularly if they feel pushed at work and are working consistently longer hours than their comfort level. As a result, they begin to feel that any time left over after meeting work obligations needs to be for the children.

Libra families experience this "time famine" to a lesser degree because both members of the couple have put up clear boundaries at work, and many have cut back their schedules or workloads to some degree. For these parents, it does not feel like such a sacrifice to spend time away from their children. It allows the couple to choose to make their own relationship a priority, to talk without interruption, to reminisce and plan, and to just have fun together.

Finding a babysitter may be difficult and expensive but it is an investment that pays huge dividends. It is amazing how an inexpensive lunch out on a Saturday afternoon or an ice cream and walk through the woods can help you connect as a couple and remember why you got together in the first place. A Libra woman described how she and her husband made time for one another in this way:

> Every semester we have to reconfigure what hours we will spend with the children and at work. The one constant is the time we spend with each other. We spend the evenings together. We don't—except in extreme cases—bring our work home. What is important here is we spend time talking or watching a show or just being together. The kids are in bed

by 8:00 or 8:30 and we stay up until 11:30 or midnight hanging out together. The conversations will range from what is going on with the kids to what do we think about what is going on in the world. We read each other's writing and talk about our projects.

In some instances, time with your children can also be the choice in strengthening your couple bond. When our older son was an infant and preschooler, Bryan and I met after work on many Friday nights at an indoor play center, a child's version of nirvana with endless balls, riding scooters, playhouses, puzzles, and toys. We would order pizza and drinks, follow Skylar around as he explored, and have some special time to let down and connect. There was something very romantic about this family get-together and we both so looked forward to our Friday evenings. When our younger son was just days old—and sleeping for much of the day but not much at night—we took a field trip (and anything qualifies as a field trip at this stage) to a wonderful inn near our house to have high tea in the middle of the afternoon. While Forrest slept beside us at the table, we laughed and complained about dealing with the intense sleep deprivation all over again.

Fulfillment

Among the greatest advantages of the Libra work and family approach is the deep bond it engenders for couples. Both men and women were consistently emphatic about this point throughout my interviews. Because Libra couples share in the myriad details required to raise a family and maintain careers, they feel strongly that they have built something important together. A Libra man with grown children characterized his and his wife's team approach:

> We believed in collaboration and dialogue. It was an ongoing thing. You did what you needed to do to be a good team in bringing up your kids. That was the idea. In my case, my wife

> hated to go to the playground. I never understood why, but I was delighted to go. It was a beautiful time for me. You fill in the cracks where you could. It was a process of discovery, of learning about your partner to see what kind of parent they were with your children.

The practice of walking in another's shoes to better understand the full range of challenges they face day to day builds closeness. Couples describe it as not taking one another for granted. In so doing, they develop a deep respect for their partner as both a parent and professional. I am not suggesting that couples in other work-family models do not and cannot also build a strong sense of partnership; they certainly can. Yet research underscores that women and men who favor a shared approach have an easier time of it. A study of new parents concluded that "in many traditional couples, the birth of a child begins a process of gradual disengagement between spouses." As the mother focuses at home, the father increases his focus at work, and "over time the community of interest between the spouses diminishes, leading to a widening communications gulf."[10] According to academic research, greater equality in sharing the economic responsibilities of the family offered benefits to marital satisfaction for both men and women, but to an even greater extent for men.[11]

A father described the mentality that flows from this shared approach and contrasted it with the traditional model of separate spheres:

> It is not as polarizing [doing it this way]. In traditional settings I see a distance created. The stay-at-home mother thinks it's her house. The father is focused at work. They can't cross talk. They don't appreciate what the other is doing. One of my colleagues says things like, "My wife has an MBA but she has been home so long that I think she is losing her mind." My wife and I can very much support one another on the

career side and on the home front. My wife will say, "Tag in. You handle these kids," and I can jump in. I have the energy and the skills to manage the situation. We block for each other when we are at the end of our ropes.

The Libra approach sets the stage for maintaining the romantic love within the marriage by showing partners they are able to count on one another. It is far easier to feel positive about a partner who is at your side in the trenches, dealing with all that is required to care for a family, than it is to feel in synch with a partner whose day-to-day world is so very different than your own. One Libra woman talked about how their partnership approach brought her and her husband closer together:

> I think there would be a lot more resentment built up [if we assumed more traditional roles]. I would not have any real perspective on what it is like to take care of my son. I can understand how challenging it can be. With both of us working we understand that as well. It really has brought us closer.

Several research studies have found shared housework to be a barometer for marital happiness. A Pew Research Center survey of over 2,000 adults found that sharing household chores ranked as the third most important factor in a successful marriage, right behind faithfulness and a happy sexual relationship.[12] Research shows that when men do more of the housework, women's perception of fairness and marital satisfaction rise and the couple experiences less marital conflict. In the U.S., couples that share in providing for the family both economically and in the home are less likely to divorce than in marriages where those roles are specialized.[13] Not surprisingly, sharing promotes intimacy, which translates into a better sex life. It makes sense. The hilarious book *Porn for New Moms* hits the nail on the head. The book has very attractive men doing the things so many new mothers long for help with: writing thank-you notes, worrying about baby food, changing diapers—basically sharing the load.

The time to begin building the parental partnership is the moment you bring your newborn—or adopted child—home. Caring for a young child is extremely demanding and can feel very isolating. A sense of shared experience helps combat the disjunction one feels after losing the structure of the workday, professional colleagues, and a feeling of efficiency. Typically the mother is at home, alone for much of this early parenting phase, and with her world turned upside down, she can feel very distant from her partner, whose daily routine has changed to a far lesser degree.

A male managing partner of a large law firm in Washington, D.C., who took a six-month paternity leave to care for his infant son, spoke vividly about his experience of adapting to this different world:

> Caring for a baby is time-consuming and stressful. My life lost its structure while I was at home full-time. I lost my ability to plan. I had thought caring for my son would be a part-time responsibility, and that I would have plenty of time to do what I wanted to do when I wanted to do it—to go hiking, to visit museums, to read, to play the piano—all with my son, of course. But I did few of those things, except when my wife was home, because my time alone with my son was controlled by his needs. I found this very frustrating at first, but I learned to adjust and go with the flow.[14]

While in many Libra families the early sharing of parental responsibilities strengthens and cements the marital partnership, other relationships evolve to this model from more traditional parenting roles. No matter how you arrive at the Libra approach, it is the commitment to joint responsibility for all that is required to care for a family that leads to deep fulfillment for women and men alike.

Flexibility

The Libra approach builds in a great deal of flexibility as couples learn from one another in both the professional and personal spheres. A Libra woman I interviewed, who had started a business several years earlier, was able to play a mentoring role to her husband during the start-up phase of his design business. Another husband and wife, who worked in consulting at different points in their careers, talked about being able to deeply appreciate both the benefits and challenges of what it meant to be on the road for work. Some Libra couples (in the same profession) have gone as far as sharing one job, providing a clear opportunity to learn from one another at work and at home.

The major recession beginning in 2008 illustrates how the Libra model, typified by two parents actively involved in the labor market, creates a financial and emotional buffer for the family. During the recession, the large majority of those who lost their jobs were men. According to the Bureau of Labor Statistics, the proportion of married college educated women aged twenty-five to forty-four working or looking for work rose in the first half of 2009, while for married male college graduates of the same age, it declined.[15] Joan Williams, director of the Center for Work Life Law at the University of California Hastings College of Law, who has written extensively about gender norms, points out that the recession "has brought home to many families that having one income places you in a very vulnerable position."[16] Even in families where both parents lost their jobs, their joint professional network was an asset in finding a new job. A *Wall Street Journal* article in May 2009 highlighted how couples that were unemployed at the same time provided extra support on several fronts. They would share their networks, review each other's resumes and correspondence, and conduct mock interviews, all of which helped them to find new positions more quickly.[17]

Libra men and women also bring their perspective as a working spouse to their partner's professional situations. Libra couples typically rely on one another as work confidantes as well as partners on the home front. One man, describing his relationship with his wife, said, "We teach each other and we learn from each other. We are role models for one another."

Bryan and I regularly talk about work challenges, seeking one another's opinion and helping the other to *think out loud* before moving forward. For example, a colleague of Bryan's bought and was spinning off one of the company's product lines, and he was courting one of Bryan's engineers. Bryan fully supported this move both because he knew it would be a great professional development experience for his employee and the colleague was in fact a friend and someone Bryan very much wanted to see succeed. The problem was the departure of this talented engineer was going to throw a monkey wrench into plans to deliver the next release of the software on time. In listening to this story—and with my expertise in work redesign—I presented a possible solution, a middle ground. I suggested Bryan approach his colleague and ask that the engineer remain on Bryan's team until the next release and then be free to move to the new company. As it turned out, this was a better solution all the way around because it gave his colleague (the president of the new company) more time to ramp up before taking on the expense of this additional new hire.

In addition to supporting one another professionally, Libra couples share the challenges and rewards of parenting, observing one another and swapping stories of confronting parental challenges—both the more dramatic and the more mundane. A mom recounted the story of her preschool son trying on pants that no longer fit. He demanded she get him another pair from the drawer. When she encouraged him to ask in a nicer way, he responded in a similar demanding fashion, and the mom walked away in frustration. Her son started crying and sought out his father, who listened to the pants dilemma and gently responded, "It makes you feel badly when your pants don't fit, doesn't it?" The mom went on to say:

I watched my husband's different type of approach. It made me relax to watch him have more compassion for my son's emotions. We both want to model being firm and being caring. We sometimes go overboard in both directions. We balance one another out. I am constantly adjusting my idea of what parenting is based on what I try, what he tries, and what seems to work.

Bryan and I rely on one another in both big and small ways, those emotional and practical, as we raise our sons. I have vivid memories of finding great comfort in comparing notes when our sons were infants and toddlers. For instance, our younger son had strong feelings about wearing particular favorite clothes to school. If that special sweatshirt had not made it through the laundry, the question became, do you let him wear it dirty (never a favorite option of mine), or do you deal with the stress of making him wear another? When he was very small, he would refuse to wear a coat en route to day care even in the dead of winter. Bryan and I would commiserate as we decided whether it was better to deal with the stares of other parents or to fight to get the coat on. The companionship provided both stress relief and great humor as we tried to figure it all out.

When our older son was in elementary school, we were able to support one another in a very pragmatic way. Over about a three-year period he needed extra support with reading, which required two appointments weekly away from school, but during school hours. We limited the impact on both our work schedules by taking turns—each managing the transportation back and forth on just one of the days per week.

Benefits for the Children

Choice

Perhaps the greatest beneficiaries of the Libra approach are the children. Parents model for their children that it is possible to be an active parent and an engaged professional. Children learn the importance of spending time on things that bring you fulfillment, see that you respect and deeply care for their other parent, and watch as you develop vital parts of yourself. Living in a Libra household helps children envision playing multiple roles as adults. Children learn that they are an important priority but that parents have other important priorities as well. The Libra model allows children to see that they—not their gender—can define the choices that make sense for them and their family. This approach helps to inculcate a deep understanding of gender equality for both boys and girls. As illustrated below, several Libra parents described the importance of role modeling for their children:

> The kids see my wife having a thriving career and being a nurturing parent. It is nice for boys to see a father involved at home and not being a workaholic.

> We are showing the kids a model of marriage that is a deep partnership based on mutual love and respect. I let them know they can find their own path, to create their own model and not have to fit into something that is predefined. We talk a lot about options and choices in our house.

> The kids got role models of flexibility. They got the life experience of seeing it could be done.

> I feel like I've been a great role model for my kids where the meaning of my life isn't them. That doesn't mean my kids don't bring great meaning to my life: I like that they see me as

someone who takes pride in my work and pride in my family.[18]

Research underscores that children value their parents taking care of their own needs. In a study of 120 men and women aged eighteen to thirty-two that explored perceptions of growing up in a variety of family structures and thoughts on ideal family models, nearly half (45 percent) of those who grew up with an at-home mother would have preferred another option. Conversely, 80 percent of children who grew up with a work-committed mother identified this as the best option. The majority of those with an at-home mother disagreed that this arrangement provided special advantages. Some experienced their mother's acute focus as overwhelming and "with strings attached." Kathleen Gerson, who conducted the research, concluded in her book *The Unfinished Revolution*, "in the end when mothers seemed unhappy at home, or too involved in their children's lives, the cost of their "sacrifices" outweighed the presumed benefits."[19] This is not to suggest that a working mother is optimal for every family, but it does underscore the importance of mothers—and fathers—pursuing the path that is right for them. In a study exploring how work affects children, when parents—and children from the third grade through the twelfth grade—were asked their biggest wish, parents identified more time with their children, while children reported they wished their parents were less stressed.[20]

In Libra families, mothers make their professional development a priority while fathers make spending time to nurture their children a priority. As a result, their children get the message that being a good parent means making choices that let you find the balance between meeting your own needs and the needs of others.

Fulfillment

The Libra model provides children with a deep sense of security. Children learn that both parents can care for them and meet their needs. Many parents in Libra families commented on how quickly their children learned to go to whatever parent was available at the time they needed someone. We find that our sons gravitate toward whichever parent they know will pay attention to their problem at any given moment. We are perhaps more direct than many, but in our house, we sometimes go as far as saying, "Dad's on tonight" or, "Mom's in charge right now." In a Libra family the benefit of a dual parental presence in children's lives is clear:

> The kids got both of us; they really got two parents.

> The kids can rely on us equally. They can go to us for anything. They know we will always be there for them.

> My kids know that we are there. They have inner security. They are connected, secure, and trusting kids.

Children also experience deep fulfillment knowing their parents' relationship is strong. According to Seth Eisenberg, the CEO of PAIRS, a preeminent marriage education program, "The relationship between parents is the foundation of children's lives. There is no comparison that is even remotely close."[21] As a child of divorce, I spent a lot of time worrying about who might be alone on any particular holiday. My mother never remarried or found another life companion, and even when I was an adult, her welfare weighed heavily on my heart and mind, as it did on the hearts and minds of several of my siblings.

Finally, because in the Libra model children spend substantive time with each of their parents, they have an opportunity to get to know their parents deeply. Several Libra men commented that they wished they had known their fathers better but work had kept him away from home a great deal. A Libra father described how his involvement with his children when they were growing up brought them all closer as a family:

> Even though the older kids are in college, living their own lives, I still feel like I really know the shape of their lives. I got to see them through each step in their development and I know I helped shape a lot of that. I wasn't a spectator but a complete participant. And they know me. Sure, the way they evaluate me may change over time as they learn more about the world, but I have a sense that they really know me. They can joke around and make fun of me; I am not a stranger to them in any way. They see the warts and also know the good parts as well.[22]

Flexibility

All parents bring strengths and struggles to the highly complex job of parenting. What is unusual about the Libra approach is that the children have greater exposure to the full array of skills because both parents spend substantial time in their day-to-day care. Different stages of a child's life bring different challenges, and multiple children add greatly to the complexity.

Libra women and men shared many stories about how they and their spouse differed in their parenting styles and strengths, and these differences were beneficial for their children. For example, one mother admitted that when she and her daughter clashed repeatedly during the middle-school years, her husband's more laid-back temperament was a better fit for handling the drama. Conversely, when her children were in high school, she far more easily adapted to their teenage biorhythms, staying up late into the night when they seemed to come alive, while her husband required an earlier bedtime.

Mothers shared several examples where their husbands brought greater skill to managing some aspect of parenting. In one family, while the mom was unable to tolerate her six-month-old crying in order to help her daughter learn to fall asleep on her own, within just a few days, while she was away on business, her husband helped their child to sleep through the night, greatly bringing down the stress level of two formerly exhausted parents. Another father proved more successful than his wife in getting his children to reliably do their chores without all the complaining and pushback. Parents provided multiple examples of the differing strengths they brought to the table.

> I felt perfectly competent as a parent but I would tire. Their dad had more staying power. When I would tire, he was able to stay with the kids in a more sustained way. I felt very appreciative of that.

> He was always better with little kids, with setting up fun things to do. I was probably emotionally more accepting than he tended to be and I was better at setting the family infrastructure, like letting everyone know we needed to go home from the beach because we were worn down.

> Fathers are just as capable [as mothers] in providing a nurturing environment, and the children involved benefit from having different points of care, not just being dependent on one person.[23]

In our household, Bryan has been the far greater resource supporting our children in learning to play musical instruments. Forrest is a child who can more easily become frustrated when he is learning something new, and the challenge of learning to play piano was very trying at times. Bryan's calming influence, his musical background, and his stories recounting his challenges learning to play piano as a boy collectively were very beneficial in supporting Forrest through the process. In addition, Bryan and Forrest would go out for dinner together after the weekly piano lesson, which became a special weekly ritual for just the two of them.

Research underscores the many benefits for children of having two involved parents. Children growing up with parents in more egalitarian marriages performed better academically, had fewer health issues, and built stronger friendships than those who grew up in more traditional families. According to national survey data, several benefits accrue to children of fathers playing a more central role in managing the home and caring for the children. These children performed better in school and had lower rates of absenteeism. They were healthier and less likely to see a child psychologist for behavioral challenges, take prescription medicine, or be diagnosed with attention deficit disorder. Interestingly, school-age children who shared in housework with their fathers reportedly had more friends and better relationships with peers. Fathers in egalitarian marriages were described as modeling "cooperative family partnerships."[24]

Benefits for the Workplace

A Libra approach to life characterized by prioritizing both work and home—and also setting limits in both domains—accrues numerous benefits to the workplace. Yet the caricature of the ideal employee—who puts up few to no boundaries, is always accessible, works long hours, and is the person who always rises up in a crisis—has increasingly become the model of the successful employee in our twenty-first century organizations. I'd like to help shed light on the other side of the story. Having spent many years talking to people about how they combine work with other life priorities, how they work daily, what gets rewarded in their organizations, and what supports versus undermines them in being most effective in their jobs, I can tell you that some of our current work norms keep us busy—painfully busy in some cases—but do little to add real value. We equate activity with productivity, and the sped-up pace of work, like the sped-up pace of life, provides precious little space to step back and assess what is actually going on in a thoughtful and measured way. This section will illustrate the many benefits for organizations of employees, including managers and leaders, who bring a more balanced approach to the workplace.

Choice

Being a manager, and especially a leader, has never been an easy job. In the modern work world, the need for managing and leading in new ways makes it that much more difficult. Yet the road forward remains learning to operate differently, in ways that remain productive and are sustainable, instead of expanding the time devoted to work as the continued default solution. Libra professionals expand the options for organizations by modeling new and better approaches for managing in the twenty-first century.

In many organizations, particularly larger ones, the leadership is comprised of the small subset of the population (less than 20 percent) who live in the traditional family structure. With someone else tending to home and children, these individuals can remain fully focused at work in a way that most employees cannot. Yet research on executives illustrates how a dual focus—on work and on home— engenders skills development in managing the complexity of modern work environments. A third of executives, including both men and women, from ten multinational companies reported ascribing equal importance to work and their lives off the job while 61 percent reportedly placed a higher or much higher priority on work.[25] In comparison to their work-centric counterparts, this dual-centric group reported numerous positive results. They worked fewer hours, felt much less stressed and more able to integrate their work-life responsibilities. They also felt more successful at their jobs. But the real surprise was that these executives who identified themselves as dual-centric were as successful as their work-centric colleagues based on classic measures such as level, compensation, and the number of people they managed. In fact, dual-centric women had advanced to higher reporting levels. Some of their reported strategies for managing it all included setting strict boundaries, being emotionally present when physically present, taking time for rest and recovery, and remaining clear about their priorities.[26]

Being solely focused on work doesn't require leaders to develop the discipline and skill to manage across these worlds of work and home. Sadly, they often don't realize what a skill this really is. The old adage "necessity is the mother of invention" is apt here. I've often said that the most effective means to combat this ridiculous notion that parents—usually women—who actively put up limits at work (on either a full or reduced schedule) are less committed to their jobs is to have the leadership of the Fortune 500 spend a week getting any typical toddler to day care. They would soon realize that not only are you committed, but you have to be that much more committed to manage everything that is required of you at home and at work. You are trying to give your best at all of it—including remaining highly responsive and effective at work and often going above and beyond to prove just how committed you are—while the feedback in many work environments remains that downsized schedules equate with downsized engagement. Women and men today, particularly younger employees, are seeking to find a way to combine the visceral desire to be deeply involved with their families with the drive to be an effective professional.

The story of an executive in one of my client companies illustrates the enormous organizational benefits that flow from a more balanced approach to leading and managing. This leader knew she needed to make some changes when over 60 percent of her team of nearly 100 employees reported dissatisfaction with their work and life balance. This individual was under great pressure to produce results and struggled with how increased balance could possibly coincide with meeting the team's deliverables. She started to collect feedback and found that lack of clarity about priorities, constant firedrills, endless iterations of reports, and lack of communication—and understanding—about the work and life challenges employees faced were core contributors to the constant sense of overload. The team made several important adaptations, experimenting with process changes, more open discussion about work and life challenges, and the expanded use of flexibility, yet several months later, despite these improvements, employees continued to report a very high rate of dissatisfaction regarding work and life balance.

This leader was understandably discouraged, and I give her enormous credit for continuing to listen and learn from employees about what was not working. What she found was that despite many improvements, employees continued to distrust that working differently was supported when she as the leader had made no changes in the way she worked. She began to experiment with changes in her own work behaviors, admitting her very weak time management skills, and began leaving the office by 6:30 on multiple nights per week and blocking off protected time, without interruptions, during the workday. The team response was enormous, with over 90 percent of team members indicating satisfaction with work and life balance, compared to less than 40 percent when they began. The team credited improvements in the productivity of the group to a far better understanding of workloads and expectations, a more streamlined approach to getting the work accomplished, and greater management understanding of team capacity and limitations. At the same time, this executive experienced important benefits in her own life, discovering how much *life* there was outside of work.

The power of leaders living more balanced lives is tremendous, and enables others in their organizations to believe they can do the same. In my consulting work, employees provided consistent feedback about the disconnect between organizational support of work-life integration—in the form of statements, programs, and policies—and the reality that very few, if any, leaders seem to make use of these supports.

During the Boston Consulting research (referenced in the chapter on current-day work norms), where consulting teams experimented with planned time off, partners and project managers at the firm were encouraged to be more transparent about taking time off for personal matters. One of the consultants shared that a senior partner's comment at a kickoff meeting for the project made a major impression on him. The partner said that while work was very important to him, it wasn't the most important thing in his life and he was not embarrassed to say so. The consultant continued, "I had never heard a partner talk like that before. My work is really important to me, too, but it is not the most important thing in my life. [His openness] made me comfortable to admit that."[27]

Keep in mind that most employees are leaders to someone else in their organization. We tend to think of the person at the top as the only one with influence, but that is far from the truth. Mid-level associates at a law firm set the tone for new associates just learning the ropes. Mid-level managers play an enormous role in enabling better work-life balance for their team when they share personal strategies for integrating work and home. I consulted to an organization planning their first-ever women's leadership conference, bringing together women from across this large and geographically diverse company. Over their three days together, these women came to appreciate the extent to which they were role models for junior level women in the organization. These women realized they had been so focused up—on the dearth of women at the most senior levels of the company—that they had lost sight of how many individuals in the organization, men and women alike, considered *them* to be company leaders.

Fulfillment/Efficacy

As it refers to organizations, I am using fulfillment to mean work efficacy or adding value. Libra professionals are highly motivated to be both effective and efficient at work because they are energized by their ability to craft a satisfying work and life fit and to ensure time and energy for their lives outside of work. Several Libra professionals referenced how this model promoted loyalty and efficacy:

> I remember seeing studies suggesting people who work part-time are happier and more efficient. I believe it on all those scores. You want to be productive and want to work harder.

People who want to adjust their schedule for their children are not going to abuse that. When an employer is flexible it engenders a strong sense of loyalty, loyalty on an emotional level. It's sort of an acknowledgement that your life outside of work matters to us. It has value to us. That is huge.

In truth we end up doing more than one person would—not two people but more like one and a third. We get involved in students' lives. We carry the teaching load of one person but we do one and a third because we can't help ourselves and we don't mind it. [From a man doing a job share in a tenure-track academic position.]

What we do to make money is the essence of who we are. We don't think of work as a stepping-stone to the next level, a raise, whatever. [It's] how can I find a way to get in a place in my current job, or another job, where I am satisfied, get good at what I do, and charge more for my skills.[28]

Libra professionals work in a wide range of professions—as lawyers and doctors, academics and business people—and with jobs of varying scope and responsibility. Many Libra professionals, though certainly not all, work on a reduced schedule for some portion of their careers. In the modern workplace, these part-time professionals (an oxymoron, because in many workplaces a part-time schedule is more than forty hours) continue to struggle with many biases such as "they are not committed professionals" and "they can only add limited value if they are not working full-time." A major Catalyst research study on part-time professionals served to dispel many myths. Over a two-year period Catalyst conducted a comprehensive study of part-time work arrangements across more than 2,000 employees in four large, highly competitive professions—law, consulting, high technology, and pharmaceutical research. The study explored the impacts of reduced arrangements on the employees working part-time, their coworkers, their supervisors, and their clients. The results were overwhelmingly positive and underscored the efficacy of reduced workloads.

More than 90 percent of employees—those working on part-time schedules as well as their full-time colleagues—indicated reduced schedules had a neutral or positive impact on delivering high quality work. In *all* cases, clients reported no negative impact from the part-time schedules, and overwhelmingly managers of those on part-time schedules reported the individuals provided outstanding client service. Part-time professionals identified an increased ability to focus, fewer interruptions, and better attention to priorities as contributing to their high levels of productivity. While working on an alternative arrangement, over half of those surveyed had received a promotion. Yet several also shared frustrations over receiving excellent performance ratings yet not being considered for promotions.[29]

I am a definite example of someone who learned to work better and smarter after having children. Working hard is what I know how to do best. As a student in college and business school, my hard work and long hours were rewarded with good grades. As a young professional, I applied this unquestioned standard of excellence to everything I did at work and was rewarded with excellent feedback. Eventually, however, as I moved up in my career, it became more challenging to bring that same level of acute mastery, the A+ job, to every task or responsibility. My ability to prioritize and match effort with value gradually became far more critical.

In the early years of my consulting career, I had the luxury of time. After my first son was born, my life became about abrupt stops. I had to interrupt a conversation to leave work for pickup at day care or I had to quickly gather necessary materials for a client meeting (via plane) the next morning. As someone who prizes completion, this was a very difficult transition for me, but learning to stop and put up a boundary has been among the most valuable lessons I've learned in both my career and in my life. For me, it has been one of the greatest gifts of being a mother. Not working on something until I got it just so represented a huge shift. I could no longer throw time at a problem or spend long hours getting everything to my standard of near perfection. The hard truth was that the incremental time and effort was often not worth the incremental benefit. My ability to say, "This is good enough," increased, as did my ability to distinguish what required going the extra mile and what did not. Also, breaking from work to become involved in something else was often just the thing I needed to get some perspective and come back to a work challenge with more clarity and often a better solution.

In addition to their laser-like focus on efficacy, Libra professionals benefit the workplace by bringing skills developed in other parts of their lives. A Libra woman reported that becoming a parent helped her to be far more effective in relating to the parents of her students. A Libra father indicated the patience he developed as a dad went a long way in helping to manage a younger coworker with a low frustration tolerance:

> I have a guy at work that I supervise who is just like a kid. He wants instant praise for good work. He wants to skip the hard parts and move on to the fun parts immediately. Now I am better at knowing when to talk with him about the situation.[30]

Living a Libra life, where work remains an important priority among many, also allows people to retain a more balanced perspective. It is similar to the notion of diversifying your investments, so that while there may be volatility in any one segment of the portfolio, over time, a balanced portfolio results in the best long-term returns. For Libra professionals, a particularly challenging day at work can be put in perspective by an intimate moment spent with your child, while the stress of your children bickering can be balanced by a quiet drive to work or a productive client meeting. A Libra professional describes the value of perspective in solving problems at work:

CHAPTER 8: THE BENEFITS OF THE LIBRA APPROACH   247

> A big positive for the workplace is you are able to be a much more balanced person at work. You are much more reasonable. I see these workaholic people who are so entrenched in their opinion. They become very counter-productive. They are not able to listen. [Time away] gave me healthy space. I think with anything you do, you need space from it.

A Libra father managing a fifteen-person team described the value of a more balanced perspective in managerial decision making:

> To me a seasoned professional is someone who is able to prioritize business-critical tasks, and that's not easy. What I value in the people that report to me is if they are able to step back and gain some perspective and make a good decision. As a seasoned professional you get better and better at that. If you can have everything, then you want everything, but like a spoiled child, it is not always good and you lose the ability to understand what will really make a difference. You don't learn as much about winning or losing. Learning from mistakes allows you to do a better job in the future. If you keep evaluating and adjusting over time, you will do much better long term.

Perhaps shockingly, twenty of the twenty-two women who have served as CEOs of Fortune 500 companies as of October 2010 are mothers.[31] They reported employing experiences and skills from their parenting role to help them in their efforts to climb the corporate ladder. Mary Dillon, chief executive of U.S. Cellular Corp. and a former marketing chief at McDonald's, said, "I learned plenty about how to be an effective executive from raising my children." She shared that her experience of raising four children contributed to her success in catalyzing a global expansion of healthier food options added to McDonald's menu offerings. Carol Bartz, former CEO of

Yahoo, indicated that being a mother helped her learn to be more judicious in picking her battles at both work and home.[32]

Shared parenting experiences can be a way to connect with clients and to strengthen work relationships. A Libra dad described taking his daughter on appointments when she was an infant. He recalled having her in a pack with his architectural drawings sticking out of his bag and said, "People were ecstatic I had a baby with me." Another father who is a screenwriter shared that at times his daughter also comes with him when he is working. He reported, "I had a meeting to pitch a story with an entertainment company and I took my baby with me. The guy was so happy with her there. He was telling me he also had a daughter and that he was sad she was going off to college soon."

I realize there are limitations and times when combining children and work does not make sense, but sharing this important part of our lives with colleagues and clients can deepen and broaden the relationships. The accounting firm Ernst & Young experimented with a highly innovative work management approach by having client teams include their personal commitments (e.g., leave at three o'clock to coach soccer on Tuesdays, away for a wedding on Friday) in the work schedule they shared with clients. The E&Y professionals found that not only did this improve their work and life balance, it also opened up new avenues for strengthening their client relationships.[33]

Flexibility

Intrinsic to the concept of work redesign introduced in the chapter "How We Work" is the idea of using work-life needs and desires as a catalyst to generate better solutions. Earlier in this chapter, I shared the story of a leader motivated by the dissatisfaction of her employees with their work and life balance to improve the communication, coordination, and work processes of her team.

Similarly, a Libra dad wanting to move to a four-day schedule in order to have more time with his wife and young children illustrates the power of the Libra approach in improving how work is accomplished. At first, this engineer's desire for a four-day schedule seemed impossible. His job, at the small company where he worked, spanned several roles, including product development, quality control, production, and research and development. He worked with the ThirdPath Institute to strategize how he could redesign his job and move to a reduced workload. When this engineer first approached the general manager of his company to propose a reduced schedule, he quickly learned how highly the company valued his contribution as well as the company's big-picture priorities. He found that, through the process of streamlining, he became nearly as effective on his reduced schedule as on his previous full-time schedule. He went on to describe how his request and the process of adapting his job were beneficial for his company more broadly:

> It's a small company that's evolving rapidly. Change is the norm around here. Because of my exercise [redesigning his job] two years ago, I did push the momentum for the rest of the company. We established more standard protocols for dealing with new products. We hired another engineer and we've been able to meet our goals with the two of us and without dropping the ball on anything. My change had a larger effect on the direction of the company.[34]

Libra professionals either have, or develop, strong managerial skills, which engenders greater fluency into the whole work system. They are strong planners, think ahead to ensure deliverables are met beforehand, do everything they can to avoid highly disruptive last-minute crises, and develop others to ensure work moves forward in their absence. Libra employees learn to communicate better about priorities and their own accessibility and they are motivated—and required—to delegate.

In interviewing a Libra professional working for a large financial services company, he shared that his manager was reluctant to allow one of his colleagues to work a flexible schedule because he was already working a 90-percent workload. This Libra professional insisted they would work together to ensure their joint work was covered. In fact it developed into a highly effective situation whereby he and his coworker provided backup for one another and it became seamless to those with whom they worked.

A leader having worked full-time for many decades adapted his schedule in order to care for his granddaughter one day per week. He described how this change was a benefit to his company and his team:

> Early on I was developing them to take more responsibility, knowing they could—to not have to come to me for everything they are doing. Now they don't come to me with things I don't need to be involved with. My being away one day per week started that process. Now they have much more confidence in the decisions they make. Before they would have used me as a crutch.[35]

Through several years of my consulting career, I worked closely with a colleague to manage multiple large client projects. On some projects we were actually named co-engagement managers. Like the fluidity that developed in my marriage, there was fluidity in the way we worked that was awesome—effective, productive, and allowing us both the flexibility we needed in our lives to care for the five children that we had between us. There were client meetings in which something came up and one of us could not go, but because the other person was up to speed on most of the details and highly familiar to the client, it was a nonevent. Or times when we were writing a major report and one of us said to the other, "I need you to take the lead here—I don't have the mind space to fully focus because of things going on at home." Our shared ownership at work created clear benefits for us, our clients, and our company.

Concluding Thoughts

In research studies, quality of life is defined as low levels of stress-related mental and physical health problems, including burnout, and high levels of life satisfaction, including satisfaction with our careers and in our roles as spouses, parents, and employees.[36]

At its core, the Libra approach is about creating a strong partnership, characterized by gender equality, to meet the full range of individual and family needs. It is also defined by intentionally slowing the pace in our personal and professional lives in order to make greater time and space for what strengthens and energizes us. Men and women who practice the Libra approach enjoy high quality of life and in so doing benefit their relationships with their spouses/life partners, their children, and their workplaces.

Chapter 9

Balance Redefined: Focus on What Works

If one advances confidently in the direction of one's dreams, and endeavors to live the life which one has imagined, one will meet with a success unexpected in common hours.

---Henry David Thoreau

The idea of work and life balance too often gets interpreted as a perfect state of alignment, one in which everything is precisely as it should be. Libra women and men, on the other hand, think of work and life balance more like a compass—one with an ever-vibrating needle—that they can refer back to for direction and inspiration. Libra women and men strive to maintain equilibrium in several areas of their lives *over the long term*. They seek to balance their professional lives with other important priorities, the role of caretaking with the role of breadwinning, the needs of children with those of the parents, and their aspirations with the pragmatic choices and decisions they need to make every day.

We suffer from a collective failure of imagination about how life could feel different for professionals raising children in the twenty-first century. The Libra life offers a vision of how to bring down the intensity and infuse more joy and sustainability into our lives at work and at home. Rather than adding more to our overflowing to-do lists, it suggests that we shed what is less important and work to reallocate the family resources of money, energy, and time in ways that better meet the needs of *everyone* in the family. Libra women and men split up the pie of responsibility more equitably, sharing *ownership* for both the domestic and economic needs of their families. They also make the well-being of each member of the family a priority. Their sense of being a team, of working together to realize their work and life vision, provides Libra women and men with great strength. They grow in their confidence and ability to rise to any challenge—be it work, children, money, whatever—and figure out how to respond. In my interviews I have discovered that, while Libra women and men *can* speak passionately about how they strive to make their shared and balanced approach work, and about the many benefits of this approach, they are not naturally vocal advocates. What keeps this approach to work and life balance such a well-kept secret?

First, we lack a common language to even describe this work and life model of sharing and moderation. Ironically, "co-parenting," which might be an apt description of the shared approach to child rearing, is a word we use to describe divorced families rather than intact ones. While the term "dual-career" captures the work focus of both members of the couple, it lacks the implication of proactive management of careers to ensure greater balance over the long term. In response to my questioning what, if anything, a father called his family's work-life approach, he said, "I don't have any magic words, but we joke that we are Team Smith and we treat it [managing careers and raising children] like a team sport." As I use the word "Libra," it stands for balance and a long-term perspective across several variables—in our careers and in our lives outside of work, in the roles of women and men at work and at home, and in our focus on the needs of children and adults.

Second, we hear little about the Libra approach because no one feels, or dares to imply, that they have the work and life balancing act all figured out. Libra women and men consider their work and life integration as an ongoing learning process rather than a final destination. They know they want both professional work and active parenting in their lives and they see experimentation, evaluation, and recalibration all as part of the journey.

Third, we are faced with constant messaging about how it is impossible to have it all—that it is impossible for women and men to jointly raise children while remaining committed professionals. On the other hand, who wants to be so arrogant as to think "Actually, I *am* doing it"? The men and women I interviewed were exceedingly humble. Their perspective was, "This is how we are making it work, and we are exceptionally grateful for what we have been able to create in our lives." They felt extremely sensitive about revealing to a friend who was complaining about a partner not pulling his or her weight either domestically or economically that they felt so lucky to be full partners in managing home and work. They hesitated to share with a coworker who was complaining about never making it home for dinner with their kids that they felt so blessed that family dinner was a regular part of their weekly routine. Libra couples are out there, making this model work in their lives. Nevertheless, those I interviewed indicated that, while they were happy to share their experiences if someone asked, they were very reluctant to imply their choices were the right way for everyone to manage their work and life balance.

While the Libra approach is not common, I also believe it is not rare. Though we encounter many stories about the difficulties of work and life balance, we hear far too little about the many women and men who are finding a different way through the work and life labyrinth—less gendered, more fulfilling, less pressured. Two books I've referenced earlier, *Equally Shared Parenting: Rewriting the Rules for a New Generation of Parents* and *Getting to 50/50: How You Can Have It All by Sharing It All,* are fabulous resources filled with many additional stories of how couples are making this work. By highlighting couples and families who are under the radar yet finding a more balanced approach, we reinforce the many ways in which women and men *are actively* writing new work and life scripts for the twenty-first century.

If the ideas for employing the Libra work and life solution resonate with you, I urge you to experiment and see how even a small step can have far-reaching effects. If you constantly lack any time for yourself, try to choose just one night every other week for you (and alternately your spouse) to have all to yourself. If you never make it home for dinner, try and pick just one night a week that you will leave the office without fail. If you feel like your weekends are filled with chores and responsibilities, try and negotiate with your manager to leave the office mid-afternoon one day per week to run errands so that you can safeguard a weekend morning or afternoon for fun. If you have been thinking about going on a special vacation with your family, set a future date, do some research, and start saving to move this goal from an idea to an actual work in progress.

Think of this process of taking small steps like steering a large ship such as the QE2. For most of us the issues inherent in work-life choices—where you live, where you work, how you care for your children—are too complex to change on a dime. But a small change in direction sets in place a shift that builds momentum through time. You start to flow on a different route, and before too long you can see a new horizon and a new destination in the distance.

The Mindset for Success

We come with many assumptions about why the Libra model is impractical at best, impossible at worst. And there are obstacles to overcome and challenges to navigate. But instead of letting dreams die without even considering the possibilities, Libra men and women seek to stay focused on what they can influence and take steps—sometimes big and sometimes small—to move closer to their work and life vision.

In my interviews, I explored what enabled Libra women and men to walk this different road. While this book is filled with their wisdom, here are a handful of key foundational elements—in the words of Libra women and men themselves—that set them up for success at work and at home.

Keep an Open Mind

> I don't think it's especially hard. The only thing I really know is you need a kind of open-mindedness about what your role is and about the organic changing nature of your role over time.

You have to be flexible and open-minded. There are a lot of societal pressures. Can I challenge these norms? Can I have the courage to do things differently?

Think Ahead

Teachers say chance favors the mind that is prepared. There was luck involved, but I had also worked to put myself in a good position.

Work and family gets looked at as a women's issue. If the couple is starting out, the man needs to be thinking about these issues, too. Men need to get a seat at the table [of work and life planning].

Think about it when you are selecting your mate. Who you choose to be in a relationship with is really important. Look at what people do, not what they say.

Build the Couple Relationship

Being supportive of one another is a calling. Couples need to talk about their philosophies, about how they want to tackle the problem of working and raising a family.

One of the things we do is talking and listening to understand rather than to respond. The conversation is to enrich the relationship rather than to be right. I am not perfect at this and neither is my husband but it helps us with difficult conversations.

The pressure is to focus on your children's development—that they are in the right activities, doing the right enrichment things. All of these are important but people neglect their relationship. Also they think they don't have to work on their relationship. That it will just happen. I believe the quality of the family environment is really important and parents could benefit from spending more time on the relationship and less time driving around everywhere.

Approach Work Strategically

The amount of work fills to fit the amount of time. If you know your limits, you end up structuring your responsibilities so you can fill them.

From the very beginning at work I was very open about "I don't do face time." You don't need to be at work to get a lot done ... I am really organized. I don't leave stuff around. I deal with things as they come in. I don't procrastinate.

The easiest thing to do is to be a workaholic. This [putting up limits] is the hardest thing to do.

It is all about finding the right situation. You may have to give it a few tries. You may not find the right organization at first. It is a matter of finding the right situation with the right dynamic. I can't think of one [work] situation that is the end all and be all. If it's not working, be prepared to move.

Live Within Your Means

I have been an investor and a saver. I'm someone who always maxed out my 401(k) not knowing what I was doing it for, and it has worked out great. We have not missed a beat [since he dialed back at work to create time to care for his infant daughter].

We are more like my grandparents than my parents—that is, you don't spend money you don't have. We save money for vacations and things like that so we are not playing catch-up.

We like to spend money on the things we really enjoy, but in our normal routine we try to pare down as much as possible.

We knew we would have to be more fiscally conservative than when we were both working more, but it is a decision we made and we thought it was well worth it to spend more time with the children and each other.

So know that balance is possible over the long term. Know that gender equality is good for women *and* men *and* families. Experiment. Keep the faith. I promise you the journey will be worth it!

ACKNOWLEDGEMENTS

Writing this book has been a wonderful, gratifying, intense and challenging experience. I have many to thank for their help on this journey.

I need to begin by thanking my husband Bryan for always believing in me, for passionately supporting my career as well as for being a wonderful husband and a powerful role model for our sons of all that a man can be – an accomplished professional and good provider, a nurturing father, and someone who is incredibly fun and enjoys life. To my sons Skylar and Forrest, thank you for continuing to teach me about being a parent, about myself, and about the joys of life. I am so excited to see the men you will become. I also want to thank my sister-in-law Alicia Jylkka D'Annolfo for sharing her talent as a design professional to design the book covers, front and back, and her professional photography skills to get some lovely photos of someone who tends to be very camera shy.

I want to deeply thank Anne Weisberg for being a great colleague and dear friend. Without her encouragement and support, this book might never have been written. In a conversation over dinner one night, Anne said, "You and Bryan have done something a lot of people want to do. You should write a memoir." From that seed grew the idea of weaving our story of walking this path with the story of many others similarly combining careers and parenting in a highly shared and intentionally moderate way. The book became an opportunity for me to wed these stories with learnings from my many years of consulting and research. Anne has provided introductions, research leads, thought-provoking discussion, and a welcoming place to stay on my many trips to New York. Her enthusiasm for this project has been unwavering and a key spark throughout this process.

I am indebted to Jessica DeGroot for articulating to me more than 10 years ago the concept of shared care, describing this deeply shared partnership approach to work and raising a family around which this book is centered. Jessica's organization *ThirdPath Institute* has been a tremendous resource and provided numerous real-life examples of men and women walking this road. Jessica has provided inspiration, encouragement and on many occasions a listening ear. Thank you for your vision and the work you do every day to support women, men, and families.

I want to thank several people who acted as advisors during the process of my writing this book including Jane Bermont, Sharon Teitelbaum, Jennifer Kohler, Bill Taussig and Marcee Harris Schwartz. They read major sections of the book and provided their reactions and suggestions. They sent many kind words as I worked through the various stages of the book writing process, and more than I suspect they know their involvement provided energy and momentum to keep me moving forward.

This book could not have been written without the generosity of many women and men who shared their stories of striving to carve out a more fulfilling path through the work and life jungle. They, in their quiet unpretentious ways, work every day to live lives where professional commitment and involved parenting are not mutually exclusive and where roles are not defined by gender. They are thoughtful and courageous as they work to be living models who challenge pervasive cultural messaging and norms. It has been intensely gratifying to hear these men and women echo so many of my experiences and sentiments as both a parent and professional. Through sharing their stories, these women and men have helped me to crystallize *The Libra Solution*.

My understanding of work-life issues, gender equality and diversity has been enriched and deepened by many colleagues throughout my professional career. I want to thank my many Catalyst colleagues who work every day to help level the playing field of our organizations and make them places where every person—man or woman, white or of color, straight or gay—has the chance to shine. I want to thank my WFD colleagues who assist organizations in creating work cultures where being a great employee and a fully engaged partner and parent are not at odds. Through my work with these colleagues over many years, I have learned a great deal which informs my thinking and this book. I want to especially thank several people who have been important mentors: Charles Rodgers, Arlene Johnson, Jane Bermont, Jo Weiss, Meryle Mahrer Kaplan and Kara Helander.

In addition to those with whom I have had the pleasure to work more directly, there are many who have made important contributions to the conversations about diversity, women's leadership and work and life integration through their research, consulting and writing. I have relied upon their work in developing many of my arguments and it is upon their shoulders that the strength of this book rests.

Writing a first book is a daunting task. I want to thank Grub Street for supporting a community of writing professionals who have greatly enhanced this book. I was told that a great editor is someone who helps you to sharpen your thinking and polish your ideas. Special thanks go to Jill Parsons Stern who has been an amazing editor and helped me to do just that. Jill's involvement has been critical and this book is far stronger because of her contributions. It was wonderful to work side by side with Jill in the writing trenches as she validated my ideas, challenged my thinking, and helped me to improve my messaging. Last but certainly not least Chip Creek has been a consummate professional in copy editing my manuscript and helping to lift the veil on precisely where all those marks of punctuation belong and the ins and outs of reference citations. I am very glad for his sharp eye and grammatical expertise.

NOTES

Introduction

[1] Brooks, David. "The New Humanism." *The New York Times,* March 7, 2011. Retrieved 4/14/2011 at http://www.nytimes.com/2011/03/08/opinion/08brooks.html.

Chapter 1

[1] Friedan, *The Feminine Mystique*, 13.
[2] Coltrane and Adams, *Gender and Families*.
[3] Gerson, *The Unfinished Revolution*, 106.
[4] Ibid., 122.
[5] Phillip A. Cowan and Carolyn Pape Cowan. "Do Babies Make Marriage Better or Worse? It All Depends," from *Unconventional Wisdom*, Issue 2, a publication of the Council on Contemporary Families, April 17-19, 2009. Retrieved on February 13, 2010, at http://www.contemporaryfamilies.org/all/unconventionalwisdom2.html.
[6] Lachs, "Desire in the Twilight of Life," c1-c2.

Chapter 2

[1] Based on the transcript from the Fem 2.0 Wake Up! radio show titled, "Work/Life and Kids: What Do Kids Really Think About Their Working Parents?" The program was aired on February 10, 2010, and was moderated by Ellen Galinsky, president of the Families and Work Institute. The guests included Lisa Belkin and Josh Coleman.

[2] Bianchi and Milkie, "Work and Family Research in the First Decade of the 21st Century," 708.

[3] Harrington et al., *The New Dad: Caring, Committed and Conflicted*, 23.

[4] U.S. Bureau of Labor Statistics, *Married Parents' Use of Time Survey 2003-2006*, press release at http://www.bls.gov/news.release/atus2.nr0.htm, Table 2. Time spent in primary activities (1) by married mothers and fathers with own household children under 18 by employment status of self and spouse, average for the combined years 2003-06:
http://www.bls.gov/news.release/atus2.t02.htm and
U.S. Bureau of Labor Statistics, *American Time Use Survey Summary 2010*, http://www.bls.gov/news.release/atus.nr0.htm, Table 11. Time spent in leisure and sports activities for the civilian population by selected characteristics, 2010 annual averages: http://www.bls.gov/news.release/atus.t11.htm.

[5] Table 2, Time spent in primary activities (1) by married mothers and fathers with own household children under 18 by employment status of self and spouse, average for the combined years 2003-06:
http://www.bls.gov/news.release/atus2.t02.htm.

[6] Aumann et al., *The New Male Mystique*, 11.

[7] Rothausen-Vange, Teresa J. "Gender: Work-Family Ideologies and Roles." *Work and family encyclopedia*. Chestnut Hill, MA: Sloan Work and Family Research Network. November 14, 2001. Retrieved March 17, 2010, at http:wfnetwork.bc.edu/encyclopedia_entry.php?id=241&area=All.

[8] Risman and Seale, "Betwixt and Be Tween," from *Families as They Really Are*, 1-28.

[9] Collins, *America's Women*, xiv.

[10] Catalyst, *The Next Generation*, 24-27.

[11] Harrington et al., *The New Dad: Caring, Committed and Conflicted*, 11.

[12] Catalyst, *Women and the MBA*, 36; Catalyst, *Women in Law*, 19.

[13] Belkin, "The Opt-Out Revolution."

[14] Moen and Roehling, *The Career Mystique*.

[15] Taken from Phyllis Moen's homepage, which provided an overview of *The Career Mystique*. Retrieved on March 9, 2010, at http://www.soc.umn.edu/~moen/CareerMystiquePage.htm.
[16] Catalyst, *Women and Men in U.S. Corporate Leadership*, 31.
[17] Catalyst, *Women in Law*, 43.
[18] Cohany and Sok, "Trends in labor force participation of married mothers of infants," 9-16.
[19] Percheski, "Opting Out? Cohort Differences in Professional Women's Employment Rates from 1960 to 2005," 497.
[20] Merrill-Sands et al., "Women Pursuing Leadership and Power: Challenging the Myth of the 'Opt Out Revolution,'" 3.
[21] Galinsky et al., *Overwork in America,* Executive Summary, 1-5.
[22] Ibid.
[23] Ibid.
[24] Based on proprietary workforce studies.
[25] Galinsky et al., *Overwork in America,* Executive Summary, 1-5.
[26] Hallowell, "Overloaded Circuits: Why Smart People Underperform," 55-62.
[27] Andersen, "The End of Excess: Why this crisis is good for America," 34-38.
[28] The book *Affluenza* by John deGraaf, David Wann, and Thomas Naylor and subsequent television program on PBS highlights the American model of overconsumption. The URL for the website, retrieved on March 12, 2010, is http:www.pbs.org/kcts/affluenza/. John deGraaf is also the leader of the *Take Back Your Time* day celebrated in October to bring attention to the issue of overwork and overconsumption.
[29] Begley, "Wealth and Happiness Don't Necessarily Go Hand in Hand," b1.; Marshall Goldsmith, "Creating a Great Rest of Your Life."
[30] OJJDP Statistical Briefing Book, Juveniles as Victims, Question: What is the trend in the child maltreatment victimization rate? Retrieved April 8, 2011, at http://www.ojjdp.gov/ojstatbb/victims/qa02105.asp?qaDate=2008; OJJDP Statistical Briefing Book: Juveniles as Victims, Question: What are the trends in serious violent crime victimization of youth? Retrieved April 8, 2011, at http://www.ojjdp.gov/ojstatbb/victims/qa02501.asp?qaDate=2005.
[31] Warner, "Mommy Madness. What Happened When the Girls Who Had It All Became Mothers?"; Haddock, "Are Modern Women Miserable?" Retrieved February 2010 at http://www.alternet.org/module/printversion/79521.
[32] Haddock, "Are Modern Women Miserable?"
[33] Galinsky et al., *Times are Changing*, 18.

[34] Shellenbarger, "If you Need to Work Better, Maybe Try Working Less," d1-d2.
[35] Keohane, "Imaginary Friends," c1, c4.
[36] Warner, "Mommy Madness."
[37] Based on a phone interview conducted by the author with Stephanie Coontz on January 14, 2011.
[38] The author conducted an oral history of Lillie Margaret Lazaruk in the spring of 2009. This quote is from the transcript of her interviews.
[39] Ibid.
[40] Ibid.
[41] Q&A with Stephanie Coontz, author of *A Strange Stirring: The Feminine Mystique and American Women at the Dawn of the 1960s*, retrieved on February 20, 2011, at http://www.stephaniecoontz.com/books/astrangestirring/.

Chapter 3

[1] Aucoin, "Family first? Athletes and politicians send a mixed message on how to balance work and children."
[2] Two studies, one published by the Families and Work Institute (Aumann et al., *The New Male Mystique*) and the second by the Boston College Center for Work & Family (Harrington et al., *The New Dad: Caring, Committed and Conflicted*), highlight the growing work-life stress for men as they combine professional work with assuming a more central role in raising their children.
[3] Aumann et al., *The New Male Mystique*, 3.
[4] Luscombe, "Marriage: What's It Good For?," 51-53.
[5] ThirdPath Teleconference, "Flexing Work During the Infant/Toddler Years," December 3, 2010.
[6] Schoppe-Sullivan, "Maternal Gatekeeping, Coparenting Quality, and Fathering Behavior in Families with Infants," 389, 391, 396-397.
[7] Jayson, "More parents share the workload when mom learns to let go."
[8] Belkin, "When Mom and Dad Share It All."
[9] Jayson, "More parents share the workload when mom learns to let go."
[10] Stone, "The Rhetoric and Reality of 'Opting Out,'" 14-19.
[11] Warner, "Mommy Madness. What Happened When the Girls Who Had It All Became Mothers?"
[12] Tugend, "It's Just Fine to Make Mistakes."

[13] Harrington et al., *The New Dad: Exploring Fatherhood Within a Career Context*, 6, 27.
[14] U.S. Bureau of Labor Statistics, Table 5. Employment status of the population by sex, marital status, and presence and age of own children under 18, 2008-09 annual averages. Retrieved on February 16, 2011, at http://data.bls.gov/cgibin/print.pl/news.release/famee.t05.htm.
[15] Levey, "Work-Family Balance—of Paramount Importance to Women," 36-37.
[16] Harrington et al., *The New Dad: Caring, Committed and Conflicted*, 22-24.
[17] Ibid., 17.
[18] Ibid., 22-24.
[19] Stone, "The Rhetoric and Reality of 'Opting Out.'"
[20] Luscombe, "Marriage: What's It Good For?," 50-51, 53.
[21] Martin Hekker, "Paradise Lost."
[22] Kreider and Ellis, *Number, Timing and Duration of Marriages and Divorces: 2009*, 6, 17.
[23] Potter Cromartie, "Labor force status of families: a visual essay," 35-41.
[24] Catalyst, *Women of Color Executives*, 29.
[25] Coontz, "Stop Blaming Betty Friedan."
[26] Luscombe, "Marriage: What's It Good For?," 53.
[27] Galinsky et al., *Times are Changing*, 14.
[28] Ibid., 18-19.
[29] Phone interview with author on January 11, 2011.
[30] ThirdPath Teleconference, "Integrated Leaders," January 7, 2011.
[31] Aumann et al., *The New Male Mystique*, 3-12.
[32] Tang and MacDermid Wadsworth, *Time and Workplace Flexibility*, 45.
[33] Harrington et al., *The New Dad: Exploring Fatherhood Within a Career Context*, 10, 12, 18, 20.
[34] Harrington et al., *The New Dad: Caring, Committed and Conflicted*, 12.
[35] Ibid., 23.
[36] Ibid., 26-30.
[37] Harrington et al., *The New Dad: Exploring Fatherhood Within a Career Context*, 22.
[38] Harrington et al., *The New Dad: Caring, Committed and Conflicted*, 8.
[39] Harrington et al., *The New Dad: Exploring Fatherhood Within a Career Context*, 19-27.
[40] U.S. Bureau of Labor Statistics, Married Parents' Use of Time Survey 2003-2006, press release: http://www.bls.gov/news.release/atus2.nr0.htm,

Table 2. Time spent in primary activities by married mothers and fathers with own household children under 18 by employment status of self and spouse, average for the combined years 2003-06: http://www.bls.gov/news.release/atus2.t02.htm.

[41] Harrington et al., *The New Dad, Caring, Committed and Conflicted*, 13.

[42] Bianchi and Milkie, "Work and Family Research in the First Decade of the 21st Century," 709.

[43] Hewlett et al., *The Hidden Brain Drain*, 14.

[44] Shapiro et al., "Optioning In versus 'Opting Out': Women Using Flexible Work Arrangements for Career Success," 1-4.

[45] Barnett and Shibley Hyde, "Women, Men, Work and Family: An Expansionist Theory."

[46] Zaslow, "Friendship for Guys (No Tears!)," d1.

[47] Ibid.

[48] Harrington et al., *The New Dad: Exploring Fatherhood Within a Career Context*, 28.

[49] Phone interview with author on January 28, 2011.

[50] Ibid.

[51] Petersen, "So Cute, So Hard on a Marriage," d1.

Chapter 4

[1] Organization for Economic Co-operation and Development (OECD), 2009 average annual hours worked per worker, retrieved on March 18, 2011, at http://stats.oecd.org/Index.aspx?DataSetCode=ANHRS.

[2] Hara Estroff Marano, "Do You Suffer from V,acation Deficit Disorder?" Special feature written for eDiets by editor of *Psychology Today*, retrieved on January 4, 2004, at http://www.ediets.com/news/printArticle.cfm?articles_id=7899.

[3] Williams, Joan, *Reshaping the Work-Family Debate: Why Men and Class Matter*. Cambridge, MA: Harvard UP, 2010.

[4] Mandel, "The Real Reasons You're Working So Hard … and What You Can Do About It."

[5] Aumann et al., *The New Male Mystique*, 3-5.

[6] Tugend, "Vacations Are Good for You, Medically Speaking."

[7] Galinsky et al., *Overwork in America*, Executive Summary, 7-8.

[8] Mandel, "The Real Reasons You're Working So Hard."

⁹ Aumann et al., *The New Male Mystique*, 5.
¹⁰ Begley, "Wealth and Happiness Don't Necessarily Go Hand in Hand," b1.
¹¹ Organization for Economic Co-operation and Development (OECD), 2009 estimates of labour productivity levels, retrieved on March 18, 2011, at http://stats.oecd.org/Index.aspx?DataSetCode=LEVEL.
¹² Olson, "The World's Hardest-Working Countries."
¹³ Based on a presentation given by Deirdre Anderson (Cranfield School of Management) titled, "Work Life Trends in Europe," on November 9, 2010, for a meeting of work-life and diversity experts at the United Nations.
¹⁴ The Energy Project website, retrieved on May 11, 2010, at http://www.theenergyproject.com/tools/key-ideas.
¹⁵ D'Annolfo Levey et al., *Beyond Flexibility: Work-Life Effectiveness as an Organizational Tool for High Performance*, 9, 16; D'Annolfo Levey et al., *Beyond Flexibility: Creating Champions for Work-Life Effectiveness*, 5.
¹⁶ Tang and MacDermid Wadsworth, *Time and Workplace Flexibility*, 12, 55-59.
¹⁷ Hewlett and Buck Luce, "Extreme Jobs: The Dangerous Allure of the 70-Hour Workweek," 4.
¹⁸ Harrington et al., *The New Dad: Caring, Committed, Conflicted*, 7-10.
¹⁹ Aumann et al., *The New Male Mystiuqe*, 5.
²⁰ Shellenbarger, "If You Need to Work Better, Maybe Try Working Less," d1.
²¹ Catalyst, Quick Takes, "Work Stress," 2009, retrieved on March 20, 2011, at http://www.catalyst.org/publications/231/work-stress.
²² Hewlett and Buck Luce, "Extreme Jobs," 8.
²³ Aumann and Galinsky, *The State of Health in the American Workforce*, 2-7, 9, 11, 30.
²⁴ Breen, "The 6 Myths of Creativity," 75-78.; Amabile and Kramer, "Inner Work Life: Understanding the Subtext of Business Performance," 74-80.
²⁵ Ibid.
²⁶ Ibid.
²⁷ Linkow et al., *Men and Work-Life Integration*, 11-12.
²⁸ Munck, "Changing a Culture of Face Time," 126-130.
²⁹ Ibid.
³⁰ Perlow and Porter, "Making Time Off Predictable—and Required," 104-107.
³¹ Ibid.
³² Schwartz, "Manage Your Energy, Not Your Time," 64-68, 70-71.
³³ Ibid.
³⁴ Tang and MacDermid Wadsworth, *Time and Workplace Flexibility*, 50-54, 60.

[35] Pascale et al., "Changing the Way We Change," 139.
[36] Wang, "How Your Schedule Can Help (or Hurt) Your Health," d1.
[37] Aumann et al., *The New Male Mystique*, 5-8.
[38] Ibid.

Chapter 5

[1] The *Wall Street Journal* published a separate section (section R on April 11, 2011) titled "Women in the Economy: The Journal Report, A Blueprint for Change," which included proceedings from a meeting of nearly 200 leaders convened to focus on the issue of women's leadership in the economy. Rebecca Blumenstein was the editor of the section.

[2] Catalyst, Quick Takes, "Women in U.S. Management," March 2011, retrieved April 5, 2011, at http://www.catalyst.org/publication/206/women-in-us-management; Catalyst, Quick Takes, "U.S. Women in Business," March 2011, retrieved April 5, 2011, at http://www.catalyst.org/publication/132/us-women-in-business.

[3] Catalyst, Quick Takes, "Women in Law in the U.S.," May 2010, retrieved April 14, 2011, at http://www.catalyst.org/publication/246/women-in-law-in-the-us.

[4] Catalyst, Quick Takes, "Women in Medicine," March 2009, retrieved April 14, 2011, at http://www.catalyst.org/publication/208/women-in-medicine.

[5] Catalyst, Quick Takes, "Women in Government," October 2010, retrieved April 14, 2011, at http://www.catalyst.org/publication/244/women-in-government.

[6] Blumenstein, "Women in the Economy," r1.

[7] Eagly and Carli, "Women and the Labyrinth of Leadership."

[8] Conan, "Is Sex Discrimination at Work Still a Problem?" retrieved on April 5, 2011, at http://www.npr.org/2011/04/05/135149194/is-sex-discrimination-at-work-still-a-problem.

[9] Eagly and Carli, "Women and the Labyrinth of Leadership."

[10] Ibid.

[11] Catalyst, *The Double-Bind Dilemma for Women in Leadership*, 8.

[12] Catalyst and the Institute of Management Development (IMD), Switzerland, *Different Cultures, Similar Perceptions*, retrieved April 20, 2011, at http://www.catalyst.org/publication/71/different-cultures-similar-perceptions-stereotyping-of-western-european-business-leaders.

[13] "From Kindergarten to the Boardroom: The Top Priorities." From "Women in the Economy," r7. (See endnote 1 for chapter 5.)

[14] Marlino and Wilson, *Teen Girls on Business*, 3-5.

[15] Ibid.

[16] Catalyst. *Women and Men in U.S. Corporate Leadership: Same Workplace, Different Realities?*, 17-22.

[17] Foust-Cummings et al., *Sponsoring Women to Success*, 1-6.

[18] "Where Are All the Senior-Level Women?" From "Women in the Economy," r3. (See endnote 1 for chapter 5.)

[19] Hewlett and Luce, "Extreme Jobs: The Dangerous Allure of the 70-Hour Workweek," 10.

[20] "Where Are All the Senior-Level Women?" From "Women in the Economy," r3. (See endnote 1 for chapter 5.)

[21] "It's Partly in Your Head." From "Women in the Economy," r10. (See endnote 1 for chapter 5.)

[22] Galinsky et al., *2008 National Study of Employers*, 6-7.

[23] Moen et al., *The New "Middle" Workforce*, 29.

[24] Brown et al., *Working in Retirement*, 4-14.

[25] Conan, "Is Sex Discrimination at Work Still a Problem?" (See endnote 8 for chapter 5.)

[26] Ibid.

[27] Catalyst, *The Bottom Line*, 1-2; Desvaux et al., "A business case for women," 2-3.

[28] "Women in the Economy: The Journal Report, A Blueprint for Change." (See endnote 1 for chapter 5.)

[29] Moen et al., *The New "Middle" Workforce*, 1-5.

[30] This overview is based on the Catalyst description of the Safeway Initiative: Championing Change for Women: An Integrated Strategy, published in 2006.

[31] Based on research with Anne Weisberg for a case study developed by the author for the Catalyst publication "Beyond Flexibility: Work-Life Effectiveness as an Organizational Tool for High Performance," 19-21.

[32] Based on a presentation given by Anne Weisberg titled, "Mass Career Customization: Building the Corporate Lattice Organization," on November 9, 2010, for a meeting of work-life and diversity experts at the United Nations.

[33] Benko and Weisberg, Mass Career Customization, 2007.

[34] Yen, "Women surpass men in advanced degrees." Retrieved May 2, 2011, at http://www.sltrib.com/sltrib/world/51699168-68/women-percent-stay-degrees.html.csp.

Chapter 6

[1] Dr. Joshua Coleman is a psychologist, author of several books on relationships and parenting, and co-director of the Council on Contemporary Families. He publishes ongoing articles on his website www.drjoshuacoleman.com. This information is taken from an article titled "Lindsey, Paris and Britney: It's All Your Mother's Fault!," published March 16, 2009. It was also published in the *Huffington Post*.

[2] Pruett, *Partnership Parenting*, xiv and xv.

[3] (See endnote 1 for chapter 6 on Dr. Joshua Coleman.) This information references an article titled "When Dads Become Dads: New Research Shows That Moms Are Not the Only Ones Whose Bodies Change," published on November 1, 2009.

[4] Based on the transcript from the radio show "What Do Kids Really Think about their Working Parents?" on Fem 2.0 Wake Up? The program was aired on February 10, 2010, and was moderated by Ellen Galinsky, president of the Families and Work Institute. The guests included Lisa Belkin and Josh Coleman.

[5] Latour, "The Bad Mother Complex: Why Are So Many Working Mothers Haunted by Guilt?"

[6] Ibid.

[7] Pear, "Married and Single Parents Spending More Time with Children, Study Finds," retrieved July 19, 2011, at http://www.nytimes.com/2006/10/17/us/17kids.html?pagewanted=print.

[8] Ibid.

[9] Barnett, "Women and Multiple Roles: Myths and Reality," 162; Pruett, *Partnership Parenting*, 83, 205.

[10] Zimmerman, F., D. Christakis and A. Meltzoff. "Television and DVD/video viewing in children younger than 2 years." *Archives of Pediatric and Adolescent Medicine*. 2007. 161 (5), 473-479.

[11] The Nielsen Company (2009)." TV viewing among kids at an eight-year high." Retrieved July 19, 2010, from http://blog.nielsen.com/nielsenwire/media_entertainment/tv-viewing-among-kids-at-eight-year-high/.

[12] Christakis, D., and F. Zimmerman. "Early television viewing is associated with protesting turning off the television at age 6." Medscape General Medicine, 2006, 8 (2), 63.

[13] Rideout et al., *Generation M2: Media in the Lives of 8- to 18-Year-Olds*, 1-5.

[14] U.S. Bureau of Labor Statistics, American Time Use Survey, Table 1. Time spent in primary activities, 2009 annual averages, retrieved April 14, 2011, at http://www.bls.gov/news.release/archives/atus_06222010.pdf.

[15] Lahart and Zhao, "What Would You Do With an Extra Hour?," d1, d3.

[16] Juster et al., *Changing Times of American Youth: 1981-2003*, 5-8.

[17] Levin, Diane., "Buy, Buy Childhood: Helping Children Resist the Lure of Today's Media and Commercial Culture," *Early Childhood: The Newsletter of the Winnetka Alliance for Early Childhood* (Spring/Summer 2008): 1-6.

[18] Holt, D.J., P.M Ippolito, D.M. Desrochers, and C.R. Kelley. *Children's Exposure to TV Advertising in 1977 and 2004*. Federal Trade Commission Bureau of Economics Staff Report (June 1, 2007): 9.

[19] Lichter, S.R. et al., *Sexual imagery in popular culture*. 2000. Washington, DC: Center for Media and Popular Policy.

[20] Blumenstein (editor), "Life Imitates Art." From "Women in the Economy," r11. (See endnote 1 from chapter 5.)

[21] Ibid.

[22] Wilson, "Media and Children's Aggression, Fear, and Altruism," 100-103.

[23] Buijzen, M. and Valkenburg. "The effects of television advertising on materialism, parent-child conflict and unhappiness. A review of research." *Applied Developmental Psychology* (2003). 24: 437-456.

[24] *Consuming Kids: The Commercialization of Childhood,* DVD, Media Education Foundation, 2008.

[25] Park, Takoma. "New poll shows marketing to kids taking its toll on parents, families." Center for a New American Dream., July, 1999.

[26] Bernstein, "Your BlackBerry or Your Wife," d1, d4.

[27] Keohane, "Imaginary Friends," c1.

[28] Finkelhor et al., *Nonfamily Abducted Children: National Estimates and Characteristics*, 1-5.; U.S. Census Bureau, Household Relationship and Family Care Status of Children Under 18 Years by Age and Sex: 2010, http://www.census.gov/apsd/techdoc/cps/cpsmar10.pdf.

[29] OJJDP Statistical Briefing Book: Juveniles as Victims, Question: What is known about substantiated or indicated child maltreatment?, retrieved April 8, 2011, at

http://www.ojjdp.gov/ojstatbb/victims/qa02102.asp?qaDate=2008&text=&print=yes.

[30] OJJDP Statistical Briefing Book: Juveniles as Victims, Question: Who are the perpetrators of child maltreatment?, retrieved April 8, 2011, at http://www.ojjdp.gov/ojstatbb/victims/qa02111.asp?qaDate=2008&text=&print=yes.

[31] OJJDP Statistical Briefing Book: Juveniles as Victims, Question: What is the trend in the child maltreatment victimization rate?, retrieved April 8, 2011, at http://www,ojjdp.gov/ojstatbb/victims/qa02105.asp?qaDate=2008.

[32] OJJDP Statistical Briefing Book: Juveniles as Victims, Question: What are the trends in serious violent crime victimization of youth?, retrieved April 8, 2011, at http://www,ojjdp.gov/ojstatbb/victims/qa02501.asp?qaDate=2005.

[33] Wilson, "Media and Children's Aggression, Fear, and Altruism," 97.

[34] Wickersham, "The myth of the Frankenstudent."

[35] Ibid.

[36] Kantrowitz and Wingert, "The Parent Trap."

[37] Shellenbarger, "How to Cram More Into 24 Hours," d1.

[38] Lecture given by Stephen Durant titled "Burnout, Staleness & Depression: Lessons from MGH Sports Psychology," September 10, 2011.

[39] Bigelow et al., *Just Let the Kids Play*, 59-60.

[40] Ibid., 23.; Wilson, "Too Long on the Playing Field?," 14-21.

[41] Ibid., 23.

[42] Wilson, "Too Long on the Playing Field?" 16-17.

[43] Shellenbarger, "A Box? Or a Spaceship? What Makes Kids Creative?," d1.

[44] Shellenbarger, "Raising an Accidental Prodigy," d1, d2.

[45] Ibid.

[46] Hartigan, "Pressure-cooker kindergarten."

[47] This information was taken from a printed conversation between the creator of the movie *Race to Nowhere*, Vicki Abeles, and Jay Mathews. "Me vs. creator of 'Race to Nowhere,'" *Washington Post* blog, April 8, 2011.

[48] Gardner Elkin, "Freedom to Play," 34.

[49] Gilliam, *Prekindergarteners Left Behind*.

[50] Author attended a lecture by Dr. Anthony Rao on February 1, 2011 on his book *The Way of Boys: Raising Healthy Children in Challenging Times*.

[51] Pruett, *Partnership Parenting*, 81, 205.

[52] Gabriel, "Parents Brace Documentary on Pressures of School." Retrieved on April 14, 2011, at http://nytimes.com/2010/12/09/education/09nowhere.html.

[53] The *Race to Nowhere* website provides information about how to access the movie. The Letter from the movie's director, Vicki Abeles, was retrieved from the website on April 14, 2011, at www.racetonowhere.com/print/1073.

[54] Alessandrini, Chris., "'Race to Nowhere' rings familiar with local youth," *Lexington Minuteman*, April 5, 2011.

[55] Gardner Elkin, "Freedom to Play," 34.

[56] Lehrer, "Why Rich Parents Don't Matter," c12.

[57] Ibid.

[58] Ibid.

[59] Chua, "The Tiger Mother Talks Back," c2.

[60] Ruan, "In China, Not All Practice Tough Love," c2.

[61] Gamerman, "What Makes Finnish Kids So Smart?"

[62] Based on the transcript from the radio show "What Do Kids Really Think about their Working Parents?" on Fem 2.0 Wake Up? The program was aired on February 10, 2010, and was moderated by Ellen Galinsky, president of the Families and Work Institute. The guests included Lisa Belkin and Josh Coleman.

[63] (See endnote 1 from chapter 6 on Dr. Joshua Coleman.) This information references an article titled "What Creates Happiness Among the Youth? Surprising New Research," published on October 1, 2009.

[64] Caplan, "The Breeders' Cup," w2.

[65] Lecture, "Burnout, Staleness & Depression: Lessons from MGH Sports Psychology," September 10, 2011.

[66] Beck, "Thank You. No, Thank You: Grateful People Are Happier, Healthier Long After the Leftovers Are Gobbled Up."

[67] Ibid.

[68] Spiegel, "Old-Fashioned Play Builds Serious Skills." Retrieved April 14, 2011, at http://www.npr.org/templates./story/story.php?storyId=19212514.

[69] Ibid.

[70] Bernstein, "Your BlackBerry or Your Wife," d1, d4.

[71] Rideout et al., *Generation M2: Media in the Lives of 8-To 18-Year Olds*, 1-5.; "Daily Media Use Among Children and Teens Up Dramatically From Five Years Ago", Kaiser Family Foundation press release, January 20, 2010, retrieved April 10, at http://www.kff.org/entmedia/entmedia012010nr.cfm.

[72] Ibid.

[73] Ibid.

[74] Wilson, "Media and Children's Aggression, Fear, and Altruism," 100-103.

[75] Galinsky, *Mind in the Making*, overview of seven core skills in introduction pages 1—11.
[76] Ibid, 351-352.
[77] Shellenbarger, "The Secret of Dad's Success."
[78] (See endnote 4 for chapter 6.) Fem 2.0 Wake Up! Blog Radio, "Work/Life and Kids: What Do Kids Really Think about their Working Parents?" Work-life series, episode 11, February 10, 2010.
[79] Phone interview with author, January 11, 2011.
[80] (See endnote 1 from chapter 6 on Dr. Joshua Coleman.) This information references an article titled "What Creates Happiness Among the Youth? Surprising New Research," published on October 1, 2009.

Chapter 7

Throughout this chapter, quotes without attribution are based on transcripts of interviews conducted by the author for this book. Small details have been altered in select instances to maintain the anonymity of the individuals.

[1] I have used selected quotes from ThirdPath profiles and transcripts of teleconferences throughout this chapter. The ThirdPath website URL is www.thirdpath.org. This quote came from a ThirdPath communication titled "Reflections on Fatherhood from Shared Care Dads," dated June 16, 2002.
[2] (See endnote 1 from chapter 7 regarding ThirdPath Institute.) This quote was taken from a ThirdPath communication titled "Following their Hearts: Laura and Robert's Transition to Shared Care," dated February 2003.
[3] Shellenbarger, "One Couple Has Mastered The Art of a Balanced Life."
[4] Catalyst, *Two Careers, One Marriage*, 7.
[5] Ibid., 8-9, 28-30.
[6] Ibid, 24, 28, 28.
[7] Ibid., 12-22.
[8] Ibid., 20.
[9] Ibid., 20.
[10] Ibid., 23-24.
[11] Ibid., 23.
[12] Ibid., 29.
[13] Ibid., 35.

[14] Moen et al., *The New "Middle" Work Force*, 2.
[15] Ibid., 22-23.
[16] Barnett and Shibley Hyde, "Women, Men, Work and Family: An Expansionist Theory," 789.
[17] Ibid., 789.
[18] Catalyst, *Flexible Work Arrangements III*, 3-5.
[19] Ibid., 8-9.
[20] Ibid., 25-27.
[21] Ibid., 40.
[22] Ibid., 31-32.
[23] Ibid., 43.
[24] Ibid., 32.
[25] Ibid., 20.
[26] Ibid., 20.
[27] Ibid., 8.

Chapter 8

Throughout this chapter, quotes without attribution are based on transcripts of interviews conducted by the author for this book. Small details have been altered in select instances to maintain the anonymity of the individuals.

[1] I have used selected quotes from ThirdPath profiles and transcripts of teleconferences throughout this chapter. The ThirdPath website URL is www.thirdpath.org. This information was from a ThirdPath teleconference on May 25, 2010, with Amy and Marc Vachon to talk about their book *Equally Shared Parenting*.
[2] Stone, "The Rhetoric and Reality of 'Opting Out,'" 14-19.
[3] Barnett and Shibley Hyde, "Women, Men, Work, and Family: An Expansionist Theory," 784-788.
[4] Ibid.
[5] Kimmel, "Has A Man's World Become a Women's Nation?" 352-353.
[6] (See endnote 1 for chapter 8.) ThirdPath teleconference, "Flexing Work during the Infant/Toddler Years: Dads and Moms Sharing Care," December 4, 2010.
[7] (See endnote 1 for chapter 8.) ThirdPath teleconference with Sharon Meers, author of *Getting to 50/50*, on March 26, 2010.

[8] (See endnote 1 for chapter 8.) ThirdPath teleconference, "Flexing Work during the Infant/Toddler Years: Dads and Moms Sharing Care," December 4, 2010.

[9] (See endnote 1 for chapter 8.), "Dads Who Have Taken Their First Step Towards Shared Care," September 29, 2008.

[10] Barnett and Shibley Hyde, "Women, Men, Work and Family: An Expansionist Theory," 786-789.

[11] Ibid.

[12] Shellenbarger, "Housework Pays Off Between the Sheets," d1, d3.

[13] Coltrane, Scott and Oriel Sullivan., "Men's Changing Contribution to Housework and Childcare," prepared for the 11th Annual Conference of the Council on Contemporary Families, April 25-26, 2008, retrieved on February 23, 2010, at http://www.contemporary families.org/marriage-partnership-divorce/menchange.html.

[14] James Sandman, "What a Difference a Dad Makes," remarks for the Working Mother Work Life Congress, October 1, 2003, that the author attended.

[15] Greenhouse, "Recession Drives Women Back to the Work Force."

[16] Ibid.

[17] Lublin, "One Household, Two Pink Slips," d1, d10.

[18] (See endnote 1 for chapter 8.) ThirdPath profile, "Weaving Family and Work for Two Decades," May 2005.

[19] Gerson, *The Unfinished Revolution*, 17-21.

[20] Galinsky, *Ask the Children*.

[21] Based on the author's transcript of a phone interview with PAIRS CEO Seth Eisenberg on January 14, 2011.

[22] (See endnote 1 for chapter 8.) ThirdPath profile, "Reflections on Fatherhood from Shared Care Dads," June 16, 2002.

[23] (See endnote 1 from chapter 8.) ThirdPath profile, "Father's Day Update," June 12, 2007.

[24] Kimmel, "Has A Man's World Become a Women's Nation?" 352-353, drawn from research by Scott Coltrane and Michelle Adams.

[25] Galinsky et al., *Leaders in a Global Economy: A Study of Executive Women and Men*, 1-6, and Galinsky, *Dual-Centric: A New Concept of Work-Life*, retrieved March 2010 at http://familiesandwork.org/site/research/reports/dual-centric.pdf.

[26] Ibid.

[27] Perlow and Porter, "Making Time Off Predictable—and Required," 108-109.

[28] (See endnote 1 for chapter 8.) ThirdPath teleconference with Amy and Marc Vachon, coauthors of *Equally Shared Parenting,* on May 25, 2010.
[29] Catalyst, *A New Approach to Flexibility*, 5-7, 43-51.
[30] (See endnote 1 for chapter 8.) ThirdPath profile, "Weaving Family and Work for Two Decades," May 2005.
[31] Lublin, "The Corner Office, and a Family," b9.
[32] Ibid.
[33] Based on the Catalyst Awards Description of the winning Ernst & Young Initiative, 2003.
[34] (See endnote 1 for chapter 8.) ThirdPath teleconference, "Flexing Work during the Infant/Toddler Years: Dads and Moms Sharing Care," December 4, 2010.
[35] (See endnote 1 for chapter 8.) ThirdPath teleconference, "Creating an Integrated Career," January 7, 2011.
[36] Barnett, Rosalind. "Reduced Hours Work/Part-Time Work." *Work and family encyclopedia,* Chestnut Hill, MA: Sloan Work and Family Research Network, January 28, 2003. Retrieved April 13, 2010, at http:wfnetwork.bc.edu/encyclopedia_entry.php?id=252&area=All.

REFERENCES

Amabile, Teresa M., and Steven J. Kramer. "Inner Work Life: Understanding the Subtext of Business Performance." *Harvard Business Review* (May 2007): 72-83.

Anand, Geeta. "India Graduates Millions, But Too Few Are Fit to Hire." *Wall Street Journal*, April 5, 2011.

Andersen, Kurt. "The End of Excess: Why this crisis is good for America." *Time* (April 6, 2009): 34-38.

Apgar, Mahlon IV. "The Alternative Workplace: Changing Where and How People Work." *Harvard Business Review* (May – June 1998): 121-136.

Aucoin, Don. "Family first? Athletes and politicians send a mixed message on how to balance work and children." *Boston Globe*, January 23, 2010.

Aumann, Kerstin, and Ellen Galinsky. *The State of Health in the American Workforce.* New York: Families and Work Institute. 2009.

———, Ellen Galinsky and Kenneth Matos. *The New Male Mystique.* New York: Families and Work Institute. 2011.

Babcock, Linda, and Sara Laschever. *Women Don't Ask.* New York: Bantam Dell, 2007.

Babits, Marty. *The Power of the Middle Ground: A Couple's Guide to Renewing Your Relationship.* Amherst, MA: Prometheus Books, 2009.

Bailyn, Lotte, Joyce Fletcher, and Deborah Kolb. "Unexpected Connections: Considering Employees' Personal Lives Can Revitalize Your Business." *Sloan Management Review* (Summer 1997): 11-19.

———, and Paula Rayman. *The Radcliffe-Fleet Work and Life Integration Project.* 1999.

Barnett, Rosalind. "Women and Multiple Roles: Myths and Reality." *Harvard Review Psychiatry* Vol. 12 No. 3 (May/June 2004): 158-164.

———, Andrew Steptoe, and Karen C. Gareis. "Marital-Role Quality and Stress-Related Psychobiological Indicators." *Annals of Behavioral Medicine* Vol. 30 No. 1 (2005): 36-43.

———, and Janet Shibley Hyde. "Women, Men, Work and Family: An Expansionist Theory." *American Psychologist* (October 2001): 781-796.

———. "Reduced Hours Work/ Part-Time Work." *Work and family encyclopedia*. Chestnut Hill, MA: Sloan Work and Family Research Network. February 28, 2003.

———. "Women's Journey Toward Equality: Where We Are and the Path Ahead." *Judith Sargent Murray's 285th Birthday Lecture*. May 1, 2009.

Bean Yancey, Kitty. "Couples retreat is an Rx for sex and intimacy." *USA Today*, February 11, 2011.

Beck, Melinda. "How to Get Your Groove Back." *Wall Street Journal*, July 6, 2010.

———. "Thank You. No, Thank You: Grateful People are Happier, Healthier Long After the Leftovers Are Gobbled Up." *Wall Street Journal*, November 21, 2010.

———. "The Sleepless Elite." *Wall Street Journal*, April 5, 2011.

———. "Why Relaxing Is Hard Work." *Wall Street Journal*, June 15, 2010.

Begley, Sharon. "Wealth and Happiness Don't Necessarily Go Hand in Hand." *Wall Street Journal*, August 13, 2004.

Belkin, Lisa. "The Opt-Out Revolution." *New York Times*, October 26, 2003.

———. "When Mom and Dad Share It All." *New York Times*, June 15, 2008.

Benko, Cathleen, and Anne Weisberg. *Mass Career Customization: Aligning the Workplace with Today's Nontraditional Workforce*. Boston: Harvard Business School Press, 2007.

Bennett, Drake. "The Next Corporate Titan: MOM." *Boston Sunday Globe*, September 2, 2007.

Bernstein, Elizabeth. "Fighting Happily Ever After." *Wall Street Journal*, July 27, 2010.

———. "She Talks a Lot, He Listens a Little." *Wall Street Journal*, November 16, 2010.

———. "Your BlackBerry or Your Wife." *Wall Street Journal*, January 11, 2011.

Bianchi, Suzanne M., and Melissa A. Milkie. "Work and Family Research in the First Decade of the 21st Century." *Journal of Marriage and Family* (June 2010):705-725.

Bigelow, Bob, Tom Moroney, and Linda Hill. *Just Let the Kids Play: How to Stop Other Adults from Ruining Your Child's Fun and Success in Youth Sports*. Deerfield Beach, FL: Health Communications, Inc., 2001.

Blumenstein, Rebecca (editor). "Women in the Economy: The Journal Report. A Blueprint for Change." *Wall Street Journal,* April 11, 2011: R1-R11.

Bond, James T., Ellen Galinsky, and E. Jeffrey Hill. *When Work Works: A Status Report on Workplace Flexibility.* New York: Families and Work Institute, 2004.

Breen, Bill. "The 6 Myths of Creativity." *Fast Company* (December, 2004): 75-78.

Brown, Melissa, Kerstin Aumann, Marcie Pitt-Catsouphes, Ellen Galinsky, and James T. Bond. *Working in Retirement: A 21st Century Phenomenon.* New York: Families and Work Institute and The Sloan Center on Aging and Work at Boston College. July 2010.

Caplan, Bryan. "The Breeders' Cup." *Wall Street Journal,* June 19-20, 2010.

Catalyst. *A New Approach to Flexibility: Managing the Work/Time Equation.* New York: Catalyst, 1998.

———. *Flexible Work Arrangements III: A Ten-Year Retrospective of Part-Time Arrangements for Managers and Professionals.* New York: Catalyst, 2000.

———. *The Bottom Line: Connecting Corporate Performance and Gender Diversity.* New York: Catalyst, 2004.

———. *The Double-Bind Dilemma for Women in Leadership: Damned if You Do, Doomed if You Don't.* New York: Catalyst, 2007.

———. *The Next Generation: Today's Professionals, Tomorrow's Leaders.* New York: Catalyst, 2001.

———. *Two Careers, One Marriage: Making It Work in the Workplace.* New York: Catalyst, 1998.

———. *Women and Men in U.S. Corporate Leadership: Same Workplace, Different Realities?* New York: Catalyst, 2004.

———. *Women in Law: Making the Case.* New York: Catalyst, 2001.

———. *Women of Color Executives: Their Voices, Their Journeys.* New York: Catalyst, 2001.

Catalyst and the Institute of Management Development (IMD) Switzerland. *Different Cultures, Similar Perceptions: Stereotyping of Western European Business Leaders.* New York: Catalyst, 2006.

Catalyst, Center for Education of Women at the University of Michigan, and University of Michigan Business School. *Women and the MBA: Gateway to Opportunity.* New York: Catalyst, 2000.

Chua, Amy. "Why Chinese Mothers Are Superior." *Wall Street Journal,* January 8-9, 2011.

———. "The Tiger Mother Talks Back." *Wall Street Journal,* January 15-16, 2011.

Cohany, Sharon R., and Emy Sok. "Trends in labor force participation of married mothers of infants." *Monthly Labor Review* (February 2007): 9-16.

Cohen, Carol Fishman, and Vivian Steir Rabin. *Back on the Career Track: A Guide for Stay-at-Home Moms Who Want to Return to Work.* New York: Warner Business Books, 2007.

Collins, Gail. *America's Women: 400 Years of Dolls, Drudges, Helpmates, and Heroines.* New York: Harper Collins, 2003.

Coltrane, Scott, and M. Adams. *Gender and Families.* Lanham: Rowan and Littlefield, 2008.

———, Oriel Sullivan. "Men's Changing Contribution to Housework and Childcare." Prepared for the 11th Annual Conference of the *Council on Contemporary Families*, April 25-26, 2008.

———. "Fatherhood, Gender and Work-Family Policies" (book chapter). Gornick, Janet C., and Marcia K. Meyers (editors). *Gender Equality: Transforming Family Divisions of Labor.* The Real Utopias Project. New York: Verso. 2009.

Conan, Neal. "Is Sex Discrimination At Work Still a Problem?" Talk of the Nation, *National Public Radio.* April 5, 2011.

"Consuming Kids: The Commercialization of Childhood." (DVD). *A Media Education Foundation Film.* Northhampton, MA. 2008.

Coontz, Stephanie. "Sharing the Load: Quality Marriages Today Depend on Couples Sharing Domestic Work." *The Shriver Report: A Study by Maria Shriver and the Center for American Progress.* (2009): 371-379.

———. "Stop Blaming Betty Friedan." *Slate,* May 5, 2010.

Corporate Voices for Working Families. *Business Impacts of Flexibility: An Imperative for Expansion.* Washington, D.C: Corporate Voices, November 2005.

Council on Contemporary Families. *Unconventional Wisdom, Issue 2: A Survey of Recent Research and Clinical Findings on Gender, Families and Equality,* April 17-19, 2009.

D'Annolfo Levey, Lisa, Meryle Mahrer Kaplan, and Aimee Horowitz. *Beyond Flexibility: Creating Champions for Work-Life Effectiveness* (Making Change series). New York: Catalyst, 2008.

———. *Beyond Flexibility: Work-Life Effectiveness as an Organizational Tool for High Performance* (Making Change series). New York: Catalyst, 2008.

De Graaf, John, David Wann, and Thomas N. Naylor. *Affluenza: The All Consuming Epidemic.* San Francisco: Berrett-Koehler Publishers, Inc., 2001.

Desvaux, Georges, Sandrine Devillard-Hoellinger, and Mary C. Meaney. "A Business Case for Women." *The McKinsey Quarterly* (September, 2008): 1-7.

Diener, Ed, and Martin E. P. Seligman. "Beyond Money: Toward an Economy of Well-Being." *Psychological Science in the Public Interest,* Vol. 5, No. 1 (July 2004): 1-31.

Eagly, Alice H., and Linda L. Carli. "Women and the Labyrinth of Leadership." *Harvard Business Review,* September 2007.

Elium, Jeanne, and Don Elium. *Raising a Family: Living on Planet Parenthood.* Berkeley: Celestial Arts Publishing, 1997.

Finkelhor, David, Heather Hammer, and Andrea J. Sedlak. *Nonfamily Abducted Children: National Estimates and Characteristics.* (National Incidence Studies of Missing, Abducted, Runaway, and Throwaway Children [NISMART]). Washington, D.C.: U.S. Department of Justice, Office of Juvenile Justice and Delinquency Prevention, October 2002.

Foust-Cummings, Sarah Dinolfo, and Jennifer Kohler. *Sponsoring Women to Success.* New York: Catalyst, 2011.

Friedan, Betty. *The Feminine Mystique.* Middlesex, England: Penguin Books, 1963.

Friedman, Stewart, and Sharon Lobel. "The Happy Workaholic: A Role Model for Employees." *Academy of Management Executive* Vol. 17 No. 3 (August 2003): 87-98.

———, Perry Christensen, and Jessica DeGroot. "Work and Life: The End of the Zero Sum Game." *Harvard Business Review,* November-December 1998.

Gabriel, Trip. "Parents Brace Documentary on Pressures of School." *New York Times,* December 8, 2010.

Gager, Constance, and Scott Yabiku. "Who Has the Time? The Relationship Between Household Labor Time and Sexual Frequency." *Journal of Family Issues* Vol. 31 (February 2010): 135-163.

Galinsky, Ellen. *Ask the Children: What America's Children Really Think About Working Parents.* New York: Harper Collins, 1999.

———. *Mind in the Making: The Seven Essential Skills That Every Child Needs.* New York: Harper Collins, 2010.

———, Kerstin Aumann, and James T. Bond. *Times are Changing: Gender and Generation at Work and at Home.* New York: Families and Work Institute, 2009.

———, and James T. Bond. *The Impact of the Recession on Employers.* New York: Families and Work Institute, July 2009.

———, James T. Bond, Stacy Kim, Lois Backon, Erin Brownfield, and Kelly Sakia. *Overwork in America: When the Way We Work Becomes Too Much.* New York: Families and Work Institute, 2004.

———, James T. Bond, Kelly Sakai, Stacy S. Kim, and Nicole Giuntoli. *When Work Works* (2008 National Study of Employers). New York: Families and Work Institute, 2008.

———, Shanny L. Peer, and Sheila Eby. *2009 Guide to Bold New Ideas for Making Work Work.* New York: Families and Work Institute.

Gamerman, Ellen. "What Makes Finnish Kids So Smart?" *Wall Street Journal,* February 29, 2008.

Gardner Elkin, Lea. "Parenting Matters: Freedom to Play." *Lexington's Colonial Times Magazine*, September/October 2010.

Gerson, Kathleen. *The Unfinished Revolution: How a New Generation Is Reshaping Family, Work, and Gender in America.* New York: Oxford University Press, 2009.

Gilliam, Walter S. *Prekindergarteners Left Behind: Expulsion Rates in State Prekindergarten Systems.* New Haven, CT: Yale University Child Study Center, May 4, 2005.

Goldsmith, Marshall. "Creating a Great Rest of Your Life." *Bloomberg Businessweek*, February 6, 2007.

Graff, E.J. "The Mommy War Machine." *The Washington Post*, April 29, 2007.

Greenhouse, Steven. "M.B.A.'s Have Biggest Penalty, Doctors the Smallest." *New York Times,* December 6, 2010.

———. "Recession Drives Women Back to the Work Force." *New York Times,* September 19, 2009.

Gutner, Toddi. "Beat the Clock: E-mails, faxes, phone calls, oh my. Here's how to get it all done." *Businessweek Small Biz,* February/March 2008.

Haddock, Vicki. "Are Modern Women Miserable?" *San Francisco Chronicle Magazine* (Posted on AlterNet on March 13, 2008).

Hallowell, Edward M. "Overloaded Circuits: Why Smart People Underperform." *Harvard Business Review* (January 2005): 55-62.

Hamilton, John. "Multitasking Teens May Be Muddling Their Brains." *National Public Radio Transcript.* October 9, 2008.

Harrington, Brad, Fred Van Deusen, and Beth Humberd. *The New Dad: Caring, Committed and Conflicted.* Chestnut Hill, MA: Boston College Center for Work & Family, 2011.

———, Fred Van Deusen, and Jamie Ladge. *The New Dad: Exploring Fatherhood Within a Career Context.* Chestnut Hill, MA: Boston College Center for Work & Family, 2010.

Hartigan, Patty. "Pressure-cooker kindergarten." *Boston Globe,* August 30, 2009.

Hewlett, Sylvia Ann, Carolyn Buck Luce, Peggy Shiller, and Sandra Southwell. *The Hidden Brain Drain: Off-Ramps and On-Ramps in Women's Careers.* Harvard Business Review Research Report, March 2005.

———, and Carolyn Buck Luce. "Extreme Jobs: The Dangerous Allure of the 70-Hour Workweek." *Harvard Business Review,* December 2006.

———. "Women and the new 'extreme' jobs." *Boston Globe,* December 4, 2006.

Hughes, Kathleen A. "He Says Maine. She Says Florida." *Wall Street Journal,* March 21, 2011.

Jackson, Maggie. *Distracted: The Erosion of Attention and the Coming Dark Age.* Amherst, New York: Prometheus Books, 2008.

Jayson, Sharon. "More parents share the workload when mom learns to let go." *USA Today*, May 4, 2009.

Joyce, Cynthia. "'Race to Nowhere' targets academic pressures." *NBC News and mnsbc.com*. March 8, 2011.

Juster, F. Thomas, Hiromo Ono, and Frank P. Stafford. *Changing Times of American Youth: 1981-2003*. Ann Arbor, MI: Institute for Social Research, University of Michigan, November 2004.

Kantrowitz, Barbara, Pat Wingert. "The Parent Trap." *Newsweek*, January 29, 2001.

Kelly, Mary Louise. "'Pre-Adulthood' Separates The Men From The Boys." Talk of the Nation, *National Public Radio*. February 28, 2011.

Keohane, Joe. "Imaginary Friends." *Boston Sunday Globe*. February 14, 2010.

Kimmel, Michael. "Has a Man's World Become a Woman's Nation?" *The Shriver Report: A Study by Maria Shriver and the Center for American Progress. (*2009): 323-357.

Kintz, Anita. "Why We Work." *Working Mother (*September 2001): 64-74.

Koch, Richard. "How Less Can Be More." *Across the Board* (Nov/Dec. 1998): 43-47.

Kreider, Rose M., and Renee Ellis. *Number, Timing, and Duration of Marriages and Divorces: 2009*. Washington, D.C.: U.S. Census Bureau, May 2011.

Laabs, Jennifer. "Overload." *Workforce Magazine*, January 1999.

Lachs, Mark. "Desire in the Twilight of Life." *Wall Street Journal*, November 13-14, 2010.

Lahart, Justin and Emmeline Zhao. "What Would You Do With an Extra Hour?" *Wall Street Journal*, June 23, 2010.

Latour, Francie. "The Bad Mother Complex: Why are so many working mothers haunted by guilt?"*Boston Sunday Globe*, March 13, 2011.

Lehrer, Jonah. "Why Rich Parents Don't Matter." *Wall Street Journal*, January 22-23, 2011.

Levey, Lisa. "Work-Family Balance—of Paramount Importance to Women." *Careers and the Woman MBA*.Vol.3, No. 1 Cambridge, MA: Crimson & Brown Associates. 1997.

Linkow, Peter, Jan Civian, and Kathleen M. Lingle. *Men and Work-Life Integration: A Global Study*. WorldAtWork and WFD Consulting, May 2011.

Lobron, Alison. "Overworked? Here's how to deal." *Boston Globe: Career Issue*, March 7, 2010.

London Business School: The Lehman Brothers Centre for Women in Business. *Innovative Potential: Men and Women in Teams*, 2007.

Lublin, Joann. "One Household, Two Pink Slips." *Wall Street Journal*, May 12, 2009.

———. "The Corner Office, and a Family." *Wall Street Journal*, October 18, 2010.

Luscombe, Belinda. "Marriage: What's It Good For?" *Time* (November 29, 2010): 48-56.

Mandel, Michael. "The Real Reasons You're Working So Hard ... and what you can do about it." *Business Week*, October 3, 2005.

Marlino, Deborah, and Fiona Wilson. *Teen Girls on Business: Are They Being Empowered?* A National Study from The Committee of 200 and Simmons College School of Management, April 2003.

Martin Hekker, Terry. "Paradise Lost (Domestic Division)." *New York Times*, January 1, 2006.

McCracken, Douglas M. "Winning the Talent War for Women: Sometimes It Takes a Revolution." *Harvard Business Review* (November-December 2000): 159-167.

McHale, James, Jason Baker, and Heidi Liss Radunovich. "When People Parent Together: Let's Talk About Co-parenting." University of Florida. IFAS Extension. Publication FCS2277. October 2007. Retrieved March 15, 2011 at http://edis.ifas.ufl.edu/fy1000.

Meers, Sharon, and Joanna Strober. *Getting to 50/50: Having It All by Sharing It All.* New York: Bantam Dell, 2009.

Mendels, Pam. "When Work Hits Home: Few CEOs seem to realize that it pays to offer a balance." *CEO Magazine* (March 2005): 51-53.

Merrill-Sands, Deborah, Jill Kickul, and Cynthia Ingols. "Women Pursuing Leadership and Power: Challenging the Myth of the 'Opt Out Revolution.'" *CGO Insights*, February 2005.

Moen, Phyllis, and Patricia Roehling. *The Career Mystique: Cracks in the American Dream.* Oxford, U.K.: Rowman & Littlefield Publishers, Inc., 2005.

———, with Donna Dempster-McClain, Joyce Altobelli, Wipas Wimonsate, Lisa Dahl, Patricia Roehling, and Stephen Sweet. *The New "Middle" Work Force.* Publication of the Life Course Center at the University of Minnesota and the Bronfenbrenner Life Course Center and Cornell Careers Institute at Cornell University. Spring 2004.

Munch, Bill. "Changing a Culture of Face Time." *Harvard Business Review* (November 2001): 125-131.

Myerson, D. and M. Scully. "Tempered Radicalism: Changing the Workplace from Within." *CGO Insights*, November 1999.

Nash, Laura, and Howard Stevenson. *Just Enough: Tools for Creating Success in Your Work and Life.* Hoboken: John Wiley & Sons, 2004.

———. "Success That Lasts." *Harvard Business Review,* February 2004.

Olson, Parmy. "The World's Hardest-Working Countries." *Forbes*, May 21, 2008.

Opdyke, Jeff D. "With This Debt, I Thee Wed." *Wall Street Journal*, April 1, 2009.

Parker-Pope, Tara. "Go Easy on Yourself, a New Wave of Research Urges." *New York Times,* February 28, 2011.

———. "She Works. They're Happy." *New York Times,* January 22, 2010.

Pascale, Richard, Mark Millemann, and Linda Gioja., "Changing the Way We Change." *Harvard Business Review* (November-December 1997): 125-139.

Pear, Robert. "Married and Single Parents Spending More Time With Children, Study Finds." *New York Times,* October 17, 2006.

Percheski, Christine. "Opting Out? Cohort Differences in Professional Women's Employment Rates from 1960 to 2005." *American Sociological Review* Vol. 73 (June 2008): 497-517.

Perlow, Leslie, and Jessica Porter. "Making Time Off Predictable—and Required." *Harvard Business Review* (October 2009): 102-109.

Petersen, Andrea. "So Cute, So Hard on a Marriage." *Wall Street Journal,* April 28, 2011.

Peterson, Richard R. "A Re-evaluation of the Economic Consequences of Divorce." *American Sociological Review* Vol. 61 (June 1996): 528-536.

Pincott, Jena. "The Masculine Mystique." *Wall Street Journal,* March 27-28, 2010.

Plumb, Taryn. "That was THEN, this is NOW." *Boston Sunday Globe,* February 14, 2010.

Pollak, Ruth (producer). *One Woman One Vote.* (DVD.) 1995 Educational Film Center, originally produced as part of American Experience on PBS.

Potter Cromartie, Stella. "Labor force status of families: a visual essay." *Monthly Labor Review* (July/August 2007): 35-41.

Pruett, Kyle, and Marsha Kline Pruett. *Partnership Parenting: How Men and Women Parent Differently—Why It Helps Your Kids and Can Strengthen Your Marriage.* Cambridge, MA: Da Capo Press, 2009.

Rideout, Victoria J., Ulla G. Foehr, and Donald F. Roberts. *Generation M2: Media in the Lives of 8 to 18 Year Olds.* Menlo Park, CA: Kaiser Family Foundation, January 2010.

Risman, Barbara J., and Elizabeth Seale. "Betwixt and Be Tween: Gender Contradictions Among Middle Schoolers," in *Families as They Really Are,* edited by Barbara Risman. New York: W.W. Norton & Company, 2009.

Roach, Stephen. "The Hollow Ring of the Productivity Revival." *Harvard Business Review* (November/December 1996): 81-89.

Ruan, Victoria. "In China, Not All Practice Tough Love." *Wall Street Journal,* January 8-9, 2011.

Schechner, Sam. "Keeping Love Alive." *Wall Street Journal,* February 8, 2008.

Schoppe-Sullivan, Sarah J. "Maternal Gatekeeping, Coparenting Quality, and Fathering Behavior in Families with Infants." *Journal of Family Psychology* Vol. 22 No. 3 (June 2008): 389-398.

Schwartz, Tony. "Manage Your Energy, Not Your Time." *Harvard Business Review* (October, 2007): 63-74.

Shapiro, Mary, Cynthia Ingols, and Stacy Blake-Beard. "Optioning In versus "Opting Out": Women Using Flexible Work Arrangements for Career Success." *CGO Insights*, January 2007.

Shellenbarger, Sue. "A Box? Or a Spaceship? What Makes Kids Creative?" *Wall Street Journal*, December 15, 2010.

———. "Avoiding the Mommy Track: This IBM Vice President Trims Her Work Week and Still Landed a Promotion." *Wall Street Journal*, February 23, 2007.

———. "Housework Pays Off Between the Sheets." *Wall Street Journal*, October 21, 2009.

———. "How to Cram More Into 24 Hours." *Wall Street Journal*, December 8, 2010.

———. "If You Need to Work Better, Maybe Try Working Less." *Wall Street Journal*, September 23, 2009.

———. "Kids Quit the Team for More Family Time." *Wall Street Journal*, July 21, 2010.

———. "One Couple Has Mastered The Art of a Balanced Life." *Wall Street Journal*, May 16, 2001.

———. "Raising an Accidental Prodigy." *Wall Street Journal*, March 30, 2011.

———. "The Secret of Dad's Success." *Wall Street Journal*, June 14, 2011.

———. "When Granny Is Your Nanny." *Wall Street Journal*, June 24, 2009.

Shor, Juliet. *Plenitude: The New Economics of True Wealth*. New York: The Penguin Press, 2010.

Society for Human Resource Management. *Workplace Flexibility in the 21st Century: Meeting the Needs of the Changing Workforce*, 2009.

Spiegel, Alix. "Old-Fashioned Play Builds Serious Skills." *National Public Radio Transcript*, February 21, 2008.

Stark, Betsy. "Dad: 'I Can't Stay for That Meeting.'" *ABC News*, June 16, 2007, retrieved April 19, 2010 at http://abcnews.go.com/print?id=3283684.

Stelter, Brian. "TV Viewing Continues to Edge Up." *New York Times*, January 2, 2011.

Stone, Pamela. *Opting Out? Why women really quit careers and head home*. Berkeley: University of California Press, 2007.

———. "The rhetoric and reality of 'opting out.'" *Contexts* (publication of the American Sociological Association) Vol. 6, No. 4 (Fall 2007): 14-19.

Stork, Diana, Fiona Wilson, Andrea Wickes Bowles, Jenny Sproull, and Jennifer Vena. *The New Workforce Reality: Insights for Today, Implications for Tomorrow.* A Collaborative Study by Simmons School of Management and Bright Horizons Family Solutions, January 2005.

Strgar, Wendy. "The Importance of Boundaries." *Huffington Post,* September 15, 2010.

Susanka, Sarah. *The Not So Big Life: Making Room for What Really Matters.* New York: Random House, 2007.

Tang, Chiung-Ya, and Shelley MacDermid Wadsworth. *Time and Workplace Flexibility.* New York: Families and Work Institute, 2010.

Taylor, Paul, Richard Fry, D'Vera Cohn, Wendy Wang, Gabriel Velasco, and Daniel Dockterman. *Women, Men and the New Economics of Marriage.* Pew Research Center, January 2010.

Tugend, Alina. "It's Just Fine to Make Mistakes." *New York Times,* March 11, 2011.

———. "Vacations Are Good for You, Medically Speaking." *New York Times,* June 7, 2008.

U.S. Bureau of Labor Statistics. *American Time Use Survey 2009 Results,* June 22, 2010.

U.S. Bureau of Labor Statistics. *Married Parents' Use of Time: 2003-2006,* May 8, 2008.

Vachon, Marc and Amy. *Equally Shared Parenting: Rewriting the Rules for a New Generation of Parents.* New York: Penguin Books, 2008.

Van Deusen, Fredric R, Jacquelyn B. James, Nadia Gill, and Sharon P. McKechnie. *Overcoming the Implementation Gap: How 20 Leading Companies Are Making Flexibility Work.* Chestnut Hill, MA: Boston College Center for Work & Family, 2008.

Waldman, Ayelet. "In Defense of the Guilty, Ambivalent, Preoccupied Western Mom." *Wall Street Journal,* January 15-16, 2011.

Walker, Marcus, and Roger Thurow. "U.S. Europe Are Ocean Apart on Human Toll of Joblessness." *Wall Street Journal,* May 7, 2009.

Walker, Marion A. "The Day the E-Mail Dies: How One Company Learned Shutting Down the PC In Box Is Easier Said Than Done." *Wall Street Journal,* August 26, 2004.

Wang, Shirley S. "How Your Schedule Can Help (or Hurt) Your Health." *Wall Street Journal,* March 29, 2011.

Warner, Judith. "Mommy Madness. What happened when the Girls Who Had It All became mothers?" *Newsweek* , February 21, 2005.

Warner, Judith. *Perfect Madness.* New York: Riverhead Books, 2005.

Weiner-Davis, Michele. "The Marriage Map." *Parade Magazine,* March 17, 2002.

WFD Consulting and the American Business Collaboration. *The New Career Paradigm: Flexibility Briefing,* 2007.

Wheatley, Margaret. "Can We Reclaim Time to Think?" The Alliance (A Publication of the Alliance for Work-Life Progress), May 2002.

Wickersham, Joan. "The myth of the Frankenstudent?" *Boston Globe*, April 15, 2010.

Wilcox, Bradford W. "Can the Recession Save Marriage?" *Wall Street Journal*, December 11, 2009.

Wilde Mathews, Anna. "So Young and So Many Pills." *Wall Street Journal*, December 28, 2010.

Willis, Claudia. "The Case for Staying Home." *Time* (March 22, 2004): 51-59.

Wilson, Barbara J. "Media and Children's Aggression, Fear, and Altruism." *The Future of Children*, Vol. 18 No. 1 (Spring 2008): 87-118.

Wilson, Deidre. "Too Long on the Playing Field?" *The Boston Parents' Paper* (April, 2006): 14-21.

Wilson, James, Q. "Hard Times, Fewer Crimes?" *Wall Street Journal*, May 28-29, 2011.

Wolf, Naomi. "What Price Happiness." *More* (April 2010): 106-109, 171-173.

Wotapka, Dawn. "Reality Check: 'Extreme Makeover Downsizes Its Dream Homes." *Wall Street Journal*, April 6, 2010.

Yen, Hope. "Women surpass men in advanced degrees." *The Salt Lake Tribune* (Associated Press), April 27, 2011.

Zaslow, Jeffrey. "Friendship for Guys (No Tears!)." *Wall Street Journal*, April 7, 2010.

Zupek, Rachel. "Will a Bigger Salary Make You Happier?" *MSN Careers*, July 13, 2007.

INDEX

Affluenza, 43
At home vs. working moms, 202-203, 235
Attention Deficit Trait (ADT), 41-42

Bad Mother Complex (mother guilt), 155
Bailyn, Lotte, 8, 111
Balanced perspective at work, 246-247
Barriers for working women, 125, 127-137
  few role models, 132
  importance of style, 128-129
  limited access to mentors and sponsors, 131-132, 137-138, 149-150
  long hours, 134
  organizational interventions, 143-147
  performance vs. potential, 127-128
  values mismatch, 129-131
Belkin, Lisa, 27
Benefits of the Libra Solution
  choice, 213-214, 216, 217-219, 226-227, 234-235, 240-243
  efficacy, 243-248
  flexibility, 214-215, 216, 224-225, 231-233, 237-239, 248-250
  fulfillment, 214, 216, 220-224, 227-230, 236-237, 243-248
Billable hours (law firms), 101-102
Boston College Center for Work and Family, 54, 63, 78-81, 85
Boston Consulting Group, 113-114
Bureau of Labor Statistics, 62-63, 80-81, 231
Business case for working women, 143

Career Mystique, 34
Career path flexibility, 205-207, 208-210, 244-245
  investment in future earnings, 82-83
  lack of, 34-37
  mature women, 36-37
  need for new models, 133-137
  new models, 145-148
Career strategies for women, 148-150
Catalyst, 11-13
  consulting, 12-13, 103, 116-117
  research, 33, 34, 54-55, 128-129, 205-207, 208-210, 244-245
Census Bureau, 62
Center for Gender in Organizations (Simmons School of Management), 35-36
Change efforts, 119-120
Child care usage, 198-200
Children
  abductions, 160-161
  and chores, 182-183
  and gendered thinking, 158
  and gratitude, 177
  and importance of fulfilled parents, 184-185
  and importance of mutual parental regard, 184-185
  and marketing, 158-159
  and materialistic values, 159
  and over scheduling, 162-165, 179
  and safety concerns, 159-162
  and violence, 158-159, 180-181
  enrichment requirements, 162-165
  go-to behaviors/ go-to people, 177-178
  importance of limits, 179-181
  life skills, 181-183
  parents as anchor, 176-178
  rising homework, 166
  screen time usage, 157-158, 179-181
  sense of security from strong parental partnership, 236
  time with parents, 155-156
  turning point in marriage, 23-24, 87-88
  youth sports, 164-165
Choices and tradeoffs, 202-211
Coleman, Josh, 72-73, 184
Collins, Gail, 31
Confluence of forces, 27-28, 51-52
Coontz, Stephanie, 48-49
Cornell Careers Institute, 207-208
Creativity
  and adults, 107-108
  and children, 165
Cyberbullying, 180

DeGroot, Jessica (see Third Path Institute), 17
Deloitte, 141-142, 146-147
Dual career couples
  research on, 205-210, 217-219
Dual centric, 81, 120, 240-241

Durant, Stephen (MGH Sports Psychology Program), 177-178

Economic dependence, 65
Education
   and stress, 166-170
   comparisons by country, 173
   early academic focus, 166
   Finnish approach, 173
   Icelandic approach, 173
Egalitarian marriage as ideal, 21, 27-28
Egalitarian parenting, benefits for children, 234-235
Eisenberg, Seth (PAIRS), 236
Employee networks, 12-13, 149-150
Employee/ employer value proposition, 32-34
Ernst & Young, 248
Erosion of parental confidence, 173-175
Experimenting, 231-233, 255-257
Extreme jobs, 104-106, 114, 134
Extreme parenting, 43-44, 61-62, 153-157, 184

Face time, 100
Families and Work Institute (FWI), 38-39, 54, 106-107, 181-182
Father's group, 51, 84-86
Fathers
   and support, 83-86
   and work, 78-82, 105
   early involvement with children, 75-76, 78-81, 193-194, 220-223, 230, 257
Fear, 45-47
Feminine Mystique, 19-22, 62, 73-74
Feminism, 21, 47-51, 63-65, 149-150
   more than choice, 48, 63-65
Financial freedom (professional freedom), 67-68, 231
Flexible work options (see career path flexibility), 35, 81-82, 104-105, 208-210, 243-245
Friedan, Betty (The Feminine Mystique), 19-22, 62, 73-74
Fulfillment/ efficacy, 243-248

Galinsky, Ellen (Mind in the Making), 28, 181-182
Gender confidence gap, 138
Gender cycle
   as self fulfilling prophecy, 139-141
   disrupting, 88-90
Gender norms, 29-31, 53-56, 87-90
   and middle school students, 30-31
   disrupting, 88-90
   how men contribute, 73-87
   how women contribute, 57-71
   intensify after children, 88
Gender pay gap, 140-141
Gerson, Kathleen, 235
Gifted children, 165
Good enough parent, 175

Happiness and money (well being and money), 43, 97
Health benefits of egalitarian partnership, 219
Home no longer a refuge, 39-42

Ideal employee, 239
Importance of open mind, 256-257
Importance of planning for children, 23-25, 87-88
Incremental change, 202-204, 255-256
Institute for the Study of Youth Sports, 164
Intelligence (nature vs. nurture), 169-170
Intensive parenting (see extreme parenting)
Investment banking, 6-9
Involvement of both parents, 183

Jackson, Maggie (Distracted), 41

Lacking sense of enough, 42-45
Lang, Ilene, 125
Language, importance of, 94, 154-155, 254
Lazaruk, Lillie Margaret, 49
Leader support for flexibility, mixed messaging, 108

Male mystique, 54
Marital partnership, 194-197, 230
Marital satisfaction, 219, 229-230
Marriage/ partnership, importance of, 58-59, 67-69, 194-197, 208, 226-230, 257-258
Marriott, 111-113
Massachusetts General Hospital Sports Psychology Program, 177-178
Maternal gate keeping, 57-59, 76-78
McKinsey, 133-134
Men and friends, 83-84
Men
 changing roles of, 20, 71-73
Mentors, 131-132, 149-150
Meritocracy, 141
Metis, 2-3
Meyer, David, 109
Moen, Phyllis (Career Mystique), 34
Money, 62-67, 78, 82-83, 89-90, 197-198, 258-259
Movement from Industrial age to Information age, 91-92
Multi-tasking, 109-111, 156

National Incidence Studies of Missing, Abducted, Runaway and Throwaway Children (NISMART), 160
New "problem with no name", 22
New normal after children, 59
New York City Dads' fathers group, 84-86
No Child Left Behind, 168

Opting out (choosing to stop working outside the home), 35-36, 61-67
Organization for Economic Cooperation and Development (OECD), 97
Overload, 37-45, 94-96, 103-106

PAIRS, 236
Paradox leading to gender norms and over busy lives, 27-28, 51-52
Parent energy meter, 156-157
Parental anxiety, 163
Parenting compass, 176
Parenting
    small moments, 221-222
Pew research, 55, 64, 72, 229
Previous parenting norms, 153-154
Primary career, limitations of (see financial freedom), 36-37, 73-74, 81-82, 224-225
"Problem with no name", 19
Productivity, 96-98
Project for International Student Assessment, 173

Quality of life/ well being, 251

Race to nowhere, 167-168
Raising feminist sons, 16
Reciprocal mentoring, 144-145
Rodgers, Fran, 8, 10-11
Role modeling
    as a manager/ leader, 241-243
    at work, 81
    for children, 184-185, 234-235

Safety concerns (see children: and safety concerns), 46
Safeway, 146
Schoppe- Sullivan, Sarah, 57-58
Schwartz, Felice, 11, 16
Schwartz, Tony (The Energy Project), 16, 115
Screen time usage
    adults, 157-158
    children, 157-158, 179-181
Self care, 222-224
Shared ownership, 67-69, 200-202, 220-222, 227-230, 236-239, 253-254
    financial, 62-69, 73-75, 221
    chores, 229-230
Sharon, Meers (Getting to 50/50), 255
Shellenbarger, Sue, 105
Simmons School of Management, 8-9, 130-131
Sponsors, 131-132, 149-150
Spouse as parent support, 232-233
Spouse as professional support, 231-232
Stone, Pam, 61, 64, 217
Strengthen work relations, 248
Super woman syndrome, 69-70
Systems approach, 2-3, 215

Technology, 37-39

Teen attitudes regarding business, 130-131
Television deregulation, 159
The Libra Appproach (see The Libra Solution)
The Libra Solution, 2-4, 17-18, 25-26, 253-259
   and parenting, 175-176, 186-188
   and work, 243-250
   benefits for children, 234-239
   benefits for individuals, 217-225
   benefits for the marriage, 226-233
   benefits for the workplace, 239-250
   core elements, 189-204
   experimentation, 231-232, 255-256
   how to get started, 255-256
   importance of partner choice, 59, 200-201, 257
   incremental change, 203-204, 255-256
   many paths to, 211-212
   mindset for success, 256-259
   moderation, 197-200
   new models of leadership, 240-243
   overview of benerfits, 213-216
   planning, 257
   pragmatism, 202-204
   priorities, 60-62, 67-69
   strategies, 256-259
The Libra Work and Life Model (see The Libra Solution)
Third Path Institute, 17, 197, 249

Tiger mother (Chinese mother), 170-172
Time with children, 155-156
Two income independence, 204-206

United Nations, 150-151
Unstrucutred time, 178-179
U.S. workforce policies, 94

Vachon, Amy and Marc (Equally Shared Parenting), 58, 215, 255

Wachovia, 114-116
Wall Street Journal, 20, 83, 105, 110, 170-171, 231
Warner, Judith (Perfect Madness), 47-48, 61-62
Weisberg, Anne, 147
Women
   career strategies, 148-150
   CEOs, 247-248
   dissatisfaction with work, 66
   educational degrees, 150
   importance of their contributions at work, 150-151
   in leadership, 126
   leaving work to stay home, 66
   of color, 70-71
   undervaluing themselves, 137-138
Women's initiatives, perceptions of special treamtment, 142

Women's movement, 21, 47-51, 63-64
Women's rights, 50
Work and mothers, 132-133
Work and stress, 106-107
Work hours, 27-28, 35-36, 94, 120, 134
  ideal, 207-208
Work norms
  challenges of modern approach, 95-96, 98-103
  changing, 91-94
  costs for individuals, 106-107
  costs for organizations, 107-108
  employee/ employer value proposition, 32-34
  modern approach, 93-96, 118-121, 239-240
  personal influence, 93, 103-106
  redefining, 78-82, 84-85
Work redesign, 111-121, 248-250
Work/Family Directions (WFD), 8, 10-11
Working smarter, 111-117, 121-123, 258
Work-life balance, defining, 1-2, 253
Work-life models, 24-25

ABOUT THE AUTHOR

As a consultant and author, Lisa D'Annolfo Levey challenges organizations and individuals to consider the environments, and behaviors, which support people to thrive at work and in their lives. Levey is a former senior director at Catalyst, the leading research and advisory organization working to build inclusive environments and expand opportunities for women at work. Levey has consulted across a wide range of industries and professions and is a recognized expert in the field of diversity, women's advancement and work-life integration. Some of her clients have included Exxon Mobil, Johnson & Johnson, KPMG, IBM, the Icelandic Ministry of Trade & Industry, the New York City Bar, and the United Nations. Levey holds a Bachelor of Science degree with distinction from Cornell University and a Masters of Business Administration with highest honors from the Simmons College School of Management. For more information on this book, visit *www.thelibrasolution.com*.

www.ingramcontent.com/pod-product-compliance
Lightning Source LLC
Chambersburg PA
CBHW032100090426
42743CB00007B/189